American Legal Processes

Viewpoints
On American Politics

EDITOR: SAMUEL KRISLOV

American Legal Processes

WILLIAM MCLAUCHLAN

Congress and the Administrative State

LAWRENCE DODD AND RICHARD SCHOTT

From Social Issues to Public Policy

ROBERT EYESTONE

Mass Media and Politics

NORMAN LUTTBEG

American Legal Processes

William P. McLauchlan
Purdue University

JOHN WILEY & SONS
New York • Chichester • Brisbane • Toronto

Library of Congress Cataloging in Publication Data:

McLauchlan, William P
   American legal processes.

   (Viewpoints on American politics series)
   Includes index.
    1. Courts—United States. 2. Procedure (Law)—
United States. I. Title.
KF8700.M3   347'.73'1   76-26579
ISBN 0-471-58560-2
ISBN 0-471-58561-0

Printed in the United States of America

10 9 8 7 6

To Ethel and Harold McLauchlan, my parents, for all the opportunities they have given me

Foreword

I am gratified to be able to inaugurate this series, *Viewpoints on American Politics,* with an offering in my own area of interest, the courts. The approach is distinctive and the focus unusual. Professor McLauchlan, a product of the University of Chicago and its law school, with its complex emphasis on both empiricism and economic theorizing, has been bold enough to attempt to pull them together. Furthermore, he has tried to bring this approach to courts at all levels, civil and criminal, so that he can introduce the notion of a standard or model structure.

For most students in most courses, "courts" has meant simply the Supreme Court. Recently, legal scholars have strongly urged a broader understanding and attention to the other courts. These, after all, make the decisions in all but a few score of cases a year and operate in ways quite different from that most atypical institution in Washington. McLauchlan's book represents that approach—to the typical and the cumulative, the daily and nearby structure. This volume describes the range of American courts in terms of the typical arrangements prevailing in the various states. Rather than swamp the student with 50 variations, it reduces the discussion to a few basic patterns. This is the first textbook effort to pull together what a decade of research in public law has been making evident.

The volume is intended for the general student of American government. Prelaw students may find it especially rewarding, but the emphasis is on broad analytic understanding, and not particular technicality. The volume illustrates that trial courts, appellate courts, and administrative tribunals all have a place in the political process.

During the past few years the emphasis on crime in the media has drastically raised the attentive public's sophistication toward legal process. Even the television detectives are more precise and more observant of legal niceties than we see in the reruns of their counterparts of a decade ago. Students bring that sophistication with them, and I believe they will find this volume takes them from where they are and gives them more of what they want.

This is the first volume of a new series, *Viewpoints on American Politics* and the first fruit of a three-year program. Our plan is to develop a set of volumes to enrich introductory courses on American government. Each volume is intended to be an elementary monograph: written on the level appropriate for students taking their first course in politics; proffer a particular point of view based on sound research data; deal with a topic of major concern; and contribute to the general understanding of American politics.

Samuel Krislov
Minneapolis, July 1976

Preface

Like most books this book has a history, and it began in the fall of 1969 in a civil procedure class taught by Geoffrey Hazard at the University of Chicago Law School. Although the book has evolved substantially from the original idea, with much of the details of the politics of civil process being lost, the core of the original idea remains. Professor Hazard might not find a great deal in this book that reflects his thoughts or perspective, but the incredible amount of interpersonal politics that occur in civil litigation continues to keep me interested in this larger subject.

Most political scientists have not dealt with this subject.[1] For several possible reasons we have devoted our time and attention to criminal justice and the variations in the politics of criminal justice systems. One reason could be a result of the injustice that occurs in such processes and the concern of many observers with these features of the criminal system. Another reason might be the political scientist's lack of training and understanding of civil processes. In any case, this imbalance is inexcusable. This book is a first attempt at redressing the balance and remedying the gaps in our understanding of the use and operations of courts, in general, not just appellate and not just criminal courts.

As an examination of the table of contents indicates, this book is only a partial effort since various chapters focus on

---

[1] Martin Shapiro, "From Public Law to Public Policy, or the 'Public' in 'Public Law'," 5 *PS* 410 (1972) presents a first statement of the imbalance in political science. See also, Glendon Schubert, "Communications," 6 *PS* 85 (1973).

criminal processes and appellate courts. This reflects the pressures of the discipline and current interests. It also reflects an effort to balance civil with criminal process systems. Such a context and perspective allow the civil process to be compared and contrasted with the other, more widely known facets of the judicial process.

I thank the many people who have contributed to this book. Sam Krislov, as general editor of the series, provided suggestions for changes and improvements in several earlier drafts of the manuscript. David Neubauer also provided valuable perspectives. My good friend Brad Canon made many very cogent suggestions for adding examples and illustrations to make the book more readable and understandable to the undergraduate. Although I have not adopted all of his recommendations, I have the "burden of proof" on those I did not accept. Allan Wichelman was the political scientist "next door" who asked questions, made suggestions, and provided a sounding board for my ideas and approaches during the later stages of the writing. We differ on the "imbalance" of the criminal justice system probably only because of different socialization processes and his stronger sense of justice. Fred Dallmayr and Martha Adams provided substantial support at crucial times during the preparation of the manuscript. Rita Lynch and Sandra Scott did the "conversion" of rough drafts to final copy.

Wives appear to be responsible for the major academic contributions of our profession. My wife is no exception. She provided support, insights, and standards, which made the product much improved at numerous points. My daughters, were "patient," each in her own way. Kendra helped by letting her mother "work on Daddy's chapters" and by requiring that I stop and think every so often, when her blanket "stuck under Daddy's chair." Alina's timing was exceptional.

None of these people are responsible for whatever errors remain in this book.

William P. McLauchlan
West Lafayette
June, 1976

Contents

List
of Tables and
Figures

Introduction

This book examines several very important questions about the legal process in this country. Although there are many such questions that could be examined, this book focuses on two sets of questions about courts. Since most cases are heard only by the court of first instance, and never reach an appellate court, these questions refer primarily to trial courts.

The first group of questions focus on *who* uses courts in this country. All people do not utilize the judicial process equally, and people may litigate for a variety of reasons, some rational, some irrational. This book surveys the factors that litigants take into account before deciding to go to court, and examines *why* these people use courts. The reasons for going to court are crucial to understanding the functions that courts serve in our political system. This group of questions cannot be treated definitively here, but consideration of it should give the reader a greater sensitivity for courts and their operation.

Another set of questions focuses on *how* American trial courts operate. Once a person has chosen to litigate, what is likely to happen to him and his case in the court? The procedures courts use to settle litigated conflicts often influence the result. In addition, the results themselves are a unique part of court processes, since what people are likely to get from a court decision might very well influence whether they choose to litigate or seek other, authoritative, or informal resolution of their dispute. Courts are one facet of conflict resolving institutions in our society, and the court processes make it unique—different from other arenas in which disputes can be settled. How procedures affect outcomes and participants is crucial to an understanding of our legal system.

More specifically, the precise procedures that are used in courts are examined. It is quite possible for someone to have a very valid claim but to lose in court for failure to proceed correctly, or because the process is biased against certain kinds of claims or parties. The actual procedures used reveal a good deal about what courts are supposed to be doing, and how they are supposed to do it, as well as what actually occurs in a court. The procedures reflect what is intended, even if practicalities prevent this from happening in all cases. The models upon which the actual procedures of courts are based also reveal something about the theoretical orientation of our courts. Furthermore, a comparison between the model or prototype procedures of a court and the actual processes used by courts will illustrate varying amounts of discrepancy. The degree and direction of real-life deviation from "perfection" are instructive. Among other things this examination will show how the system accommodates a wide variety of disputes that the model of procedure did not anticipate or was not designed to deal with.

The processes involved in court operation range from very rigorous and formal to very lax and informal. While all institutions operate by processes, the legal processes are nearly as variable as those of most other political institutions, despite the historical, adversary model that is well known, and that has been frequently ascribed to by many observers as the best procedure available.[1] The one primary characteristic of processes is their flexibility. Despite whatever may be expected or anticipated about procedural regularity, courts have the power to adjust their procedures, and many judges, individually, or court systems, generally, do adjust procedures from time to time in order to deal with the particular problem before the courts.

These questions are empirical ones, and it would be best if there were adequate empirical data to provide definitive answers to the questions. However, this book is not based on empirical

---

[1] Jerome Frank, *Law and the Modern Mind* (Garden City, N.Y.: Doubleday, 1930); and Jerome Frank, *Courts on Trial* (New York: Atheneum, 1949).

data since there is very little of the right kinds of data available for analysis. Instead, this book is largely based on a variety of material that others have discovered and presented. As a first attempt at answering these questions, this book describes what is currently known, and raises questions that can be investigated with empirical data and analysis at a later time. This is an overview of the processes existing in American courts today, and it provides a perspective by which these courts can be understood. The discussions in this book may not be definitive, but they are intended to be comprehensive.

The descriptive chapters present a necessarily nonexhaustive picture of how courts actually proceed. Not all of the possible courts and processes found in our country are discussed. If the reader were to examine the court system that operates in the area in which he lives, he is not likely to find all of the courts that are discussed, and he may find variations from the procedures described in this book. The problem with comparing a model procedure with reality is that the reality is so varied and complex that it is impossible to get a sharply focused picture of what really happens in any given situation. What is set forth below is a generalized picture about the court and the process. However, even this generalized picture gives some idea of the richness and variations of American legal processes.

The variations of real procedures from the theory, and the variations among various actual procedures are the result of any number of factors that are outlined here. The reasons for the differences among processes are multifarious, and it is not possible to isolate causal factors in this sort of descriptive and summary work. Some fundamentals may be sketched, however.

Probably the most important influence on legal process is the substantive law involved in a case. Obviously, the rules of contract, or tort law, or probate law, contribute greatly to the procedures used by courts in resolving cases involving contracts, torts, or probate. Unfortunately it is not possible to give a precise exposition of the substantive law on each subject in order to show the connection, although the effort has been made in some cases here. Where substantive law is discussed, it should be remembered that the law is not the same in all jurisdictions.

Some variations are also due to the people involved in the

processes. Judges, lawyers, and parties influence procedures by their objectives, their perceptions about the legal system, their styles of behavior, and their skills. Local political and social conditions affect the types of individuals available for different roles.

The structure of a court system will also directly influence the procedures involved. Each state creates, by its constitution and/or its statutes, its own court structure, and provides for the operation of its courts in whatever fashion is deemed appropriate. That means some courts will not even exist in some states, although their functions are probably performed by other courts. In addition, each state, adopts its own written rules of procedure, which means that every one of the 51 court systems in this country differs in some respects.

A general outline of court structure in this country is presented in Figure A. The traditional court system is more common and is described in some detail in this book. Both systems are discussed in Chapter 8. Both of these organizations do perform nearly the same tasks, but utilize different courts and judicial personnel.

Figure A Alternative trial court structures.

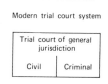

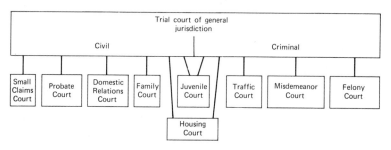

Figure B shows the two prevalent structures of appellate courts in this country. The closer discussion of them appears in Chapter 6. There is nothing sacred about any particular court structure or organization. Yet there are several considerations that arise because of the use of one or the other structures at either the trial and appellate levels. Whether one structure is better than the other is a matter of conjecture, although empirical study could certainly treat how these structures affect the court's decisions.

There are several questions posed and discussed in the following chapters. These focus on how trial courts are supposed to proceed, and how, in fact, they do process the cases brought to them. There are a number of additional questions that surround these and that provide a substantial amount of the discussion in the book. First, there are several questions relating to the use of

Figure B Alternative appellate court structures.

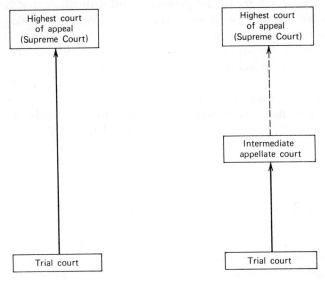

Key: —————— must hear appeals (manditory jurisdiction)

———————— may choose to hear appeals (discretionary jurisdiction)

courts generally and what factors contribute to the decision to litigate. Under what circumstances do people choose alternatives to litigation, such as bargaining, and what function do courts perform? These questions are discussed, along with the literature that relates to answering these, in the first two chapters. Chapters 3 and 4 focus on the civil and criminal trial courts in this country, respectively. There are questions of what procedural models are supposed to operate in each of these two arenas, and how do the actual civil and criminal courts differ from the model. What variations from the model are permitted, and why are different procedures necessary? The courts emphasized in these two chapters are specialized ones, which are often not considered by scholars. However, the variations in functions and procedures are most evident in these courts of limited jurisdiction and, thus, the comparison of the model with reality is best done in relation to such courts.

Chapter 5 treats the problems and difficulties that have appeared in the operation of trial courts. What effect do judicial selection problems, jurisdictional overlap and inadequacies, and resource limitations have on the operation of these courts? These clearly do affect the "success" courts have with some functions. Chapter 6 looks at how appellate courts operate, and how they differ in procedures from the trial courts discussed earlier. How do appellate courts proceed, and how do they decide cases? The effect of court decisions is covered in Chapter 7. What impact does a court decision have, and why? The last chapter, Chapter 8, focuses on the question what difference court organization and procedures have on the operation of the judicial system in any state. While no conclusive answers can be provided, it seems that these questions warrant attention and, hopefully, substantial research in the future.

The general thesis of this book is that there is no single legal process operating in this country. The processes utilized by the legal system are the result of the function being performed by it, and the result of the particular substantive law it applies. This means the law and legal-system functions are both products of numerous social relationships. Law is neither God-given nor completely socially determined. It is the purposive rules enacted by legislatures, interpreted, and applied by governmental agents (of all kinds) and accepted as legitimate by society. Law is important for keeping society in existence and operating, and while law may change, even drastically, it does serve as a guide to behavior.

We ask our legal system to do a great many things for us. The questions we ask it to answer, and the disputes we ask it to resolve, involve very difficult, complex, even impossible, human difficulties. The court system may be very ill-equipped to resolve many of the disputes that are presented to it. Court procedures are intended to frame all conflicts in a single form (a case) and to process them in identical fashion. This tendency to resist innovative conflict resolution processes increases the difficulties that arise in our legal system. However, it has not prevented some courts and some legal systems from adapting new and unique means of dealing with many kinds of problems.

1
Some Theoretical Observations About Legal Systems

All courts in America do not proceed in identical fashion. This book studies these variations and seeks to explain why they occur. This chapter focuses on some important theoretical concerns about the operation of courts. The functions courts perform and a theoretical analysis of the procedures used by courts are important in gaining a perspective for examining actual court operation. A simple economic model is used to describe the basic relationships between the structures of courts and their procedures.

The Functions of Judicial Processes

The functions of courts are generally to settle disputes through an acceptable, authoritative (governmental) means. The disputes a court settles may involve a variety of parties, subject matters, and relationships. The result of the court's resolution also varies although it is limited to a few, commonly used methods of redressing relationships, such as money, imprisonment, or specific behavioral orders to prevent unique injury.

Only conflicts that have reached certain levels of disagreement and have been framed in certain, acceptable legal terms can be presented to a court for an authoritative decision.[1] There are many disputes arising every day that never reach the point of litigation, such as traffic jams in which drivers contest crowding into lanes, or who should proceed first. There may be laws involved, and legal rights are affected, but the people involved do not think the dispute needs to be settled by a court. Usually such difficulties are forgotten by the end of the day.

A variety of factors can turn a disagreement into a legal dispute, but major influences might be the stakes (what is at issue), the inclinations of the disputants (emotional and attitudinal), and social pressures (the community's interest in the case). There are many disputes that are settled without going to court, and even court resolution may involve processes used outside courts to achieve a settlement.[2] Many disputes are negotiated between the parties, or mediated by a third party, rather than litigated. Other disputes, which do not go to court, are never settled because they are momentary and neither party considers the conflict important enough to contest. Thus courts and court processes should be viewed as one segment on a continuum of settlement processes rather than as a distinct variety of institution.

The kinds of conflicts that are presented to courts fall broadly into two categories—civil disputes and criminal disputes. Civil disputes generally involve conflicts between two private parties and are tied closely to the relationship between the parties. The parties involved in such private disputes can be individuals or groups of individuals who share a particular interest that the opposing party has allegedly injured. An example would be an individual homeowner who resides next to an industrial plant that is polluting the air, or a group of home owners all of whom are affected by the same pollution, and who want to litigate the

---

[1] See Richard Abel, "A Comparative Theory of Dispute Institutions in Society," *8 Law and Society Review* 217 (1973); P.H. Gulliver, "Case Studies of Law in Non-Western Societies," in Laura Nader, ed., *Law in Culture and Society* (Chicago: Aldine, 1969), pp. 13-15; and Vilhelm Aubert, "Courts and Conflict Resolution," *11 Journal of Conflict Resolution* 40 (1967) for discussions of the legal ethnography literature on dispute settlement and conflict resolution.

[2] See P. H. Gulliver, "Negotiations as a Mode of Dispute Settlement: Towards a General Model," *7 Law and Society Review* 667 (1973).

issue. However, most civil litigants are corporations. (But see Table 2.1.) Businesses may litigate in the name of individuals, as when insurance companies actually litigate automobile accident cases. The government also litigates civil matters. The government is a major contractor and many disputes arising from such business activities find the government litigating, as plaintiff or defendant in civil courts.

In a civil dispute, courts are called upon to define, adjust, or establish the relationship between litigants. The realtionships in dispute can involve terms of written contracts (or unwritten, oral agreements), personal injuries caused by the negligence of one party, property disputes between two parties, or some other aspects of the private relationship between two parties.

When a civil case is presented to a court and decided by the court, the disputed, interpersonal relationship may be defined or redefined. For example, the court may define the rights and duties between two strangers, as when it decides who has a prior claim on the assets of a debtor. To make this decision the court must rank these two strangers and thus establishes their relationship with one another. The court can also adjust an already existing relationship if the law requires such a readjustment. Thus, the court outlines the physical relationship between two adjoining property owners when it determines the property line between them. Certainly when the court grants a divorce, the relationship between husband and wife has been adjusted. Finally, the court may make no adjustment in the relationship at all, if it concludes that the parties should stand as they are and suffer their own losses. The importance of this alternative is that the status quo has been maintained by an authoritative decision of the court against an asserted right or injury.

Civil litigation also involves the court in allocating or reallocating various resources among the parties. Such an allocation occurs when one party is ordered to pay his opponent damages (money) for a wrong caused by the payer. This reallocation is done if the injured party has proven to the court's satisfaction that he has suffered injury that the other party caused. The most common allocation made by the judicial system is money, and this requires the translation of the claim into a monetary amount by the court system.[3] In disputes where money is an inadequate remedy, but where one party has suffered or will suffer irreparable injury because of the actions of the other party, a court may provide an equitable remedy, requiring a party to do or refrain from doing something. This type of case involves the "King's conscience" and is derived from English common law where the King's equity was always available to do justice when the regular courts—using money damages—could not provide satisfactory remedy. In modern times, for example, if a homeowner wishes to prevent a nearby factory from emitting fumes that will destory the owner's beautiful lawn, as well as injure his family's health, he would seek a court-ordered injunction against the company. In this case, monetary damages for the ruined lawn might be adequate. However, monetary damages for the impaired health of his family would not be adequate, and the court's equity jurisdiction would provide a remedy. The burden would be on the homeowner to prove that the fumes were injuring the family's health, but if the court were convinced of this irreparable injury, the remedy would be to require the factory to cease and desist from its injurious pollution.

The second category of disputes—criminal—involves the definition or adjustment of the relationship between an individual and society as a whole. The conflict here is based on behavior of the individual that society has defined as criminal or antisocial.[4] Society possesses the power to punish such individual deviant behavior. In our society, the judicial system has been given responsibility for the application of this societal power upon the deviants. This judicial responsibility is an effort to limit abuse of this power, and is shared with other governmental agencies, executive and legislative, that play different roles (apprehension or enforcement and definition, respectively) in this criminal process. The essential conflict here is one between soci-

---

[3] Richard Posner, "A Theory of Negligence," *1 Journal of Legal Studies* 32–36 (1972).

[4] See J. Heinz, R. Gettleman, and M. Seeskin, "Legislative Politics and the Criminal Law," *64 Northwestern University Law Review* 277 (1969); and Herbert Jacob, *Urban Justice: Law and Order in American Cities* (Englewood Cliffs, N.J.: Prentice-Hall, 1973), pp. 16–20.

ety and the individual, and it involves defining or adjusting that social relationship by authoritative means.

The relationship adjustment that occurs in criminal cases usually involves the imprisonment of a person designated as a criminal by the judicial system. A frequent sentence is to place the convicted individual on probation, which means that he remains free from incarceration, but must report to the authorities periodically. This penalty serves as a threat to the individual that if he does not behave, he will lose his freedom, but he can remain free as long as he behaves himself. Penalties in the criminal justice system also include the allocation of resources. Fines can be assessed by the sentencing judge for some kinds of crimes. Thus, the penalty for the misdemeanor of driving while under the influence of intoxicating beverages where no one is injured in Indiana is 5 days to 6 months in jail or a $25 to $500 fine.[5] Some crimes do not carry this interchangeable penalty. The Supreme Court has recently held that a traffic offender who could not pay the usual fine could not be imprisoned instead, because such treatment denied equal protection of the law guaranteed by the Fourteenth Amendment of the U.S. Constitution.[6] The allocation process in criminal cases involves the transfer of money only from the defendant to the state. However, there have been proposals made recently to provide compensation from the state to the victim of some crimes. This would involve the transfer of funds from society to the individual who suffered from the crime.

In some cases, the judge will impose imprisonment or a fine, and then suspend it. He may suspend sentences for several reasons. For example, he may feel that the defendant is really sorry for what he did and will gain more from being released than from being incarcerated. The judge may think that fairness requires that the defendant be released. In such an instance the defendant is not threatened with later punishment if he misbehaves. Variation in penalties may be due to rehabilitative objectives, since punishment is not the stated purpose of convicting a criminal. The variation may also be due to a number of irrelevant

[5] Burn's Indiana Statutes Annotated, 9–4–1–54(b) (2) (1973).
[6] *Tate v. Short,* 401 U.S. 395 (1971).

factors,[7] such as age, race, sex, or social status of the defendant. The accused may be set free if the trier of fact does not find him guilty beyond a reasonable doubt. This is the equivalent of the status quo alternative mentioned above in civil cases. However, the imposition of no penalty may actually involve some deprivation of individual liberties during the judicial process.

In addition to resolving civil and criminal disputes, courts play a role in the formation, definition, and application of certain public policies, despite whatever remains of the "nonpolitical" aura surrounding courts.[8] In a sense, this function occurs in all cases, although the policy impact of an individual case may be quite insignificant to everyone but the immediate litigants. However, the scope of such a policy may be broadened if the case is decided, on appeal, by the federal or state court of last resort and it becomes a precedent. Thus one decision can be used (usually *is* used) to guide future decisions by trial courts and by appellate courts on similar questions or similar fact situations. This precedential value of a court decision is an important policy aspect of the judicial function, because it provides a pattern for future courts' decisions.

The judicial process seeks to define or alter disputed relationships of people, companies, groups of people, and society as a whole. The relationships involved are often interpersonal, com-

[7] See, for example, M. Levin, "Urban Politics and Judicial Behavior," *1 Journal of Legal Studies* 193 (1972); E. Green, *Judicial Attitudes in Sentencing* (New York: St Martin's Press, 1961); A. Somit, J. Tanenhaus, and W. Wilke, "Aspects of Judicial Sentencing Behavior," *21 University of Pittsburgh Law Review* 613 (1960); and Robert Dawson, *Sentencing: The Decision as to Type, Length, and Conditions of Sentence* (Boston: Little, Brown, 1969).

[8] See, Kenneth Dolbeare, *Trial Courts in Urban Politics* (New York: Wiley, 1967); K. Dolbeare, "The Federal District Courts and Urban Public Policy: An Exploratory Study," in Joel Grossman and Joseph Tanenhaus, eds., *Frontiers of Judicial Research* (New York: J Wiley, 1969); Herbert Jacob, *Justice in America* 2d ed. (Boston: Little, Brown, 1972); Sheldon Goldman and Thomas Jahnige, *The Federal Courts as a Political System* (New York: Harper and Row, 1971); David Neubauer, "Policy Outputs of Illinois Trial Courts: An Exploratory Examination," (paper prepared for delivery at the 1972 American Political Science Association Meeting, Washington, D.C.); and Richard Wells and Joel Grossman, "The Concept of Judicial Policy-Making: A Critique," *15 Journal of Public Law* 286 (1966), for treatments of these aspects of court functions.

mercial, or criminal, and are in some way related to the scope of law. There are many kinds of adjustments that courts can provide, but most court resolutions of disputes involve money or freedom.

The Model of Judicial Conflict Resolution

The processes by which American courts resolve the issues presented to them have evolved, historically, from English law that developed around a singular method of resolving disputes—an adversary proceeding. Early in the English development of law, a person charged with an offense could clear himself of the charge by bringing in a fixed number of people who would swear to the judge that the individual had not done what he was charged with. The attestation process supposedly indicated the truth of the individual's claims. If the challenging party also brought in a number of people who swore that the defendant had offended in the alleged manner, there was no basis for the judge's decision.

This means of resolving the dispute was not the only adversary process in England. In some instances, the two contending parties—especially in a conflict that arose when one person had allegedly insulted the other—could settle their dispute on the battlefield, either by hiring a champion or by engaging in the physical battle themselves. In a sense, dueling is a more recent form of this kind of adversary dispute settlement.

These primitive forms of dispute settlement seem barbaric and irrational today. However, they were viewed as an appropriate and fair means of arriving at the truth of accusations when they were instituted and used. They have certain similarities with the modern adversary process. They allowed the two sides to the dispute to bring some form of proof—oath takers and physical prowess, for example—to bear on the allegations in the case. The processes supposedly involved an objective process in which neither party could unfairly influence the outcome. Oath takers were not supposed to be bribed, although the possibility of this is clearly present. The strengths and skills of the champions hired to do battle were supposedly not an unfair influence, since the decision rule in these cases was "might makes right." If one party could afford to hire the strongest knight in the realm, then his case must have been stronger and, thus, he rightly prevailed over the weaker case, and champion.

The modern, adversary process uses several refinements on this ancient adversary scheme, but it is still based on the same contending between the two sides to the dispute, and the same efforts by both parties to present a "case" that establishes the rightness of each side's contentions.[9] The modern system still expects the parties to the case—rather than the judge or presiding officer—to bring forward whatever information or proof supports the contentions of its side. The judge then, cannot inquire on his own into the merits of the case but must wait for the disputants to present their cases.[10] Each side (party), through its chosen representative (lawyer), presents all the evidence supporting that side's factual assertions, and the trier of fact (judge or jury) decides the facts that are most clearly proven or it weighs the evidence against a standard to determine which facts have been "proven." This adversary trial process is really one step removed from the battlefield. It does involve hired champions, collecting and marshalling all the evidence, supporting their side in an effort to win the case. However, in addition to this adversary contest, the process is supposed to produce an objective decision, based on the true facts (discovered by the trial) and the law (statutory or common law establishing the rule to be applied to the facts). The outcome (decision) is not precisely predictable, but the parties can expect the decision to be made objectively, on the basis of the evidence presented, and consistent with previous decisions. This paradigm process is the one upon which the wide

[9] See Lon Fuller, "The Adversary System," in Harold Berman, ed., *Talks on American Law* (New York: Viking Press, 1961).

[10] The inquisitorial system used in many European countries structures the process, so that the judge plays the central role in developing all of the case. He calls the witnesses and questions them himself. The parties, in this process, sit by and watch, giving the judge names of witnesses, and suggesting questions for him to ask. See, for example, Arthur Von Mehren, *The Civil Law System: Cases and Materials for the Comparative Study of Law* (Englewood Cliffs, N.J.: Prentice-Hall, 1957).

variety of processes available in courts today is based. This model is important because this book will outline a number of variations from it in the following chapters.

Several points should be noted about this model of the process. The process is self-initiated by the parties, whether it is a civil litigant or the public prosecutor. The court does not seek business, and judges almost never create their own business, as legislators do when they introduce proposed legislation. The courts exist as an available avenue for the solution of conflict. Society provides this arena for people who feel they need such assistance in their particular case. The process is designed to yield objective results based on the empirical evidence submitted in court, a set of technical decision rules (the technical, procedural steps that a trial is required to exhaust), and the law that is the basis for the decision. In the model, you cannot buy a decision or obtain a favorable decision by dishonesty or deception. Another important aspect is that the court decision is authoritative. Society and government have endowed the process with a high degree of legitimacy that requires obedience to the court decree.[11] Furthermore, people are willing to accept the court's decision as final in many cases, even though they are dissatisfied with the decision or have additional avenues for resolution open to them.

A most important characteristic of this model, for purposes of this analysis, is that one party wins what the other party loses. Each party is subjecting his own resources (time, money, and freedom) to the resolution of the conflict, and when a party loses a case, he has lost his resources or some portion of them. In game theory terms, this is a zero-sum game,[12] which means that the parties are fighting each other and each other's resources. This is in contrast to arguing about some external source of resources, such as happens in interest group activity before legislatures where the debate is over the expenditure of tax money (paid into the government by *all* taxpayers). In a zero-sum game one party loses what the other party wins.

---

[11] Theodore Becker, *Comparative Judicial Politics* (Chicago: Rand McNally, 1970), p. 13.

[12] R. Luce, and H. Raiffa, *Games and Decisions* (New York: Wiley, 1957).

In a civil case, the defendant either loses and pays the plaintiff damages, or the defendant wins, and pays nothing. In some cases, the actual payment might be made by the defendant's insurance company. The defendant in this case has already paid some premium to the company to accept the risk of his being required to redress an injury. In a few instances, a court may find a creative solution that may benefit all concerned, but these are rare exceptions to the rule that one party gains at the expense of the other.

In criminal cases the zero-sum nature of this process is less precise than in the civil case, where the resources usually dealt with are tangible. The defendant in a criminal case does risk his money but he also risks his freedom and prestige. The prosecution must expend money and time in the prosecution of the offense. However, society and the victim are also involved in a general way. That is, the "cost" of the crime to the victim and society is tied to the prosecution, even though it may be impossible to place a monetary value on these costs. Thus the resources involved, from both the perspective of the prosecution and the defense are intangibles such as prestige, freedom, fear, and some money. The defendant's loss may be zero-sum, as in the case of his freedom. However, society's gain or loss in a criminal case is quite inexact.

Table 1.1 outlines the basic characteristics of the formal, adversarial model of dispute settlement. These characteristics will be compared with other processes that are used to settle disputes in America. These other processes are outside the judicial system but play an integral role in litigation and the settlement of disputes, and may parallel this litigation pattern.

The adversary model outlined here raises some problems for the settlement of some disputes. As a result, the process may be avoided for some conflict resolution. For example, many of the conflicts presented to the courts for solution cannot be resolved by such an adversary process. Some problems are exacerbated when they are forced into an adversary format, such as divorce proceedings. As American society places increasing demands on courts to handle more kinds of problems, in greater numbers, these added conflicts may become less amenable to the traditional, adversary process than most others. In addition, in prac-

Table 1.1
Characteristics of the Formal, Adversarial Model of Dispute Settlement

Characteristic	Description
1. Adversary	Self-initiated; burden on parties to come forward with evidence; judge is passive
2. Objective	Outcome cannot be obtained by illegal or inappropriate means; decision based on evaluation of materials presented by the parties
3. Zero-sum	Winner wins what the loser loses; all or nothing outcome
4. Authoritative	Judgment carries force of law; losing party forced to pay compensation, not take anything from opponent, or serve social penalty

tice the adversary system does not always work as planned. Judges may be biased, some lawyers are better than others, and facts may not be so precisely discoverable in a competitive process of discovery and proof, as the adversary model presumes.

Several alternative arenas are available for the resolution of conflicts that share all or some of the characteristics of the judicial arena. Disputes obviously can be settled by force, but there are several less or nonviolent means of settling disputes that are just as binding or final in zero-sum terms. There are quasi-judicial processes that involve private disputes in which the parties have agreed to a private process of binding settlement by arbitration. This procedure can result in an all-or-nothing resolution or the arbitrator can "split the difference" between the parties in a compromise solution. While arbitration decisions are binding on the parties, they have no value as precedents for other parties in other cases, and they do not have official sanctions or power of enforcement that a court verdict and judgment have.[13] Mediation

---

[13] Soia Mentschikoff, "Commercial Arbitration," *61 Columbia Law Review* 859 (1961); and Louis Mayers, *The American Legal System* rev. ed. (New York: Harper and Row, 1964).

and conciliation are less formal than arbitration, but they involve a third party, who, unlike a judge, seeks to mediate and persuade the parties to reach their own agreement over the dispute.[14] Beyond these third party processes, there are informal, dyadic (two-party) negotiations between legal representatives or directly between the parties in an effort to reach an agreement. Some kinds of problems have been withdrawn from the jurisdiction of courts. For example, workman's compensation cases involving injuries to workmen on-the-job were legislated out of courts and into various administrative agencies by many states in the first third of the twentieth century.[15] Currently there is a widening debate about removing automobile accident cases (personal injury actions) from court litigation through the enactment of no-fault insurance. Since a major function of courts in these personal injury cases is to determine whether the defendant was at fault for plaintiff's injuries, not having to prove fault would remove many of these cases from courts.

Litigation and Bargaining

There are alternatives to litigation that channel many cases away from the formal court arena during various stages in the conflict resolution process. There are a variety of zero-sum resolution procedures, but there are also some procedures that involve a minimax solution. This latter group of procedures is marked by the single characteristic that the parties resolve their dispute by reaching a mutually agreeable solution. This involves a compromise or other solution in which neither party wins all that he might win, but settles for something less, in the process of limiting the likelihood of extreme losses. Rather than run the risk of losing the zero-sum game in court, where the judgment, if against the party, might be for the maximum loss possible, a litigant may agree to lose a lesser amount in an out-of-court settlement.

[14] Stewart Macauley, "Non-Contractual Relations in business." *28 American Sociological Review* 55 (1963).

[15] J. Croyle, "Tort Law Doctrine, Courts and Social Expenditures: The Courts as Primary Policy Makers," (paper prepared for delivery at the 1975 American Political Science Association Meeting, San Francisco).

In order to bargain, following the minimax strategy, there must exist a settlement range.[16] Unless there is some zone of outcomes in which there is at least one mutually agreeable solution that both parties recognize as more agreeable than litigation, there is no reason to bargain. The range is the amount of money encompassed between the minimum acceptable amount to the plaintiff and the maximum acceptable loss to the defendant. While money (the amount of damages) is the resource most likely calculated and dealt with in bargaining, attorneys may discuss dropping some counts in a criminal indictment, that is, reducing the number of charges against the defendant, or civil litigants might bargain over the number of claims contained in the plaintiff's original complaint that will be ignored in settling the case. Other kinds of nonmonetary items may be discussed between the parties such as the strength and amount of evidence that might be put forward by one of the parties in litigating. Such questions of law as what amount of evidence is necessary to prove a particular point of the plaintiff's case or defeat it can become relevant items of bargaining.

The bargaining process is dyadic, which means that there is no judge or third party who makes the decision.[17] The parties talk directly with each other or use lawyers as representatives who talk directly to each other. If there is no settlement range, or if one or both parties' expectations move outside the range, then litigation is the likely result, since there is no area in which parties can mutually agree to a compromise. However, the decision regarding when and if to negotiate and when to begin the litigation process are made by the two parties, rather than by a judge or other outsiders. In some situations the judge may seek to have the

---

[16] R. Walton and R. McKersie, *A Behavioral Theory of Labor Negotiations* (New York: McGraw-Hill, 1965); Richard Posner, "An Economic Approach to Legal Procedures and Judicial Administration," *2 Journal of Legal Studies* 399 (1973); John Gould, "The Economics of Legal Conflicts," *2 Journal of Legal Studies* 279 (1973); and Alan Friedman, "An Analysis of Settlement," *22 Stanford Law Review* 67 (1969). Note especially the discussion in H. Lawrence Ross, *Settled Out of Court: The Social Process of Insurance Claims Adjustment* (Chicago: Aldine, 1970), ch. 4.

[17] Vilhelm Aubert, "Law as a Way of Resolving Conflicts: The Case of a Small Industrialized Society," in Laura Nader, ed., *Law in Culture and Society* (Chicago: Aldine, 1969), pp. 282–289; and P. H. Gulliver, *supra* footnote 1.

parties reach a compromise settlement rather than litigate. Whether the judge enters into the bargaining depends largely on his own perceptions about what his proper role is. The judge is not necessary to a bargained settlement. If he does enter the bargaining process, it is usually after the parties have nearly reached an agreement. He can then make suggestions for minor changes that the parties can agree to or reject, and he might well be able to narrow the range of disagreement or suggest other points upon which the parties can agree. This is much like what a mediator does between parties.

The bargaining process interacts with the trial process, and each process provides parameters within which the parties negotiate and the processes take place. Figure 1.1 shows graphically what this parallel scheme looks like. The case can move simultaneously along both paths. The resolution, reached by either process, can occur at a number of points, except that the negotiated settlement may occur before the litigation process begins, and settlement cannot occur after the process yields a verdict and judgment. Also, there is no necessary correspondence between particular events in the litigation process and events in the bargaining process. The only correspondence that might arise would take place because, as the litigation proceeds, the parties may be pressured into negotiation more earnestly to avoid the litigation outcome.

The general characteristics of negotiated settlements are outlined in Table 1.2. Comparing Table 1.1 (the formal, adversary pattern) with Table 1.2 shows the substantial differences that exist between the two settlement processes. Yet, these two processes parallel each other in many of the disputes that arise in American society. The fact that two such diverse processes can occur simultaneously suggests the potential for great variations in procedures used for settling disputes in America.

AN ECONOMIC MODEL OF THE DECISION TO LITIGATE

The first decision that a potential litigant must face is whether to litigate at all. Many factors may influence the decision to litigate in particular cases. Some of these influences are quite irrational.

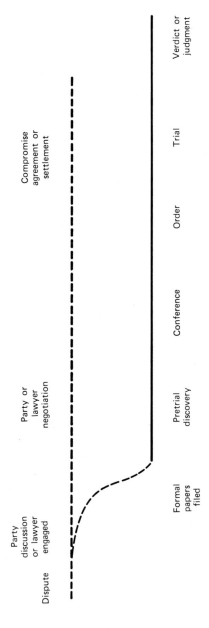

Figure 1-1 Bargaining and litigation processes portrayed on a time continuum.

Table 1.2
Characteristics of Negotiated Settlements

Characteristics	Description
1. Communication	Outcome depends on accurate calculations and precise and honest communication of information; cooperation between parties
2. Subjective	Bargain for result acceptable to parties in this case; no regard for precedential value of outcome
3. Minimax	Minimize likelihood of maximum loss; both parties give up maximum gain to obtain something
4. Dyadic	Results depend on parties bargaining directly with one another; no third party can force a settlement on disputants

Some deal with emotions, and some concern inaccurate information that leads to miscalculations of settlement zones. These psychological and "human" factors will be dealt with in a later chapter.[18] Here the decision to litigate is analyzed in economic terms.

The decision to litigate may be made on the basis of real world costs. Anyone who litigates must be prepared to pay (or have some source that will pay) the costs (monetary) of a lawyer, court fees, and possible loss of pay, as well as nonmonetary costs such as losses in time, prestige, and psychological strain. In addition, a civil defendant who loses the litigation may suffer the costs of damages. This loss is usually the greatest monetary one. It is in the context of costs and probabilities that the potential litigant can assess the situation and decide whether to litigate.

The realities of litigating, presented in a formula, illustrate something of the calculations a completely rational party might make before he decides to go to court. For a plaintiff to be willing

[18] See Vilhelm Aubert, *supra* footnote 1 for a discussion of such psychological factors.

to litigate rather than do nothing, the expected benefits of winning must exceed the possible costs of losing. Expressed as a formula, it would look like this:

$$Lp = P(D) - Cw > 1 - P(D) + Cl \tag{1}$$

Where

Lp = for the plaintiff to decide to litigate

P = the probability of the plaintiff winning

D = the amount of gain expected from litigating (damages)

Cw = the plaintiff's cost of winning

Cl = the plaintiff's cost of losing

The crucial element of the formula is P (the probability of winning), which is composed of various objective and subjective estimates. The higher P is (as it approaches 1.0 or certainty) the greater the term $P(D) - Cw$ will be. The probability estimate, involving multiplication, has much more effect on the litigation calculation than does the cost element. Estimating one's chances of winning is done on the basis of precedent, governing substantive law, and the evidential and factual strength of one's case. Objective case evaluation is part of what a lawyer is supposed to do when he gives advice and counsel to his client. However, part of the probability may also be the product of the party's subjective evaluation of his own case. Even though this factor may be anything but objective, it undoubtedly influences many parties' decisions to litigate.[19] In addition, the probabilities may change for a party as the bargaining process progresses, his perceptions change, and his evaluation of the opponent change.

Further problems in dealing with probability of winning one's case comes from the uncertainty surrounding what the judge and the jury might do in the trial. This uncertainty can only partially be reduced, by the educated guess of the attorney who is dealing with the case. However, the probability of winning one's case (P) can at least be estimated with some degree of confidence by the litigant before he decides what to do with his dispute.

As an example of this formula, assume that the Widget Company estimates that it has a 70 percent chance of winning a

[19] *Ibid.*

contract action against the Able Company for Able's failure to deliver a product to Widget by the date specified in a contract between Widget and Able. Widget has lost $1000 worth of business by this failure, and is seeking that amount in damages. The company expects that winning the case will cost $300 in fees, while the cost of losing would be $200 in attorney's fees. Under this situation, the Widget Company would choose not to litigate since the potential benefit would be $400 [.70 ($1000) − $300] while the potential loss would be $500 [.30 ($1000) + $200]. If the chances of winning went up to 75 percent, the potential loss would be equal to potential benefit. To litigate either the chances of winning would have to be higher that 75 percent, or the costs of winning would have to be reduced.

The calculation for a defendant involves the same kind of formula but, the defendant's calculation is different. Once a defendant has been served with a complaint, he is under some compulsion to respond by filing an answer and engaging an attorney. Yet, some defendants do not go through this process —they do not even appear in court. Rather than litigate, they decide to have a default judgment entered against them. Therefore, the defendant's calculation involves deciding whether to contest the case, and this decision is made on the basis of least loss. If a defendant chooses not to contest the case, he will incur none of the costs of losing *(Cl)*. However, in such cases the probability of losing (P) becomes 1.0 or a certainty so that the defendant's loss will be the damages sought by the plaintiff *(D)*. The cost of winning for the defendant, if he does choose to contest the case *(Cw)* is the money he will *have* to pay to win. The defendant's calculation here may be expressed by this formula.

$$Ld = D > Cw \tag{2}$$

Where

Ld = for the defendant to decide to litigate.

D = damages sought by the plaintiff

Cw = costs of winning (not being held liable)

In those cases where the damages sought are greater than the cost of the defendant winning the suit, the defendant will choose to litigate. In most cases the defendant would be better off defending (litigating) unless the costs of defending and winning are quite high (greater than the damages). Using the example above, if the Able Company thought it could pay something under $1000 for attorney's fees and successfully defend the law suit, it would choose to do so, using the formula presented above.

The calculations outlined above are made by the plaintiff and the defendant, independently of one another. They would make this calculation in order to decide whether to litigate a dispute or do nothing about the conflict, and these two formulas can be used to determine each party's initial stance regarding the conflict between them. Many disputes probably never go beyond this first calculation by the plaintiff, who decides that his possible gain is not large enough to justify continued efforts against the defendant. The precision with which parties make these calculations varies with the quality of legal advice, the emotional or psychological state of the party, and other, less precise factors that will be discussed later.

NEGOTIATIONS MODEL: CIVIL LITIGATION

If both parties have decided that it is economically wise to litigate rather than do nothing with the case, then the choice between litigating and bargaining can be made in an effort to determine whether it is wiser to litigate the case, seek the zero-sum solution, or negotiate a compromise agreement—that is, to reduce the risk of maximum loss by accepting a lesser loss.

The formula for negotiation is based on the existence of a zone (X in the formula below) in which the defendant's highest offer exceeds or is equal to the plaintiff's lowest acceptable offer. The formula is:

$$P_1D_1 - (C_1 - S_1) \leqslant X \geqslant P_2D_2 + (C_2 - S_2) \qquad (3)$$

Where

P_1 = the plaintiff's probability of winning
D_1 = plaintiff's expected gain (damages)
C_1 = plaintiff's costs of litigating
S_1 = plaintiff's costs of settling
P_2 = defendant's probability of losing
D_2 = defendant's expected loss (damages)
C_2 = defendant's costs of litigating

S_2 = defendant's costs of settling

X = settlement range

Several points about Formula (3) are important. Each member of the formula is separate, and each party's calculation of the opponent's portion may or may not correspond to the other side's calculation. For example, each party's estimate of the costs of litigating and settling that face the other side may be little more than a guess, even though the lawyers may be able to make that calculation with some accuracy. The probabilities $(P_1$ and $P_2)$ are independent of one another, although if both parties are reading the same precedents, have similarly qualified lawyers, and are fairly divorced from the psychological pressures of their case, P_2 should approximate P_1. The litigation costs $(C_1$ and $C_2)$ for each party are fixed in this calculation. In the formula used to calculate whether the plaintiff will litigate (1) the party used two different cost factors $(Cw$ and $Cl)$ since he could choose among lawyers. It might be expected that the cost of winning would be higher than the cost of losing, since better lawyers who would make more effort to build a strong case might cost more than less energetic and poorer quality lawyers. In Formula (3) each side has chosen their lawyer, so C_1 and C_2 are fixed. In contingent fee cases, where the lawyer's fee is an agreed-upon percentage of the amount won by the client, the cost factor is more difficult to calculate for Formula (3).

Using the example discussed above, whether Widget and Able litigate or negotiate a settlement will depend on their calculations in Formula (3). If we take Widget's probability of winning as 75 percent and the damages as $1000, and assume that the cost of litigating for Widget will be $300 and the cost of settling will be $100, then Widget's minimum acceptable offer would be $550 ($750 − $200). If Able expects a 75 percent chance of losing $1000, and the company's cost of litigating is $300 and the expected cost of settling is $150, then the maximum offer Able would make to settle would be $900 ($750 + $150). The bargaining range between these two parties is $350 ($550 to $900). If any offer is made between these two extremes by either party, the other could be expected to take it, rather than to litigate.

It should be noted that Formulas (1) or (2) and (3) present a sequence of calculations. First, a person must determine whether it would be worthwhile to litigate in his case—Formula (1) to (2). If he decides it would be worth litigating rather than doing nothing, then he can calculate whether he should try to negotiate and bargain with the other party to reach a compromise settlement—Formula (3). If litigation is dictated and Formula (3) indicates there is no settlement range *(X),* then the parties should begin formal litigation immediately.

However, because positions are not always clear with regard to Formula (3), most parties at least begin negotiations in an effort to gain a more accurate picture of the situation so they can decide whether they should seriously bargain, and this gives rise to the simultaneous existence of the two settlements path, as outlined in Figure 1.1. This initial pressure to talk probably eventually yields more settlements than would occur if the parameters in Formula (3) were explicitly known by the parties at the outset. Roughly, an average of only 10 percent of the cases filed (begun) actually go to trial. This suggests the usefulness of beginning the litigation by talking to the other party. It is not possible to tell exactly how much the trial figure is reduced by negotiating.[20] Many other factors pressure parties to settle, such as tactical maneuvers and socioeconomic matters that press some parties toward a settlement. However, undoubtedly, some of the settled cases do not appear amenable to settlement on the surface, and only after the parties begin talking to each other does a settlement appear more advantageous than litigating.

One of these factors to be worked into the formula is court delay. Court delay can cause some parties to settle when they would otherwise have litigated immediately.[21] Plaintiffs must discount the eventual value of their expected win by its present value, and this reduces the value of the win so that it is perhaps better to accept a smaller settlement now rather than wait for a

[20] See William Landes, "An Economic Analysis of the Courts," *14 Journal of Law and Economics* 67 (1971); and Richard Posner, *supra* footnote 16.

[21] Richard Posner, *supra* footnote 16; William Landes, *supra* footnote 20; Martin Levin, "Delay in Five Criminal Courts," *4 Journal of Legal Studies* 83 (1975); and Hans Zeisel, Harry Kalvin, Jr., and Bernard Buckholz, *Delay in Court* (Boston, Little, Brown, 1959).

later court judgment in their favor.[22] Defendants benefit from such delay because they enjoy the use of the money that might be lost in litigation; they can earn interest on such money and, thus, their present value of a future damage judgment against them is higher, and their settlement range position would be adjusted accordingly.

In addition, less quantifiable factors may also arise as a result of delay and affect litigation. Delay can force the defendant to settle since evidence will become less available over time—witnesses die, disappear, or forget. If the defendant has the burden of proving a certain point, the delay will pressure him to settle. Since the burden of proof is usually on the plaintiff, the loss of evidence tends to pressure the plaintiff more than the defendant. The exact amount of delay in a court may not be easy to determine or may not be public knowledge. However, most parties, in calculating, probably make at least a rough approximation of the effect of delay on their case.

Negotiations in civil cases are probably normal procedure since most parties seek to learn the other party's position. The actual calculations may be rather rough or approximate rather than precise such as set forth above. However, any sort of calculation such as this probably leads to a good many settlements or negotiated outcomes rathe than litigated ones. While these economic calculations are not the only ones which a party might consider before settling, they do indicate the kinds of considerations that parties weigh in reaching settlements of their disputes.

NEGOTIATIONS MODEL: CRIMINAL LITIGATION

The same kinds of calculations can be made before prosecuting or bargaining a criminal case, as for civil cases. However, the calculations in criminal cases are much less precise (quantifiable) and therefore more difficult to make. Certainly plea bargaining has become a widespread element of the criminal justice system, and this indicates that some sort of minimax calculation is made

---

[22] Richard Posner, *supra* footnote 16, at 420–421; and William Landes, *supra* footnote 20, at 105.

frequently by prosecutors and defense attorneys, and often they choose to bargain rather than litigate the case. The plea bargain is a form of minimax settlement in which the accused minimizes the possibility of maximum loss (maximum prison sentence or fine if found guilty) by agreeing to plead guilty in return for assurance from the prosecution that the charge will be reduced or that the prosecutor will recommend a lighter than maximum sentence. As a second expectation, the defendant anticipates that the judge, in accepting the plea to the lesser offense or in assessing the penalty, will be lenient or take the prosecutor's recommendation as binding.

The difficulty in making calculations in these cases occurs in many instances when the benefits and costs are not monetary. What the parties stand to win or lose is much less precise. What is the monetary value of a person's freedom, or what is the gain for society of imprisoning someone for a period of time? These are very imprecise factors. The cost of winning or losing is generally less specific for criminal than for civil actions. However, there may be a good deal of such calculation in the criminal justice system even if it is highly imprecise.

What is likely to occur in terms of calculations in criminal proceedings is that costs that can be quantified, such as the probability of winning or the per-case cost of the prosecutor's seeking a grand jury indictment, and proceeding through a trial might be put into the formula, while the less quantifiable items, such as the social benefits from incarcerating a person for 10 to 15 years, are not calculated in monetary terms. Thus, the determination of whether to litigate or plea bargain is done on the basis of a few quantifiable factors, which do not account for many of the important considerations that society, as well as the accused, may think are important. The result is that the legitimacy of plea bargaining is much more suspect for criminal cases than for civil cases.

Whereas bargaining in civil cases has occurred widely for some time, and can be viewed as a parallel to the trial process, the same bargaining process occurs in the criminal process with much less acceptance. In civil cases, bargaining is considered to be an appropriate means of private conflict resolution. In fact, in civil litigation the bargained result can be viewed as superior to the litigated outcome since the parties will be more satisfied with the result, which is quicker, and there may be less cost to the parties and to the government that pays the costs of providing the court for civil litigation. However, in criminal matters, plea bargaining has been attacked for a number of reasons, which include its fairness to the accused, its failure to comply with constitutional due process requirements, and its rejection of the trial question of the guilt of the accused.[23]

Conclusions

Figure 1.2 presents a continuum on which various resolution processes might be viewed, as they are examined throughout this book. At one end of the process spectrum there are flexible, informal, minimax procedures where the parties negotiate between themselves to settle the dispute. At the other extreme is the formal, adversarial judicial process that involves the third party—judge and/or jury—who will make various decisions regarding the dispute and its resolution. This end of the continuum involves the parties giving up control of the dispute to the third party, and accepting what decision that authoritative outsider makes, based on the submissions presented by the disputants. Somewhere near the middle of the spectrum is a mixed procedure that may involve a third party—judge, mediator, or conciliator—who is interested in getting the parties to agree to a bargained solution. This seems to involve some elements of each extreme procedure, but to be somewhat different from both. The discussion in this chapter indicates that disputes can move along this continuum, usually from left to right, and that they can be resolved at various points along the way by various processes. Most disputes are likely to be settled near the left end of the continuum, and only a relatively few reach the right side and become court cases.

Chapter 2 examines the many factors that influence the operation of the legal system. They help shape judicial processes, as

[23] Albert Alschuler, "The Prosecutor's Role in Plea Bargaining," *36 University of Chicago Law Review* 50 (1968).

Process	Negotiation	Courtroom negotiation	Courtroom adjudication
Characteristics	Two—party, informal, compromise solution	Third party, informal, mediation, compromise solution	Third party, formal, adversarial, zero—sum solution

Figure 1-2 Continuum of dispute-settling procedures available to litigants.

well as the selection of resolving processes by disputants. These outside factors might be classed as political, social, and psychological pressures; they structure the procedures and the effect of the processes on disputes. They are numerous, but they are also quite different from the precise calculations that have been discussed in this chapter. These additional, external factors may completely submerge the economic factors. The discussion of these important influences on the operation of the legal system is really about the environmental factors that determine who goes to court, when, and with what effects.

2
The Legal Environment

Many factors influence the operation of the legal system in America. This chapter focuses on external factors that influence the demand for court solutions and supports. These provide some of the "authority" that courts, as other political institutions, need to operate effectively. In addition, some attention will be paid to the communications processes that shape demands and supports for the court system. Although this setting of the courts is only part of a systems model of the judicial process and no precise model is developed here, these influences are crucial in regulating the flow of cases, they influence the decision to litigate, and they affect how the courts handle the business brought to them. These influences may be described as the social and political environment of the legal system, and that is the focus of this chapter.

The Demand for Courts

Litigating involves more than a person *wanting* to use the courts to resolve a dispute. Courts have established several preliminary requirements that must be met at the outset, before a court will hear and decide a "case." Courts require that the litigant establish that the court has jurisdiction over the case. Jurisdiction means that the items at issue (property, contract, or events) must be within the subject matter areas the court, by statute, may consider and that the defendant, physically, must be within the geographic control of the court. Courts require the issue be "justiciable"; that is, the dispute must be one that the court can resolve or remedy by deciding the case. The plaintiff must have standing to sue, which requires that he establish that he is the injured or endangered party who would benefit from any remedy that the court would provide at the end of the litigation. A person may be interested in a dispute but not have standing to sue if the resolution of the dispute will have no effect on him. These factors have been used by courts at various times to exclude some cases. They are not precise concepts, nor are they absolute. There are occasions when one of these preliminary requirements has not been fully met, but a court has heard and decided the case anyway. Generally, the lawyers who represent each party either establish that these requirements are met or argue that one of these factors is missing. However, if one of these issues is raised by a litigant in the case (usually the defendant), the burden falls on the opposing party (plaintiff) rather than on the court to establish the court's right to hear and decide the case. These initial considerations are only some of the factors that affect demands made on the courts.

THE LITIGIOUSNESS OF PEOPLE

Litigiousness is another factor that influences the numbers and types of cases presented to courts. Litigiousness is the propensity of people to use court procedures to settle social disputes rather than using alternative means. It is a matter of degree and involves economic, political, psychological, and social-cultural factors.[1] The measurement of it is difficult, if not impossible. However, it is possible to examine the litigation patterns of various parties to gain some insight into the nature and impact of these factors.

One recent study found that organizations (led by banks and other commercial organizations) litigate more as plaintiffs than

---

[1] Austin Sarat and Joel Grossman, "Courts and Conflict Resolution: Problems in the Mobilization of Adjudication," *69 American Political Science Review* 1200 (1975); Joel Grossman and Austin Sarat, "Political Culture and Judicial Research," 1971 *Washington University Quarterly* 177; and Joel Grossman and Austin Sarat, "Litigation in the Federal Courts: A Comparative Perspective," *9 Law and Society Review* 321 (1975).

do individuals.[2] Most large corporations either have in-house counsel, which is a group of lawyers within the company, organized to handle all the legal matters relating to the company, or they have retained counsel, which is an outside law firm paid an annual retainer fee by the company to handle any legal problems that arise. These permanent relationships for legal service facilitate litigation by these groups. On the other hand, individuals and other occassional litigants are unlikely to have such a continuing tie to legal service and thus may find it much more difficult to litigate.

The kinds of plaintiffs that bring court actions clearly influence the kinds of actions brought. In one study most plaintiffs were commercial institutions of one sort or another, and the primary kind of actions were related to the collection of debts.[3] The next most frequently litigated issue was contract actions seeking money damages. Nearly one half of the civil plaintiffs were made up of three groups of commercial interests—banks and commercial lenders, hospitals, and home construction and maintenance.[4] This suggests the relatively heavy use of courts by such corporations seeking resolution of disputes that arise in the course of doing business. Individual people were the next most frequent plaintiffs, and the actions they brought were related to personal injury actions or debts.[5] The kinds of actions brought are generally determined by the kinds of plaintiff involved, so that the use of courts to settle commercial disputes is structured largely by what interests bring actions. The use by organizations, with their established mechanism of in-house counsel or retained counsel, and their substantial economic insterests indicate a good deal about how civil courts are used, and by whom. The kinds of defendants involved in these same kinds of cases are different from the plaintiffs. Individuals are the most frequently named

---

[2] Craig Wanner, "The Public Ordering of Private Relations Part One: Initiating Civil Cases in Urban Trial Courts," *8 Law and Society Review* 423-430 (1974).

[3] *Ibid.*, at 422.

[4] *Ibid.*, Table 3.

[5] *Ibid.*, Table 4.

defendants, both for individual and organization plaintiffs.[6]

One study of litigiousness has recently outlined some of the society-wide indicators of the propensity to litigate, but with much less conclusive results than the study examined above.[7] It appears that the rate of litigation is not directly correlated with the degree of industrialization in a state. There is some indication that litigation rates may be related to subcultural patterns in the United States, although, at this time, there is little empirical support for that expectation.[8] Ethnic groups, such as blacks or foreign-born, might be expected to litigate at different rates than would native white, Anglo-Saxon Protestants. These general variations in litigation resulting from social factors should be weighed in any examination of the litigiousness of a population.

Table 2.1 indicates the plaintiff and defendant combinations for one fiscal year in one of the major federal district courts in the country. These data pertain only to cases that were filed during the fiscal year, and settled or closed within a year and one half. Some cases that had not been closed might establish a different pattern. However, these data do suggest some variation from the other empirical studies discussed above. The primary plaintiff was individuals, rather than corporations or any other civil litigant. A primary target of the individual plaintiff was the government, and most of these cases involved habeas corpus petitions, and other civil rights claims. The next most frequent plaintiff was small or intrastate corporations, and altogether, corporations accounted for just over 25 percent of the actions initiated and settled during the year. In terms of defendants, the government and small corporations accounted for over 60 percent of the cases, while large corporations, and individuals accounted for 18 percent and 16 percent of the cases, respectively. These differences might be due to the jurisdiction of the federal courts, which does not allow certain kinds of cases, and encourages other kinds of actions. Among these cases, the means of disposition were

---

[6] *Ibid.*, Table 6 and accompanying discussion.

[7] Joel Grossman and Austin Sarat, "Litigation in the Federal Courts" *supra* footnote 1.

[8] *Ibid.*, at 343-344.

Table 2.1

Categorization of Types of Plaintiffs and Defendants in Civil Cases Filed in Federal District Court for the Northern District of Illinois, Fiscal Year 1971, and Closed by October 30, 1972*

	Defendant					
Plaintiff	Individual	Interstate Corporation	Intrastate Corporation	Government	Other	Total
Individual	190	157	212	542	24	1125
Interstate Corporation	18	46	53	6	6	129
Intrastate Corporation	47	95	194	17	11	364
Government	50	33	110	2	27	222
Other	0	8	21	10	3	42
Total	305	339	590	577	71	1882†

*Source. The District Court Docket Books for Fiscal Year 1971.
†This total does not include approximately 100 cases in which there was no defendant named, and none required by law.

37

predominantly dismissal at the request of the parties (62.2%) while judgment was entered in 30.8 percent. The cases terminated by judgments included some involving a trial, and many involving default judgments, summary judgments, or other nontrial dispositions.

Political objectives and considerations are one dimension of litigiousness, although this factor is not involved in large numbers of cases. Courts are available as one political arena in which policy can be made or altered if the litigant is skillful in framing the question in such a way as to present a case for the court to decide. As political instruments, courts are somewhat limited by tradition, procedure, and power, yet even their restricted position does not prevent courts from making some policy decisions for people.[9] One interpretation of *Brown v. Bd. of Education*[10] is that no other political arena was available to blacks seeking to invalidate the separate but equal doctrine in public education, and so the NAACP developed a strategy to present the issue to the Supreme Court. Also the reapportionment cases[11] can be viewed as an effort to have the court treat an important issue that the urban populations of this country could not get malapportioned state legislatures to act upon. Thus, particular kinds of interest groups may find a friendly forum for their policy demands in the courts.[12] These cases may be unique, as public interest groups in general litigate very few civil suits.[13]

The role of economic factors in litigiousness has been outlined in Chapter 1. Here the components of the economic factor and their impact on the demands made on courts will be examined in more detail. Court costs (filing fees) are generally not great. The

---

[9] Clement Vose, *Caucasians Only* (Berkeley: University of California Press, 1959) treats this strategy in *Shelly v. Kramer,* 344 U.S. 1 (1948); and David Manwaring, *Render Unto Cesear* (Chicago: University of Chicago Press, 1962) deals with this in terms of the flag salute cases. See J. Woodford Howard, "Adjudication Considered as a Process of Conflict Resolution: A Variation on Separation of Powers," *18 Journal of Public Law* 339 (1969).

[10] 347 U.S. 384 (1954).

[11] *Reynolds v. Sims,* 377 U.S. 533 (1964).

[12] See Clement Vose, *supra* footnote 9; and Clement Vose, "Litigation as a Form of Pressure Group Activity," *319 The Annals* 20 (1958).

[13] Craig Wanner, *supra* footnote 2 at 424–425.

cost of lawyers is the largest monetary cost a potential litigant has to consider. The actual cost of an attorney will depend on the locality involved and the work that needs to be done in the case. In a medium sized midwestern community an uncontested divorce might cost $300, while a contested one could cost $500. The eviction of a tenant by a landlord might cost only $10 in filing fees. The cost depends on whether the work can be done in the office by research and completing the necessary forms, in which case an hourly rate would be charged, or the work requires a court appearance. The cost of a lawyer might be $50 an hour for out-of-court preparation and $75 to $100 per hour for court time. An attorney may take a case on a contingency fee, which is an agreed upon percentage of any award obtained from the opponent. In such a case the attorney might receive 33 percent of the damage award. If the lawyer does not think the case is one strong enough to guarantee some award in his client's favor, he may require a down payment by the litigant, possibly of filing fees or $100 for time and effort.[14] Some cases may also involve the costs of acquiring evidence and witnesses and investigating a case. For example, interviewing witnesses to an automobile accident, or to a crime, takes time and effort; they must be located and it must be learned if they can contribute useful evidence or information to a client's case. These costs may be high if the case is very complex or if this is a case that requires an extensive amount of preliminary work. These latter costs are probably greatest in cases involving corporate litigants or in patent or antitrust cases, although expert witnesses in personal injury cases can also be expensive.

There is no empirical evidence on how many people decide not to litigate because of economic considerations. The costs have varied impact on litigation depending on the wealth of the party. Certainly the quality of legal service provided will vary with the amount of money a person is willing or able to pay. It can be

---

[14] Recently the Supreme Court held that minimum fees schedules for attorneys were subject to the antitrust provisions of the Sherman Act, and that such fee schedules were price fixing. *Goldfarb v. Virginia State Bar,* 95 S. Ct. 2004 (1975). The effect of this may be to produce more diversity in legal fees within a community.

expected that the higher the fee, for a particular service, the better a job the attorney will do. Although this may not always be the case—some high paid lawyers may do very little work, of poor quality—the expectation is not unreasonable.

In some situations the costs can be passed on to others, so that these economic factors are a small part of the decision to litigate. Corporations, which rely on in-house or retained counsel, can often pass legal costs on to the customers who buy the company's product, so these considerations are not likely to weigh heavily on a corporation's decision to litigate. There are several kinds of payment arrangements that are emerging for individual people who seek to litigate. The most well-known would be in personal injury suits where the insurance company pays the legal fees, if not supplies the attorney, or an attorney takes the case on a contingent fee basis. In criminal cases, public defender offices, supported out of tax funds, or appointed counsel, paid out of public money, provide indigents accused of crimes with legal representation at no cost to the accused. Legal aid services, as part of the War on Poverty in the 1960s, provided low-cost or free legal advice and service to people who qualified. These services were largely paid for by the federal government or local contributions, rather than by the user. Prepaid legal service plans are based on regular payment of a small fee by the potential user (just like an insurance premium) in return for which he has his legal needs taken care of by a lawyer, possibly of his own choosing, who is paid from the pool of money collected from the premium payment.

Cultural and subcultural factors also influence litigiousness. In some cultures such as Japan the resolution of disputes by negotiation is considered preferable to resolution by a third party, particularly if that resolution requires formal confrontation.[15] Even within the United States some subcultures may prefer alternatives to litigation. Poor people and racial minorities may litigate

---

[15] See for example, T. Kawashima, "Dispute Resolution in Contemporary Japan," in von Mehren, ed., *Law in Japan, The Legal Order in a Changing Society* (Cambridge: Harvard University Press, 1963), p. 41; and Jerry Cohen, "Chinese Mediation on the Eve of Modernization," *54 California Law Review* 1201 (1966).

less than other groups not only because of economic factors but also because of a general unfamiliary with the legal system and suspicion of lawyers and judges in general. For these groups some informal resolution may be just as acceptable, and much quicker and cheaper than litigation. For example, desertion may be just as satisfactory as obtaining a full-fledged divorce in a court. For the more advantaged socioeconomic groups, cultural values encourage litigation.[16] Some studies suggest that people in highly urbanized and congested living conditions may be much more willing to litigate a dispute than is someone is a rural area.[17]

The impact of the social and cultural factors on litigation is not precise, and is reflected mostly in the general litigation levels for a geographic area or community. Thus, a jurisdiction with many blacks or other minorities may have low litigation rates because alternative dispute settling processes are developed. People's expectations dampen their use of courts. However, how this variable will affect a particular individual's decision to litigate is even less precise. Clearly what does happen is that these factors provide a general disposition on the part of members of these subcultures toward or against the use of courts. This predisposition shapes the outlook of any member when a dispute arises that might be litigated.

In criminal cases, cultural factors may play a substantial role in litigation. This is reflected in the willingness or reluctance of victims of crimes to report them and to swear out a complaint. The first stage of a criminal case is reporting the offense. Thus, if the victim of a burglary does not report the loss, the crime never comes to the attention of the system. In some subcultures, where the police are not trusted, or the courts are viewed as biased, against the interests of the victim, the offense may never be reported. One means of initiating a criminal prosecution is for a

---

[16] See Roger Hunting and Gloria Neuwirth, *Who Sues in New York City? A Study of Automobile Accident Claims* (New York: Columbia University Press, 1962); and Craig Wanner, *supra* footnote 2.

[17] See Craig Wanner, "The Public Ordering of Private Relations Part Two: Winning Civil Court Cases," *9 Law and Society Review* 293 (1975); and Richard Posner, "A Theory of Negligence," *1 Journal of Legal Studies* 72 (1972), especially Tables 4, 6–9, 12–14.

citizen to report a crime, and swear out a complaint that becomes the legal basis for an arrest warrant and the eventual trial of the accused. Many criminal cases are based on complaints signed by the police, but for certain crimes—such as rape, or intrafamily violence—the prosecutor is unlikely to prosecute unless he is assured that the victim will testify in court. Thus, if the victim reports the crime but does not want the offender tried or the victim wishes to remain unknown, the prosecutor will be unable to proceed with the case.

At the individual level, psychological factors may govern the decision to litigate. This element is probably the most irrational and the least measurable empirically. It is generally not tied to a realistic appraisal of the chances of winning. Psychological pressures that influence litigating include the pleasure some people get from the risk of gambling (with whatever odds of winning) in court. People may wish to "get even with" or harass an opponent by threatening litigation or beginning that process. This is exemplified by the so-called "nuisance suits," which some people make a practice of instituting. Other people may not be willing to admit defeat on their own but would accept an adverse court decision, so they press for litigation in weak cases to "save face." Other examples of the psychological factors involved include a tinge of "moral righteousness," or some litigants may persist in litigating, against all odds, because they feel that their case is representative of the claims of many others. These people may view themselves either as "spokesman" for a position or as a "martyr" for a cause. This factor may apply either to individuals or to organizations.

It is unclear what the precise impact of these psychological considerations are on individual litigants, beyond indicating that these probably influence some litigants in their decision to litigate. Predicting which potential litigants will pursue that course on the basis of a particular psychological outlook would require psychological study of individuals, and that is not possible. However, at the broad level of the judicial system, the number of cases and the rate of litigation undoubtedly are magnified somewhat by these factors. It may be that only small numbers of "marginal" people are likely to be controlled by such factors. Yet, it should be acknowledged that these may influence some litigants.

Such psychological factors are most likely to operate in civil litigation where there is substantial freedom for individuals to initiate cases. In criminal litigation, the process is more controlled by system parameters that discourage litigation based entirely upon one's feelings. However, some "sensational" cases may be prosecuted because of the public visibility of the case rather than the strength of the evidence, or a crusading prosecutor may make some decisions on an emotional, personal basis. Many criminal cases are generated by the police. They exercise substantial discretion to apprehend suspects, overlook some violations, and harass minorities. This clearly permits psychological factors to influence the cases prosecuted. In addition, personal psychology operates in criminal cases when the initiation of the case requires a complaining witness. Without this person, often the victim of the crime, the prosecutor is unable to proceed with the prosecution. Thus the reluctance of the victim to appear, or to press the charge, will prevent a case from being presented to the court. This reluctance can be the result of embarassment or emotional reaction to the unpleasantness. Criminal litigation factors will be outlined more specifically below, but as in civil disputes, there is some opportunity for individual idiosyncracies and irrational behavior in the decision to proceed with a criminal prosecution.

These factors—cultural, economic, and psychological—are present in American society and influence decisions to litigate to varying degrees. They are not precisely known or even measurable with the current state of knowledge. However, the continual increase in the rate of civil and criminal litigation is partly due to some of them. Identifying one or more as causal in a particular case would be very difficult to do. Hopefully our understanding of these variables will increase with further research.

POLITICAL SYSTEM CONTROL OF THE USE OF COURTS

Various factors that operate in the political system, institutions and actors, play a major role in channeling or structuring litigation. These might be classified as "gatekeepers" and the major effects of them are to influence the shape litigation takes, block or foster the bringing of suits, and shape how the judicial system will process the cases. These may be conscious policy efforts of the political system, designed to deter or encourage litigation. However, it is more likely these are not consciously designed to influence litigation. Rather they have the side effect that derives from the performance of other, related functions.

Lawyers act as a professional screening system for the court system. Lawyers are considered to be officers of the court, as well as hired representatives of clients. Thus, the screening functions they perform may create conflict between service to the client, and assisting the court in attaining justice. However, the lawyer's first loyalty is to provide his client with the best possible advice. This screening system alters the amount and kinds of cases through accurate advice against litigation, through bargaining or negotiating the case to settlement before litigation, or through providing an inaccurate evaluation of the case that either fosters or dampens the party's interest in litigation. This screen acts like a prism, breaking up a stream of cases and filtering them to different processes.

There are a large number of lawyers in the United States. Currently, there is well over 310,000 lawyers, which is more than double the number in 1900. This suggests something of the litigation orientation of our society, and it suggests the likely variation among lawyers that can be found—in quality, specialization, and social characteristics. Exactly what this growth means for purposes of litigation is unclear, given the growth in population that has accompanied the increase in lawyers.[18] However, it is clear that the availability of lawyers for most people has increased, until it is relatively easy for anyone seeking legal advice to find it. The cost of that advice and its quality are still important variables; however, the availability permits more people to utilize courts for the resolution of disputes if they so choose.

The advice or professional evaluation given by a lawyer may have a good deal of impact on what the client decides to do with a "case." All legal advice is not equally competent and some lawyers may give incorrect or slanted advice to encourage or discourage

---

[18] Joel Grossman and Austin Sarat, "Litigation in the Federal Courts" *supra* footnote 1, at 328–333.

litigation, even though such activity is a violation of the professional code of ethics. Like any profession, there are strata of attorneys. That means that there are some lawyers who practice very specialized kinds of law, have more than enough business to keep them occupied full time, and earn very large incomes. At the other extreme are lawyers who have little business, will handle any kind of case that comes to them, and may not make enough money to support themselves and their families. Lawyers in different strata or levels of the legal profession may very easily give clients and potential clients different kinds of advice on identical problems because of the circumstances in which they find themselves. Some lawyers need business and will give advice according to their own needs rather than the needs of the client, while other lawyers may give inaccurate advice to exclude cases they do not wish to become involved with, no matter how meritorious.[19] Even within a fairly homogeneous community, differing socioeconomic groups of lawyers appear, and the behavior and advice of a lawyer will be governed by his education and social and professional position.[20] Most lawyers probably give their best, professional advice. However the accuracy of such advice is bound to vary just as training, intelligence, and competence of lawyers vary. This system screen is neither uniform in objectivity nor uniform in quality.

One unique aspect of legal-profession control of case flow is the creation and government support of neighborhood law offices in the mid-1960s as part of the War on Poverty.[21] The clients of these offices are supposed to be poor or disadvantaged people who have legal problems but do not have the financial means or awareness to seek out a lawyer for assistance.[22] This

---

[19] Erwin Smigel, *The Wall Street Lawyer* (Bloomington: Indiana University Press, 1969); and Jerome Carlin, *Lawyers on Their Own* (New Brunswick: Rutgers University Press, 1962).

[20] See Joel Handler, *The Lawyer and His Community* (Madison: University of Wisconsin Press, 1967).

[21] Earl Johnson, Jr., *Justice and Reform: The Formative Years of the OEO Legal Services Program* (New York: Russell Sage Foundation, 1974).

[22] See, generally, Harry Stumpf, "Law and Poverty: A Political Perspective," 1968 *Wisconsin Law Review* 694; Harry Stumpf and R. Janowitz, "Judges and the

program was oriented toward the poor as a class. However, the litigation which surfaced was not unique to that clientele. Many cases appeared to be problems with neighbors, children, or spouses, and these, although magnified by ghetto poverty, are not reserved only for poor people. Not all offices handled these cases since they did not meet requirement of problems relating to the poor as a class. Some of the cases that arose were unique, such as welfare problems and some kinds of consumer fraud. These cases did not come to the surface until these legal services facilitated their visibility. Many of these cases involved challenges to federal, state, or local governmental agency policies and procedures. For some critics, this raised the question of whether it is appropriate for the government to finance litigation against itself. This is certainly a debatable question, and as system-generated litigation, it places special demands upon the legal system that have not been raised before. In a sense this shows that lawyers (the facilitators) can magnify or downplay demands depending on system-provided resources (money) and policy. It suggests that lawyers are not likely to take cases unless there is money to be made with them, no matter how justified or meritorious the claims.

A major dimension of system control of courts focuses on criminal cases and the participants in the criminal justice system, especially police,[23] and public prosecutors.[24] Police are crucial to

Poor: Bench Response to Federally Finance Legal Services," *21* Stanford Law Review 1059 (1969); Note, "Neighborhood Law Offices," *80 Harvard Law Review* 805 (1967); Kenneth Fisher and Charles Ivie, "Franchising Justice: The Office of Economic Opportunity Legal Services Program and Traditional Legal Aid." (Chicago: American Bar Foundation, 1971); F. Raymond Marks, "The Legal Needs of the Poor: A Critical Analysis," (Chicago: American Bar Foundation, 1971); and Barbara Curran and Sherry Clark, "Use of Lawyer's Services by Low-Income Persons," (Chicago: American Bar Foundation, 1971).

[23] See, for example Wayne LaFave, *Arrest: The Decision to Take a Suspect into Custody* (Boston: Little, Brown, 1965); and Neal Milner, *The Court and Local Law Enforcement* (Beverly Hills, Sage Publications, 1971).

[24] See, for example, Donald Newman, *Conviction: The Determination of Guilt or Innocence Without Trial* (Boston: Little, Brown, 1966); Richard Engstrom,

the initial screening of potential criminal defendants through their discretionary power to arrest or not, and to charge or not. Most criminal cases are generated through law enforcement efforts of the police since private citizens who are potential complainants often do not wish to sign complaints accusing persons of crimes. The success of controlling police behavior (administratively, or by legal requirements) has varied but control has been exerted on some sorts of police behavior in recent years through wide visibility of the problems, and judicial efforts to prescribe certain kinds of behavior.[25] Obviously, as the visibility of police activity has increased, more concern about the filtering effects of police behavior is voiced and more effort is made to measure and control police behavior and discretion since these factors obviously have a great impact on people and on the courts.

The public prosecutor possesses great discretionary power to prosecute or not prosecute people accused of crimes.[26] The prosecutor's discretion is contained in his authority to charge and prosecute alleged criminals. The choice of what offense to

---

"Political Ambitions and the Prosecutorial Office," *33 Journal of Politics* 190 (1971); Duane Nedrud, "The Career Prosecutor," *51 Journal of Criminal Law, Criminology and Police Science* 343 (1960-1961); and James Eisenstein, "Counsel for the United States: An Empirical Analysis of the Office of the United States Attorney," (unpublished Ph.D. dissertation, Yale University, 1969).

[25] For example, *Miranda v. Arizona*, 384 U.S. 436 (1966) and subsequent literature on the impact of *Miranda* on police and courts, Neal Milner, *supra* footnote 23; Neal Milner, "Comparative Analysis of Patterns of Compliance with Supreme Court Decisions: Miranda and the Police in Four Communities," *5 Law and Society Review* 119 (1970); Michael Wald, et al, "Interrogations in New Haven: The Impact of Miranda," *76 Yale Law Journal* 1521 (1967); and Richard Medalie, Leonard Zeitz, and Paul Alexander, "Custodial Police Interrogation in Our Nation's Capital: The Attempt to Implement Miranda," *66 Michigan Law Review* 1347 (1968). See also, *Mapp v. Ohio*, 367 U.S. 643 (1961). There is also a growing literature on the effects of *Mapp* on police behavior.

[26] See Note, "Discretion Exercised by Montana County Attorneys in Criminal Prosecutions," *28 Montana Law Review* 41 (1966); John Kaplan, "The Prosecutorial Discretion—A Comment," *60 Northwestern University Law Review* 174 (1965); Frank Miller, *Prosecution: The Decision to Charge a Suspect with a Crime* (Boston: Little, Brown, 1969); and Sarah Cox, "Prosecutorial Discretion: An Overview," *13 American Criminal Law Review* 383 (1976)

charge, or whether to charge at all, is essentially up to him. He also has the choice of charging multiple offenses, where the facts contain elements of more than one crime. The prosecutor also has discretion over choice of sentencing recommendations after a conviction. It is these decisions of the prosecutor that provide him with a large amount of the discretion he has over what cases enter the judicial system, and in what form. Although the prosecutor does not have omnipotent control over the decision—he must deal with defense counsel, appointed or retained, the presiding judge in the case and the defendant—he does have a great deal of influence on how and when cases are presented to the courts for resolution.

This discretionary control over the introduction of criminal cases in courts may be influenced by personal factors, the particular case involved, or the political climate in which the prosecutor operates.[27] For example, whether a prosecutor charges a suspect with armed robbery or a lesser crime such as assault may depend on whether the individual has been brought before the prosecutor on earlier charges, and whether he has cooperated with the prosecutor in bargaining a plea of guilty or pressed the state to go to the full route of charging and trial in the earlier case. The prosecutor may decide whether to prosecute and what to charge, depending on how visible the crime is to the community, so if the crime is a particularly heinous one—bloody and front-page material—the prosecutor may feel he *has* to prosecute without bargaining and he *must* charge the highest possible crime under the circumstances. The prosecution's decisions may also depend on how many men he has in his office to handle cases, and how many other cases he must process at that particular time. The prosecutor's decision may well not be based on the merits so much as the economic costs and benefits of handling the case through trial or plea bargaining.

[27] See Herbert Jacob, "Judicial Insulation—Elections, Direct Participation, and Public Attention to the Courts of Wisconsin," 1966 *Wisconsin Law Review* 801; Herbert Jacob, "Politics and Criminal Prosecution in New Orleans," *8 Studies in Judicial Politics*, Tulane Studies in Political Science 77 (1963); and Richard Engstrom, *supra* footnote 24.

The prosecutor's behavior may depend on whether he is running for reelection to office, and whether the election is next week or next year. The prosecutor cannot afford to make a decision on prosecuting a highly visible case during the campaign that will antagonize substantial numbers of his constituents. Although he may be able to make such a decision a year before the need to campaign for reelection, his exercise of discretion is much more constrained by the political costs and benefits as election day draws closer. This kind of control over discretion is not a long-term and dependable means of limiting prosecutor decisions.

It should be evident from this discussion that there are some official structures such as police and prosecutors that regulate some use of the courts. Furthermore, there are universal, unofficial institutions such as the legal profession that also influence the use of courts. These kinds of social structures influence what cases are brought to courts and in what forms.

POLITICAL SYSTEM USE OF THE COURTS

There are cases generated by the political system itself; they require a decision by the courts in the United States either as constitutional questions relating to the operation of the government or as regular legal questions in which the government is one party. Thus, courts operate to define the exercise of political power, and control the political—governmental actors in the system. Despite the visibility of constitutional cases, which is due in part to the appellate court structure, most of the business of courts does not involve these demands, which require definition of how the political system is to operate. Most government-generated cases present legal problems just like other litigants, involving contracts, torts, property actions, and a large group of cases that are unique because they involve litigation under a statute.

The concept of judicial supremacy, which gives courts authority to examine the legality of system actions is very crucial, but it is also limited. The limitations (often self-imposed by courts) are that courts will not deal with certain kinds of these cases except in extreme circumstances, if at all, and courts will not decide certain kinds of questions. In *Fletcher v. Peck*,[28] for example, the Supreme Court refused to hear evidence that the legislators of Georgia had been bribed to pass the grant of land involved in the case, even though it had become a major scandal.[29] Laws, once passed, were to be accepted at face value, though individual legislators could go to jail for bribery. Otherwise, courts would become a new chamber of the legislature. These self-imposed, technical restraints are adhered to in varying degrees and are more important in appellate courts than in trial courts.

The reason for such limitations as these, especially in court examination of disputes involving the political system, is the great reluctance of most courts to involve themselves directly in running the government and making overt policy decisions that courts see as constitutionally left to the other branches of government. The most significant power that courts possess in regards to examining the political system is the power of judicial review, that is, the power to examine the constitutionality of a law and declare the law invalid and inoperative if the court determines that it violates the Constitution of the United States. Even though this power may be exercised rarely and with great caution, it remains a great potential that restrains what legislatures and executives seek to accomplish by means of enacted law. The trial court, which is the major focus of this book, is not frequently called upon to use this power. These courts are usually too busy, and ill-adapted to deal with complicated or esoteric legal arguments that are involved in challenging the constitutionality of a law.

Mention should be made of the government as a civil litigant. All levels of government participate in various commercial activities involving contracts, personal injury claims, and other civil actions. The result is that the government acts as plaintiff or defendant in a substantial number of court cases. However, as a civil litigant, the government acts like any other civil litigant in choosing to litigate, and in bargaining or litigating. The govern-

[28] 6 Cr. 87 (1810).
[29] C. Peter McGrath, *Yazoo: The Case of Fletcher v. Peck* (New York: Norton, 1966).

ment is represented in such cases by the attorney general, state's attorney, or county or city attorney, rather than by private lawyers. Thus, the government is similar to a company with in-house counsel when it seeks legal advice in civil actions.

Table 2.2 outlines the components that might be considered in exploring litigiousness, and what relation each of these factors has to the litigation decision. What these items indicate is that a good many of the decisions to litigate may be made on the basis of determinants other than the merits of the case.

Table 2.2
Components of Litigiousness

Mental–Physical	Actors	Institutional
Cultural Geography Socioeconomic status Political Economic Psychological	} → Lawyers Police }	→ Court doctrines → Litigation

Support for Court Operation

For any public institution (political body) to exist, that body must have enough support to provide its decisions with authoritativeness. In other words, the court's decisions must be accepted by the political system and by society, or else its functions will cease to have relevance for the system, and people will seek other processes for handling their disputes. The authoritativeness of courts and their decisions depend on a mixture of respect for the court[30] on the one hand and agreement with the decision on the other.

From a traditional perspective courts are viewed as objective institutions that are to decide cases in terms of "the law." Some respect for courts is due to this aura or as some have termed it "the

---

[30] See Gregory Casey, "The Supreme Court and Myth: An Empirical Investigation," *8 Law and Society Review* 385 (1974).

cult of the robe."[31] This mystique of authoritativeness or respect for tradition can be eroded by unpopular or blatantly biased court decisions. Courts have traditionally tried to avoid decisions that might greatly injure the prestige and respect that people have for courts, by refusing to decide "political" questions, or by taking a general restraint orientation toward the exercise of judicial authority. However, individual parties who lose cases may become antagonistic toward the courts in general, and seek to reduce the general level of respect that courts view as important. Courts may not be able to counter the dissatisfaction of individual litigants, and generally the judiciary makes no overt effort to satisfy parties or to make "popular" decisions.

Most individual losers are willing to accept the court decision even when it is unfavorable to their interest. This is because most people who are willing to litigate do so because they feel they can get an objective and "correct" decision from the court even if unfavorable. Thus, those who are not likely to accept a court decision as authoritative are *not* likely to *litigate* in the first place. Although some observers feel that political decisions by courts, especially recent Supreme Court decisions, are very detrimental to its image and to the respect that the population has for the Court, courts may still be given business when respect among some litigants is low. The controversial decisions may not injure the court as much as some would believe.[32]

After the trial court resolution of a conflict, the loser has an alternative set of opportunities on what to do next. The loser may accept the decision, may appeal it to a higher court with appellate jurisdiction over the trial court, or may seek resolution of the dispute in an alternative political arena. Most losing litigants choose to accept the trial court's decision as final and not pursue the dispute to another arena. This solution may be based on a lack of funds, time, or inclination, or a lack of political force to obtain such an alternative resolution. It may also be based on a lack of merit—the appeal may not be meritorious. However, for most

---

[31] Jerome Frank, *Courts on Trial* (New York: Atheneum, 1949), ch. 18; and Gregory Casey, *supra* footnote 30.

[32] Philip B. Kurland, *Politics, the Constitution, and the Warren Court* (Chicago: University of Chicago Press, 1970), ch. 5.

litigants who lose, the court's decision is acceptable and they see no need to get a reversal. This kind of acceptance of the initial decision involves some costs to the loser—money, time, and psychological—but these seem to be relatively small for most litigants.

Although acceptance may involve only the two parties connected with a case, a number of court contests directly affect larger segments of society. Examples include school desegregation decisions that involve changing attendance patterns among all of the schools in the community. The school desegregation cases, whether at the local, trial court level, or at the U.S. Supreme Court level, do relate to and affect a large portion of the American population. Acceptance of a decision by an aggregate involves the likelihood of individual variation. A group with a narrow interest may react in fairly unified fashion. A large group, with diverse or general interests, may produce a wide variation of acceptance of a court decision, and may yield more overt acts of noncompliance among some pockets than would either an individual litigant or a unified group. At the same time it is likely that a large, diffuse membership group will also contain some apathetic people that produces some acceptance and support for the decision. Probably the most important factor in group acceptance of court decisions, and group support for the judicial system is the intensity of the group's position. The more intensely held an adverse position is the more likely the group will display some opposition to a court decision. However, even intensely held positions may be muted, if the group is generally supportive of the political and judicial systems.

Although a general respect for courts exists, the reality that courts (and judges) err, and are not always objective, apolitical forums, undoubtedly reduces this consensus of support among those who believe they are disadvantaged by the biases.[33] The underlying consensus may change over time, in degree, and in

---

[33] Herbert Jacob, "Black and White Perceptions of Justice in the City," *6 Law and Society Review* 69 (1971); see also J. Croyle, "Tort Law Doctrine, Courts and Social Expenditures: The Courts as Primary Policy Makers," (paper prepared for delivery at the 1975 American Political Science Association Meeting, San Francisco).

membership. Thus, the "socially acceptable" means of conflict resolution may change from courts to private means as parties feel courts are unnecessary or less favorably disposed to their claims, or if parties feel they can create better resolution institutions by agreement. One example of this might be the growth of commercial arbitration since the first decades of this century. This occurred as many commercial concerns became suspicious of some court decisions favoring laborers and their interests, or favoring interpretations of contracts that were contrary to established nineteenth century usage.

In any society there is bound to be a segment of the population that will not accept court decisions. However, this group of people who do not accept the courts as legitimate is small in number and not likely to have a substantial impact on court operation unless they seek to use violence to change dispute resolution processes. Some of the antiwar groups in the late 1960s in America became generally dissident to the point of openly rejecting court decisions and other governmental decisions, for example, the Weathermen. When a significant portion of the population rejects the authoritativeness of the decision, that is, fails to give the decision support or fails at least to acquiesce in the decision, then the system is in jeopardy. Until that occurs, individual rejections, even if numerous, are not likely to destroy or incapacitate the system. Such small-scale rejections can create difficulties and cause changes to be made in the system, however.

The components of support for the judicial system indicate that the individual (single person or organization) is the narrowest source from which support or opposition can derive. The "Group" either as litigants or the affected community, provide an intermediate sized target for court decisions, and source of support. Many of the groups that may oppose unfavorable court decisions are also likely to look to the courts as one of the few arenas that give their causes legitimacy, since usually they have little social or political strength. As a result they derive great benefit from favorable court decisions, and have a very difficult time repudiating unfavorable decisions, given the legitimacy they give the courts on favorable decisions. The general public is the most diffuse, and may provide little, but widespread support for the courts and their decisions. The kinds of response that are provided vary a good deal. Although any of these sources can accept an adverse decision directed at them and thus provide support, many opportunities exist for variations in behavior and compliance, and partial (or symbolic) acceptance of a decision. Here even when litigants or others who are opposed to a court decision seek to circumvent or blunt the impact of a decision, they may give symbolic support (in the form of lip-service or other statements or acts that indicate acceptance and compliance), because overt noncompliance or defiance is not generally accepted as appropriate.

Communication in the Judicial Process

Communication is very important in the political system because it provides information on how society absorbs policy decisions, as well as informing society of what policies are being pursued by the system. These two separate kinds of communication also exist in the judicial system. On the one hand the court's decisions are communicated to the general population and to particular litigants. This process is called feedback since it is essential for the political system to inform the population of the outputs of the political processes. On the other hand the population and litigants communicate with the judiciary by various means. This latter communication is usually in the form of inputs (demands and supports) for the judicial system. However, each of these types of communication are important to the functioning of the court system.

COMMUNICATION TO THE COURT

The court system learns about problems through the kinds of cases that are brought to it. However, there are several difficulties in terms of accurate communications. Certain kinds of disputes *must* be litigated, so the court learns little, except how many such cases there are, by means of litigation. Examples of such cases are divorce and probate. On the other hand, where the law is not well developed or where there are alternative means of settling a conflict, litigating the dispute signals to the court that either the alternative mechanisms are failing, or that the court should clarify the law on the subject so that there will be less confusion, and less need to litigate the issue. An example of these kinds of cases is school desegregation cases that literally flooded the federal courts after the 1954 school desegregation decision of *Brown.* Throughout the 1960s and up to the present, local school districts continue to litigate the issue of desegregation and the procedures which are judicially acceptable to eliminating segregation—such as busing, neighborhood schools. The continued litigation of this issue should suggest to the courts either that their original pronouncements of desegregation policy were unclear, or that many school districts disagree with court orders, or wish to find alternative solutions to those the court has put forth.

At the trial court level, there may be no opportunity for the judge to get a perspective on the business brought to him—he is too busy processing the cases to analyze what they are telling him. On the other hand, an appellate court judge, who has time to reflect on judicial business may be getting only a select portion of such business. The result of these difficulties is that the communication to the judicial system by this means is not always precise or accurate. Furthermore, what reaction the judicial system produces to these kinds of communications, either at the trial or appellate levels, is not necessarily uniform. Some judges may try to accommodate various claims and cases, and fully realize the problems which are being communicated, others may recognize the problems but feel unable to respond, and still others may neither recognize nor wish to do anything about the problems that are repeatedly brought to the court.

In contrast to communication by litigation, public comment on judicial decisions is overt and widespread. This appears in newspapers—on the editorial page and in the news columns—in scholarly journals, and in popular magazines. The accuracy and expertise of these publications in treating court decisions, as well as the selectivity of such treatment, may raise questions about this form of communication. However, no communication is without some warpage or "noise" and the result is that any political body—courts included—must attend to such information and reaction as it sees fit. Courts, of course, are supposed to be above politics, which means they do not have to consider criticism, but many courts and individual judges may be quite concerned with acceptance of their decisions.[34] What impact such comment has on court decisions is not clear, and it is likely to have little overt impact. However, it is likely that judges may think carefully about a decision and the public's reaction to it, if they feel it may cause repercussions or opposition.

COMMUNICATION FROM THE COURT

A central and important mechanism in communication with courts is the legal profession. The lawyer provides information about individual cases to clients, other lawyers, and even the general public. Lawyers may provide more or less accurate information, and their own preferences about the case will shape how they translate the decision to the litigant. Since the information lawyers provide shape a litigant's reaction to court decisions, lawyers obviously are important in terms of future litigation as well as reaction to decisions.

Beyond lawyers' affect on feedback, the most universal influence is the press; certainly this is a widely functioning, general communication mechanism. The press interprets and channels court decisions with greater or lesser fidelity.[35] Either because of technical shortcomings or for political reasons, the press may not accurately translate court decisions. Communication by the press certainly does not cover all court output. Rather, only highly visible court decisions make the front pages of newspapers or the editorial pages. Few newspapers regularly publish the

---

[34] Mr. Dooley said, "No matter whether the constitution follows th' flag or not, th' Supreme Court follows th' iliction returns," from Peter Finley Dunne, *Mr. Dooley's Opinions* (New York: Harper, 1901).

[35] David Gray, *The Supreme Court and the News Media* (Evanston, Northwestern University Press, 1968); Chester Newland, "Press Coverage of the United States Supreme Court, *17 Western Political Quarterly* 15 (1964); and Chester Newland, "Legal Periodicals and the U.S. Supreme Court," *3 Midwest Journal of Political Science* 58 (1959).

winners and losers in civil cases, as they do the baseball scores, and the press obviously does not interpret or analyze these cases. In recent years some newspapers have published the daily events in courts—the civil and criminal actions processed in court that day, as well as the police and fire calls for the day. The effect of these is generally in terms of "gossip" among various members of the community, rather than as information about the functioning of the judicial systems. Furthermore, the reaction has been not in terms of the court's work, but in terms of the particular individuals who are involved in the cases. In cities where the litigants are anonymous except to those who already know of them and their dispute, such publication probably is insufficiently newsworthy to justify printing the daily court events at all.

Normally, press coverage is most likely of U.S. Supreme Court decisions—in the national press—or the local press will cover local or state cases that concern local policies or politics. Certainly, sensational criminal trials are covered, as are "political trials" when they occur. Some civil suits such as noteworthy personal injury cases (and awards) may receive some coverage, but these are not very numerous, and their coverage is based on some element of uniqueness (newsworthiness). News coverage can affect litigation through accurate or inaccurate coverage, especially at the local level, which causes local officials or inhabitants to choose a particular litigation strategy as a result of the news reporting.

The information provided by lawyers and the press may structure future litigation by fostering or discouraging appeals or additional litigation. The information may shape or influence the perceptions and expectations that the litigants have toward the judicial system. Also, information may suggest to potential litigants that a case might be worth litigating now, which previously was not. For example, if a court changed landlord-tenant law, many tenants might be more willing to litigate disputes with their landlords. If a court changes the criminal law pertaining to persons accused of crimes, some convicted criminals may petition for habeas corpus, or other forms of relief, after learning of the change in the law. These communication processes may not provide accurate information to the public. Yet, they will shape individual perceptions and the information can generate or discourage various kinds of litigation activities.[36]

Courts in recent years have had increased visibility. Although in the past decades nearly the only people concerned with a court decision were the parties involved in the case, today many more people are interested, and in some cases, affected by the decisions. Court decisions, relating to group actions and interests, now involve the courts in many policy areas, especially areas that affect the civil rights and duties of all citizens rather than narrow, commercial law interests. Such issues as landlord–tenant cases, taxation questions, and consumer fraud disputes all are of wider public interest than most of the traditional contract, tort, and property cases that used to be litigated.

There are now more "listeners" who, though not involved, are concerned about courts and court outputs. One example of this is a "court watcher" program that involves interested citizens in an effort to sit in court, usually criminal, observe the proceedings, and publish their observations.[37] This has brought to light some court practices that are questionable to say the least. It provides informal control of courts, and the information source is completely unofficial and unassociated with any vested interest. In addition, the participants in such a program are interested, although not involved, in litigation, and their observations generally lead to much greater understanding of the process.

As more people become aware of courts and court decisions, and more people see courts as viable political arenas for the settlement of disputes, this is reflected in the growth of cases initiated in courts in recent years. The data contained in Table 2.3 illustrates this growth for civil cases, in the Federal District Courts. The various studies of litigiousness discussed above suggest that litigation is growing much faster than population, and that this indicates something about the inclinations of people.

---

[36] Herbert Jacob, *supra* footnote 33.

[37] A noncriminal court watchers program formed a partial basis for a major study and publication in the area of small claims courts: The Small Claims Study Group, *Little Injustices: Small Claims and the American Consumer: A Preliminary Report to the Center for Auto Safety* (Washington, D.C.: The Center for Auto Safety, 1972).

Table 2.3
Number of Civil Cases Initiated in Federal District Courts, by Year

Year	1940*	1950*	1960*	1970*	1972†	1974†
Number of cases	34,734	54,622	59,284	87,321	96,000	103,600

*Source. Appropriate editions of Annual Report of the Director of the Administrative Office of the United States Courts (U.S.G.P.O.).
†Source. *Management Statistics for United States Courts 1974,* Report of the Director of the Administrative Office of the United States Courts (U.S.G.P.O., 1974), p. 120.

Evidently more people know about courts, think the judiciary might be receptive to their claims, and are able to afford the time and money for litigation. This change in the orientation of people toward the judicial system is due, in part, to the communication process.

Conclusions

This chapter has presented the context in which litigation takes place. The factors that bring the courts business and give the courts support with which to operate can be viewed clearly. Although our empirical knowledge and understanding of many of these forces are imprecise and in need of further exploration, this environment is useful in understanding what courts do, and why they are presented with certain kinds of cases and supports. Figure 2.1 suggests an outline of these forces to indicate their relationships with one another and their impact on the judicial system. This diagram is inexact but it points out the major elements discussed in this chapter and it should provide a perspective from which to view judicial processes.

The litigants in this diagram can be individuals, corporations, groups, or governmental bodies that litigate or defend civil or criminal cases. Litigants are the group most directly affected by the judicial process, and the ones most likely to place specific demands and provide specific supports for the judiciary. The factors that influence demand for judicial resolution of conflicts are set forth, and are drawn largely from Table 2.2 and the

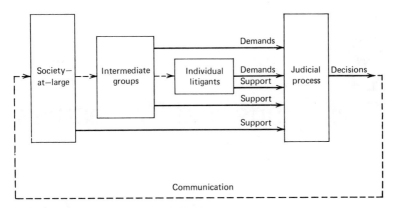

Figure 2-1 The structure of judicial inputs.

accompanying discussion. The supports that exist are drawn from the individual litigants (winners *and* losers), from intermediate groups (such as local communities, or interest groups concerned with the question being litigated such as the NAACP), and from society at large, which provides both the diffuse support for the system, and the pool from which individual litigants and interested groups are drawn. These three sets of participants can be viewed as differentially affected by judicial decisions, and probably differentially informed about them. However, the attentive public is increasing in size, and is providing more litigants as time goes by.

Important parts of this rudimentary system diagram are left open at this point. The output and feedback loop will be discussed in some detail in Chapter 7, which deals with the impact of judicial decisions. The processes by which the "judicial process" accommodates demands and produces outputs will be examined extensively in the following two chapters. Chapter 5 provides some perspective on difficulties that exist in the processing of cases through various judicial channels. Thus, the remainder of the judicial process will be outlined in subsequent discussion.

3
Civil Courts and Procedures

The basic thesis of this book concerns the variety of procedures that operate in the legal system in America. The standard procedure will provide us with a model against which we can compare differences that emerge in various courts, and it will provide some understanding of the elements of procedure that are important or even crucial to litigation. The civil litigation model will show the full-blown legal process as an arena for the settlement of private disputes. The criminal process differs significantly from this pattern and will be explored, in detail, later. The model process that will be described assumes that the initial calculations and negotiations described in previous chapters have occurred, and that the parties decide to litigate the issues.

In addition to the model that is developed here, a description of a number of specialized, civil courts will be presented. This is done to examine how particular courts compare with the model. These particular courts do not exist in all court systems in the country, and their procedures vary from one system to another where they do exist, but these procedures will illustrate the diversity of variation from the model.

The Litigation Model

For purposes of understanding civil processes in American courts it is necessary to outline two somewhat different model procedures. The first, and most widely known is for actions involving monetary damages. The second is equity procedures, where the remedy is not monetary. Since the 1930s when equity procedures were "merged" with civil damage procedures, the differences have not been great. There are no specific or unique procedural provisions for federal courts to follow in dealing with equitable matters as opposed to traditional, civil matters. Some states have maintained separate equity courts and procedures, however. Part of the discussion below focuses on equity powers separately from civil process, in an effort to distinguish the two where the differences are important.

CIVIL DAMAGES MODEL

Most cases begin with the plaintiff contacting a lawyer. Although lawyers may not be essential to litigation, it is rare that a party will try to proceed in court without a lawyer, or for a private party to be permitted by the judge to proceed without an attorney. The role the attorney plays at this stage is to analyze the plaintiff's case and assemble it into a formal Complaint. When the plaintiff, or most likely his attorney, files the written Complaint with the trial court, the pleading stage of a case begins. The Complaint is a formalized document that contains the allegations of fact about the occurrence, the allegations of injury caused the plaintiff by the defendant's behavior, and specifies the damages or remedy that the plaintiff is seeking to compensate for the injury. The Complaint must establish that the court has jurisdiction over the case and that venue is properly in the court. Venue means that the event or the injury occurred in the geographic area over which the court presides. Thus an action must be brought in the same area where the event took place.

It is crucial that the plaintiff's Complaint constitute a cause of action, that is, it must contain a clear outline of the acts that caused the injury, and the legal basis for claiming that this injury should be repaired by the defendant. Unless the plaintiff can later prove these alleged facts upon which relief can be granted at the trial, he will not have established his legal right to damages, and will be vulnerable to a motion by the defendant to dismiss for failure to state a claim. The lawyer's job in framing the Complaint is to state precisely a claim for damages so that the court will permit the case to proceed to a later stage of the process.

The Complaint must be served on the defendant in order for the defendant to be informed of the action against him. In civil litigation, the plaintiff may have the legal duty to serve the complaint, although in most jurisdictions, the sheriff or other officer of the court will be given the task of serving process. Although service may be an easy matter, it can be difficult if the defendant is not in the jurisdiction, avoids service by "disappearing," or never receives the service because it was dumped down the "sewer" by a commercial process serving company that will allege service without making it effective. The problem with failures of service are that most states require certain procedures for serving process, and these procedures are verified by filing an affidavit with the court. The affidavit does not prove service, but only swears service and, if a defendant was not served in fact, he has no notice of the action against him and, thus, he may never show up in court to defend. This can lead to a default judgment against him, although most courts are reluctant to enter such judgments.

Once service of the Complaint is completed, the defendant is given time to prepare an Answer. This is a formalized, written document presented by the defendant that either denies the allegations of the Complaint or admits them. Normally the defendant will deny all the allegations of the plaintiff, except those over which there can be little contest (such as what day of the week the 14th of August was). The purpose of the Answer is to present the court and the Plaintiff with a statement of those items that the defendant denies about the plaintiff's claims and would contest at the trial. Not only does the Answer contain denials, it may also contain affirmative defenses, which are legally sufficient claims of the defendant that exempt him from legal liability in the case, even if all the facts are as the plaintiff states them. An affirmative defense would be something like the Statute of Limitations, which bars the plaintiff's recovery of various claims if he fails to bring the claim within the statutory time period—such as one or two years from the time of the accident. The defendant may also present a counterclaim against the plaintiff. This is a claim made by the defendant, growing out of the same set of facts, that alleges that the plaintiff owes the defendant certain damages or caused the defendant certain injuries. In either of these cases—affirmative defenses or counterclaims—the plaintiff will be given an opportunity to complete a Reply, which is a formal statement explaining why the defenses or the counterclaims should not be allowed.

The purpose of the pleading stage of a case is to serve notice on the defendant of the nature of the claims alleged against him, and to notify the court that a potential case is being formulated. In addition, the pleadings provide the plaintiff with whatever arguments or justifications the defendant has for avoiding liability in the case. The issues in the case are defined much more precisely later, in the pretrial process. However, some general outlines of the case should be apparent by the time the pleadings are closed. The pleading stage may take some time, depending on the kind of case, and the amount of time the parties devote to negotiations during these initial stages of a trial. Also, the trial judge may contribute to delay or prompt pleadings depending on whether he will permit delay or postponements in filing the Answer, the Amended Complaint, or the Reply. The delays or time requirements at this stage are usually not too pressing since the case is still a long way from trial, and there is a great deal of work that has to be done by the lawyers before the case is firmed to the point of being calendared for trial. Delays at this point may also foster bargaining between the parties and, if successful, this may eliminate the case from any further judicial proceedings.

This pleading stage generally involves the last major efforts by the parties to bargain a settlement. The case can always be removed from the court, if they agree to another solution. However, the filing of a Complaint and an Answer suggest that the positions of the parties are becoming hardened and less flexible. Empirically, a substantial proportion of the cases filed in court are settled during the pleading stage. As the discussion of Table 2.1 indicates, the large percentage of dismissals (over 60%) involved voluntary dismissals during the pleading stage because the parties had settled their dispute.

The kinds of disputes that usually emerge from the pleadings are questions of liability and damages. Liability pertains to the legal responsibility for injuries suffered by the plaintiff. Obviously the plaintiff claims that the defendant is liable for the damages (having caused the plaintiff's injury) and thus he must be forced to pay the plaintiff's losses. The damage question is a question of fact that can be determined separately from the liability question. Damages relate to the amount the plaintiff has lost as a result of the injury to him. This may be an exact amount that can be carefully specified, by submitting the plaintiff's doctor and hospital bills, for example. However, it can also involve conjecture, as when the plaintiff seeks damages for "pain and suffering" in a personal injury case or when a contractor alleges that he suffered the loss of his business reputation because of defendant's failure to deliver goods on time. These kinds of damages are very imprecise, and may allow the jury or the judge to include an amount as a "fudge factor" in an otherwise precise setting.

The stage between the pleadings and the trial, commonly known as the pretrial stage, involves two basic functions. First, the issues are clarified and eventually are set down in the Pretrial Order of the judge for resolution at the trial. Second, the pretrial stage is the point at which the lawyers gather their evidence, and prepare for trial on the matters in dispute. This stage involves a number of possible activities on the part of the lawyers, the parties, and the court, aimed at developing the facts and preparing for trial. The most important procedural aspects of this period are Discovery and the Pretrial Conference.

Discovery involves the processes of learning something about what the opposing side has in the way of evidence, what their arguments will be and, in many cases, the gathering of evidence for one side through questioning and examining the other party or his witnesses, if he has control of the evidence. For example, if the opposing party is the manufacturer of a commercial product that the plaintiff purchased and that injured the plaintiff while he was using it, the plaintiff may have a very difficult time trying to prove that the manufacturer was negligent because the defendant manufacturer has control over all the information that exists about the production of the item. Discovery rules permit the plaintiff to present the opposing party with questions (called

Interrogatories) and to demand that the defendant provide answers to these. Since the judge must be convinced that the information sought is essential to the plaintiff's case and that the defendant (or his employees) can provide that information, Interrogatories can be limited by judges. But Interrogatories do allow the gathering of important information. During this stage, the lawyers for both sides may take Depositions from the witnesses of the other side, so that each party will have some idea of what the case for the other side looks like, and how strong it is. Again, since Depositions are supervised by the judge, and since the opposing lawyer is present, it is unlikely that the questioning party will gain any major admissions from the opposing side.

Both Interrogatories and Depositions are taken outside of court, by the opposing attorneys. If a witness or party refuses to answer the questions posed, a court order may be obtained, if the judge is convinced of the appropriateness of the questions, which forces the party to answer the question. The Interrogatory is written (usually a large number of these are presented, as a list) and the answers are written out. A Deposition involves oral questioning, and oral responses, which are usually recorded, in transcript form. The purpose of Discovery is to learn the basic parameters of the opponent's case and to acquire evidence that is controlled by the opponent and that is essential to the requesting party's case.

The Pretrial Conference comes at the end of the Pretrial stage, when the parties are prepared to go to trial. Usually the Conference is presided over by the judge, and the Conference largely depends on his views and efforts. Initially the Conference was suggested as a means of bargaining or a final negotiating stage—a last ditch effort to avoid the trial. In fact, few judges require the parties to bargain at this stage, so the Conference becomes the proceedings at which the issues to be tried are set down in a written, formal order.[1] This serves the function of cutting out the excess points that cannot be disputed because of whatever evidence the Discovery stage turned up and the points upon which

[1] See Maurice Rosenberg, *The Pretrial Conference and Effective Justice* (New York: Columbia University Press, 1964).

the parties agree. Although the pleadings can be general or vague, the Pretrial Order is a specification of the particulars of the plaintiff's claims and the defendant's defenses.

The time required for the Pretrial Stage varies a good deal. It can take a long time, if the case is complex, or if the parties are earnestly seeking to settle the case and the negotiations are taking a long time. Judges may often not push parties during this stage, since the possibility of settlement is present, and preparation of one's case may take a good deal of time and effort.

There are a variety of safety-valve procedural mechanisms under the control of the judge, during these early stages of a trial, that would exclude the case from court, or produce a final judgment without the necessity of a full-fledged trial on the merits. The Summary Judgment Motion permits a court to enter final judgment if the pleadings and other supporting materials such as affidavits, depositions, answers to interrogatories, and other items obtainable through the discovery process indicate there is no "genuine issue of material fact." The judge rules on the motion by evaluating the materials for an issue of material fact. This process involves the judge's exercise of his discretion in close cases. For example the parties may agree on the facts but dispute whether an insurance company's contract with a person covers a given situation. In that case, the parties may submit the insurance policy (the contract) and simply ask the judge to decide the legal question of whether the company must pay the insured person under the set of facts in the case. The judge can decide the issue by reading the insurance contract and examining the agreed-upon facts. A Motion for Judgment of the Pleadings is like a summary judgment motion, except the judgment on the pleadings utilizes no supporting materials other than the Complaint and Answer. It is available earlier in the pleading process than the Motion for Summary Judgment. These motions are not frequently successful unless it is quite clear that no issue of fact need be tried, but parties often seek to use such a motion as a means of circumventing the trial proceeding. Such a motion can be used as a delaying tactic to prolong the period of pretrial or to delay going to trial, and it should be kept in mind that some parties use it only for that purpose. The general use of such motions, however, is probably not to serve dilatory ends.

The Pretrial Order contains a statement of the issues in dispute and it sets a date upon which the trial will begin. The Trial is the formalized procedure for determining the facts in a particular case and then having the judge apply the law to those facts to resolve the dispute between the parties. The trial includes the selection of the fact finder: either the judge, in a bench trial, or a jury. The choice is usually open to the defendant, and his decision to have a jury trial or a bench trial may be governed by the kind of case, the complexity of the issues, or the amount of time a jury trial is likely to take. The fact-finder (judge or jury) is supposedly an objective party who has no bias in favor of either party, and who has little, if any, information about the case. Thus he is supposedly open to the presentation of evidence as the only basis upon which he may decide the case that is tried.

There are two stages to jury selection. The first involves the composition of the jury panel, which is a group of 50 to 100 prospective jurors. This is drawn by some random procedure from the population of the jurisdiction, and is the group from which the particular jury (petit jury) is drawn for any case. Often voter registration roles are used to draw the panel—which excludes local residents who have not registered to vote. A practice of drawing panels from the telephone directory was invalidated because it excluded the people who did not have telephones at that time, and this introduced a systematic bias into the jury panel.[2] The panel supposedly cannot exclude any identifiable group of citizens, but there is still some chance for particular groups to be systematically excluded from the panel process.

The selection of the 12 jurors can be a very difficult process —called the voir dire—if the case is notorious, or if the attorneys feel that the jurors are biased despite what they say to the contrary. For example, it may be impossible for a black defendant to get an unbiased jury in some communities, whether blacks are systematically excluded from the jury panel or not, because the jurors would probably not admit to any racial bias even if asked directly. It is quite possible that they may not realize that they are biased, but yet have formed opinions and impressions about the litigants during the empanelling process. While bias may not be

[2] *Thiel v. Southern Pacific Co.,* 328 U.S. 217 (1946).

avoided and it may be difficult to discover, the empanelling process is designed to control or minimize the likelihood of a great amount of overt bias. The selection process is supposed to insure randomness. However, some lawyers seek to get certain kinds of people on the jury panel and either exclude them or insure they are included.[3] The kinds of categories sought depend on the trial issues. For example, in a trial involving a young person, it may be to that party's advantage to select jurors of comparable age rather than much older. In the trial of a business company, that party would like to have middle class, or upper, middle class business executives and wives on the jury. These kinds of preferences cannot be articulated in the voir dire, and depending on the panel of prospective jurors, it may be very difficult to get people with particular characteristics.

Various prospective jurors can be excused on their own request, such as doctors, lawyers, and other professionals whose time on a jury could create great hardship for them. Some judges tend to excuse certain kinds of individuals, depending on their dress, their demeanor in the courtroom, or their requests, and being excused is up to the judge's discretion. The result is that with some selectivity in the panel, the judge's excusing of some jurors, and the attorney's exclusions for cause in the voir dire, the jury may be skewed toward one side's interest, or it may be composed of people of one general type—middle class housewives who cannot convince the judge that they have a valid reason to be excused.

Once the jury has been selected, the plaintiff is called on to present his case-in-chief, which is the primary case to prove the points in the plaintiff's case. This is done through witnesses who testify, under oath, to the questions posed by the plaintiff's attorney. Because of the nature of proofs and the adversary process, it is necessary to call witnesses who can testify to very basic things that many people would assume have occurred. For example, if the plaintiff suffered a broken arm in an automobile accident, a doctor must testify to that fact, and show the kind and extent of

[3] Hans Zeisel, "Dr. Spock and the Case of the Vanishing Women Jurors," *37 University of Chicago Law Review* 1 (1969).

damage. The plaintiff's presence in the courtroom with a cast on one arm does not prove to the court or jury that he has a broken arm. (The cast is not even evidence.) Another example would be in a civil action for assault and battery; the plaintiff must produce witnesses who saw the defendant physically hit the plaintiff, or else the plaintiff's allegation that the defendant caused his injuries has not been proven.

The presentation of evidence, by either side, involves a technical set of rules of evidence. These rules, which vary from one jurisdiction to another, have developed over time, or have been enacted into statute, and are designed to exclude material that is immaterial, irrelevant, and nonprobative from the trial. This information screen is a particularly complex one, and the rules of evidence permit only certain kinds of evidence to be presented. One famous rule of evidence is the rule against hearsay, which excludes statements offered as proof of the assertion made in the statement. Thus a statement by a witness that the defendant told him that he was driving too fast for conditions, and that he knew he couldn't stop in time to avoid an accident, could not be used to prove that the defendant was going too fast (unless it falls within one of the exceptions to the rule). It is hearsay because it is offered to prove the defendant was going too fast. A variety of technical exceptions do exist, including admissions by the defendant. Thus the defendant's statement to the witness could be offered as proof of the matter asserted—the defendant was going faster than would reasonably be expected under conditions. It is an admission by the defendant, which is contrary to his interest, and its probative nature is increased because he said it about his own actions. This undoubtedly restricts many parties' presentation of cases. However, the rules are designed to shield the trier of fact from all extraneous matters that are not relevant to the issues at trial. Of course, many, if not most, trial judges apply this technical set of screens as they interpret them. This permits a good deal of variation from court to court or even from one trial to another conducted by the same judge.

The parties have varying burdens in the trial. The plaintiff usually has the burden of going forward with evidence. This means he must come forward with evidence that establishes his claim against the defendant. It is also usually the case that the plaintiff has the burden of proof, which requires that the plaintiff's evidence establish the essential elements in the plaintiff's case to the satisfaction of the fact finder. In civil trials, the burden of proof is usually the 'Preponderance of the Evidence,' which means that in order to win, the plaintiff must establish, to the jury's satisfaction, that he is more likely to be right than wrong. The defendant should win if the plaintiff failed to carry this burden.

Occasionally, the defendant may end up with the burden either when the defendant is alleging an affirmative defense, or when the plaintiff succeeds in transferring the burden of proof to the defendant through the presentation of adequate evidence to cause the shift. In theory, if neither party submitted any evidence, the party with the burden of proof would lose the case for failure to carry the burden. However, in some civil cases, the party with the burden of going forward with the evidence may, upon the presentation of some evidence (often not enough to satisfy the burden of proof), shift the burden to the other party, who must then successfully establish his factual position or lose the case.

At the end of the plaintiff's case-in-chief, the defendant has several options. He can present his case in defense of his position. Alternatively, he can rest his case to the trier of fact without presenting any evidence, alleging that the plaintiff failed to prove his case adequately. The defendant can also utilize a Motion for a Directed Verdict, which alleges that the plaintiff failed to present substantial evidence to raise a question of fact for the jury to decide. If the judge grants this motion he instructs or directs the jury to return a verdict for the defendant, and the trial is over, completed, with the defendant the victor. Obviously this motion, and the result of granting it, have drastic results, and it is rarely successful, but it is available, procedurally, to the defendant.

Assuming that the defendant chooses to present his case, the procedure is similar to the plaintiff's case-in-chief. The defendant's witnesses testify as to the facts that the defendant alleges prevent liability in the case from being attached to him. This would include evidence establishing the defendant's affirmative defense, if that exists, as well as evidence relating to the same facts as the plaintiff's evidence but which tends to contradict that of the plaintiff's. The defendant's efforts are to sow enough doubt in the mind(s) of the trier of fact so that the plaintiff's case will not have been proven sufficiently to satisfy the burden of proof. The same rules of evidence that govern the plaintiff's case presentation control the material that the court can allow the defendant to present into evidence. There are some differences in what the defendant can use as evidence and in what the plaintiff can present in some cases, but these concern mostly some criminal prosecutions, some states, and are under sharp attack at this time.

Part of the trial process of presenting evidence involves the opposing party's cross-examination of witnesses. This process, a major aspect of the adversary process, is designed to attack the credibility and certainty of the witnesses, and to suggest to the jury that the testimony is not reliable because the witness is less certain than he appeared during direct testimony, or that his memory is not as precise as it appeared at first. The scope of cross-examination is limited to the matters that were raised on direct testimony. The defendant cross-examines the plaintiff's witnesses, individually, when the plaintiff's attorney is finished asking questions of each of the witnesses. The plaintiff's attorney cross-examines the defendant's witnesses in similar fashion immediately after the defense attorney has finished the direct examination. Obviously the value of this process is to permit the trier of fact to compare the witness for both sides of the case, to see how reliable each witness is, and to weigh whether the trier should believe what the witness has testified to on the witness stand.

Each party is permitted, after all the evidence is presented, to give some sort of concluding arguments on the case each has presented, to the trier of fact. In a jury trial, at the end of these statements the judge will give the jury any formal instructions that are necessary before the jury retires to deliberate. The jury instructions are formal statements of the applicable law, if that is necessary for the trier of fact to consider during their deliberations. The attorneys for both sides may have major differences over what instructions should be given, and the judge will decide what final instructions will be given. Usually, jury instructions are much more important in criminal prosecutions than civil cases. However they can become a point of major contention in a civil trial as well.

At the close of the defendant's case, the plaintiff may move for a directed verdict, on the same grounds as the defendant would have moved at the close of the plaintiff's case, that is, no issue of fact has been raised. A similar motion, for a judgment notwithstanding the verdict (judgment n.o.v.), can be made after the verdict is returned by the trier of facts. These motions permit the judge to rule on the merits of the case without regard for the verdict of the jury, because there is no real issue for the jury to decide. For example, if the plaintiff failed to prove, or introduce any evidence, supporting his claim that the defendant was driving in a negligent fashion, the judge could grant a directed verdict for the defendant, or a judgment n.o.v. for the defendant even if the jury returned a verdict for the plaintiff.

The processes of jury operation are designed to shield the jurors from outside influence during their deliberations. The jury may take written copies of the instructions into the jury room but nothing else. How they proceed, once isolated, depends on the jury. However, they usually have elected a foreman at the beginning of the trial, or they are instructed to do that when they begin deliberating. Their deliberations are secret, and no outsider, except the court's clerical personnel, who supply requests for paper, food, and other items, can have contact with the jury. The jury can ask to see the judge again, if they do not understand an instruction, or would like to obtain some of the trial evidence for closer examination. The jury gets to review the trial transcript if the judge allows, and some states allow, others do not, jurors to take notes. If the jury is deadlocked—cannot reach the required decision, by the required majority—the judge can give them a "dynamite charge," which is a fixed instruction, traditionally designed to get the jury to work harder to reach the decision. Juries must be unanimous, unless the parties stipulate they will accept a specific majority vote as a verdict. The jury has 12 members unless the parties agree to a smaller number.[4] What factors the jury considers in its decisions are controlled by the evidence provided at the trial, and the guidelines of the instructions. However, it is possible, and in some cases, evident, that the jury considers extraneous factors, or decides because they misunderstand the law.[5] It seems that no amount of control can determine what mental processes the jury will follow and, while the judicial system seeks to confine jury deliberations to the evidence presented, there is no certainty that that is accomplished.

A more widely used procedural means of circumventing the trial process, once it has begun, is best categorized as a general motion to dismiss the case. This motion may be made at any point in the process if dismissal is sought. The basis for such a dismissal varies widely depending upon when it is raised. Such a motion, if granted, dismisses the case "with prejudice," which means that the party against whom the case is dismissed is not free to reinstitute the case. The most frequently used motion to dismiss, however, is a voluntary motion, which means that the parties themselves wish to have the case dismissed. This motion is available at any time prior to the return of the verdict by the jury or the judge makes the findings of fact. A voluntary dismissal signifies that the parties have negotiated a settlement, even while the trial has proceeded, and they would like the trial to be terminated since their dispute has ended, by the alternative bargaining process. The voluntary dismissal is without prejudice, which means that the case can be reinstituted at any time by one of the parties agreeing to the dismissal. Such a reinstitution would only occur if the agreement between the parties falls through at a later date, and one of the parties decides that a completed trial would be the best way to resolve the conflict. If the case is reinstituted, the trial begins anew, rather than where it left off. In addition, the court

---

[4] Some states permit a criminal jury of less than twelve. See *Johnson v. Louisiana,* 406 U.S. 356 (1972). The Fed. R. Civ. P., Rule 48 permits the parties in a civil suit to agree to have a jury of less than 12 members, and to accept a less-than-unanimous verdict.

[5] Harry Kalvin, Jr., and Hans Zeisel, *The American Jury* (Chicago: University of Chicago Press, 1971).

order entering the dismissal may include the settlement terms that the parties have agreed to. This may encourage the parties to comply with the settlement since it is part of the record, and the judge may try to get the parties to reaccept that settlement rather than to begin new litigation if one party wishes to reinstitute litigation.

The Judgment is the final entry by the court at the close of the trial. It is the order of the court requiring the losing party to take nothing if that is the plaintiff, or to pay the assessed damages if the defendant loses. The judgment is based on the jury verdict, unless the court grants a judgment notwithstanding the verdict. Failure of a losing defendant to satisfy the judgment permits the winning plaintiff to have the court declare him a judgment creditor (and the defendant a judgment debtor), and it is possible in such a case for the court to force foreclosure of the debtor's property and belongings until the judgment is satisfied. If the judgment is that the plaintiff take nothing, then the issue is barred from further litigation in a court. Since the defendant has a concluded trial and judgment to support his claim, the matter is *res judicata,* already settled, and therefore closed to further adjudication.

The time required for the trial varies a great deal. Probably it is most likely determined according to the complexity of the issues to be tried, the amount of evidence available to the parties and how much of it must be presented by them. If the issue is simple, the presentation of evidence may be finished in an hour or two; complex issues and cases may involve weeks of testimony. The average presentation of all the testimony might safely be put at between one and five days, but that is open to many exceptions, and certainly there is a pretrial waiting or preparation period that involves some time. The jury deliberations may take 15 minutes, or three or four days, again depending on the issues, on the evidence presented and, sometimes, on the members of the jury. The problem of delay in court procedures is probably most relevant when the parties are not adequately prepared to present their cases at trial, and when they seek to use procedural motions as dilatory tactics simply to achieve delay. The actual presentation of evidence and the jury deliberations may involve a minimum of time, once the parties are ready to present their cases, and have finished with whatever motions they wish to present to the judge in an effort to circumvent the trial itself.

With the entry of judgment by the trial judge, the court, as a conflict resolving arena, has done all that it is capable of doing for the disputants. The dispute between the parties has been officially resolved by the governmental, authoritative body that has been designated for such proceedings. There are posttrial motions that the losing party can make, such as a Motion for a New Trial. This motion asks the trial court to correct an alleged error that it made in the original trial by granting a new trial. Generally, the trial court will not grant such a motion, unless there has been a very major error, which the trial judge becomes convinced was an error on the basis of the new trial motion papers. However, despite this last motion, generally the trial is completed with the entry of judgment. An appeal of a legal error to a higher court is always possible; this will be discussed in Chapter 6.

The process model, which has just been outlined, is generally used in American trial courts, although there are variations in terms of procedures. Figure 3.1 presents the basic civil process framework. This civil process usually operates regardless of the subject matter of the trial. Whether the case involves a property lot line, a contract for the delivery of goods, or an automobile accident, the procedure molds the issues into the same form, and requires that the trial proceed in similar fashion.

EQUITY MODEL

There are several unique considerations that make equity procedures somewhat different from the civil model outlined above and in Figure 3.1. For discussion, the federal rules pertaining to equity and injunctions are discussed.[6]

There is a major difference between civil damages and equitable relief; equity involves injury that cannot be remedied by the payment of monetary damages after the fact of injury has been proven. In various kinds of injury, such as pollution, school

---

[6] See Fed. R. Civ. P., Rule 65.

Defendant	Procedural Steps	Plaintiff
Motion to dismiss for failure to state a claim upon which relief can be granted	*Pleading stage*	Complaint
Answer		
	Motion for judgment on the pleadings	
	Pretrial stage	
	Discovery	
	Interrogatories	
	Depositions	
	Motion for summary judgment	
	Pretrial Order	
	Trial stage	
	Selection of the jury	
		Witnesses and cross-examination
Motion for directed verdict		
Witnesses and cross-examination		Motion for directed verdict
	Post-trial stage	
	Concluding arguments	
	Instructions to jury	
	Jury verdict	
	Motion for judgment n.o.v.	
	Entry of judgment	
	Motion for new trial	

Figure 3-1 Process model of civil litigation.

segregation, or other problems where money will not repair the injury and the injury is "permanent," there may be a need for an injunction. The plaintiff has a heavier burden than in civil cases, because it must be proven that the injury is "irreparable," that is, the injury is permanent and not subject to "repair" by the payment of damages. Irreparable injury is not a precise set of circumstances and the judge has substantial discretion in determining whether the plaintiff has provided an adequate basis for finding such injury. Given the usual need for speed in the granting of equitable relief, a set of temporary, and quick procedures have been developed for the plaintiff seeking such court assistance.

Equitable relief is provided in one of two forms, either an injunction prohibiting behavior or a court order specifying that some positive act shall be done. There are three processes for providing injunctive relief. The Temporary Restraining Order (TRO) can be issued by a judge, without the defendant even being given notice of the proceeding. The judge, on motion, with supporting papers from the plaintiff, may issue a TRO for any period of time up to 10 days. During that time, the defendant is notified and given opportunity to move for dissolution of the TRO. The purpose of this injunctive relief is to preserve the status quo until a more detailed examination can be made by the court. The plaintiff must convince the judge that the actions of the defendant are so injurious that the TRO should be issued without any presentation by the defendant. Although the defendant can be notified and can participate in the TRO hearing, this procedure is used primarily in *ex parte* (one party—plaintiff) fashion.

The second form of equitable relief is the Preliminary Injunction, which can be issued only after notice and hearing to the defendant, but which can extend for any period of time that the judge sets. The Preliminary Injunction is designed to prevent irreparable injury until the full trial can be held on the matter; this may require a substantial delay under some situations. The plaintiff must, again, convince the judge of the need for such relief, but the defendant is present and can present contrary arguments and materials to the judge. The procedure for dealing with the request for a Preliminary Injunction is a hearing at which both parties are permitted to present the arguments, motions, and supporting materials in adversary fashion. It is not a trial, but is held in open court and, if an injunction results, it is a court order against the defendant.

The ultimate equitable remedy is the Permanent Injunction and is issued only after a complete trial on the matter. This may take the form of a regular trial, with the submission of oral and written evidence to support the claims of the plaintiff and defendant. There is no jury present to hear the evidence, as the equity power of the court is in the "judge's sound discretion" and thus a jury has traditionally not been considered appropriate. The usual procedure does not involve much preliminary pleading and pretrial processes. Generally, because the pleadings and pretrial materials have been developed in the proceedings for TRO or Preliminary Injunction, the trial on the Permanent Injunction usually proceeds without much delay and without many procedural hindrances.

The other form of equitable remedy—a positive court order —is rendered by the same procedures as outlined above for regular injunctions. In fact, the positive remedy is also an injunction. It merely orders the party to commit a particular act—such as delivering title of the property to the new owner, or desegregating a school system quickly, following a particular, court-devised plan. The only difference is the positive acts required of the defendant when the court issues it. The positive directive involves the same hearing and trial stages. In fact, often, the devising of a positive court order requires a much more detailed trial and presentation of evidence by witnesses, before the court will issue such an order, than a negative injunction.

Specific Court Procedures

Many variations from these models occur in American trial courts. These variations arise from several factors, such as the purpose for which a particular court is created and operated, or the subject matter of the court, which requires a unique procedure for handling the disputes that are brought to it. The courts and the procedures that are described below illustrate the texture of variations from the model processes. These courts may not proceed by means of the adversary model that has been outlined, but they may rely on a core of standard procedures no matter how diverse they appear in operation. These courts process a large number of cases—probably many more than the model outlined above. These courts are specialized and are of limited rather than general trial jurisdiction. The negotiation mode of settlement, outlined above, is the informal and predominant model of handling disputes. The procedures followed by many of these trial courts tend to mix or combine the formal model of procedure with the bargaining model, so that there are many hybrids of procedure.

SMALL CLAIMS COURT

Small Claims Courts are intended to operate much differently from the traditional, adversary process. The court is designed to provide a simple, speedy, and easily available arena in which small claims can be settled. The court process is intended to be inexpensive and thus provide a court where official determinations of disputes can occur, but with a minimum of difficulty or delay.[7]

The procedure of a Small Claims Court is not complicated, and is designed to allow rapid processing, and a minimum of delay from the filing of the complaint to the resolution of the conflict. Dilatory tactics by parties are usually not permitted or are at least not encouraged by complicated procedural frameworks. The costs of bringing an action in such a court are minimal, possibly from $1.00 to 3.50 and this is the clerical cost of record keeping and filing the complaint. No lawyer is required to proceed in Small Claims Courts, and in some states, lawyers are specifically excluded.[8] This reduces the costs that a litigant has to incur to

---

[7] "Small Claims Court: Reform Revisited," 5 *Columbia Journal of Law and Social Problems* 47 (1969); Michael Minton and Jon Steffanson, "Small Claims Courts: A Survey and Analysis," 55 *Judicature* 324 (1972); and Beatrice Moulton, "The Persecution and Intimidation of the Low-Income Litigant as Performed by the Small Claims Court in California," 21 *Stanford Law Review* 1657 (1969).

[8] "Small Claims Court," *supra* footnote 7, at 57; Beatrice Moulton, *supra* footnote 7, at 1658; and Small Claims Study Group, *Little Injustices: Small Claims and the American Consumer A Preliminary Report to the Center for Auto Safety* (Washington, D.C.: Center for Auto Safety, 1972), pp. 95-110.

bring the action. The procedures are easy to initiate by a layman. The courts are supposedly easy to use and easy to get to,[9] although they may not be as available as was intended.

Generally, the jurisdiction of Small Claims Courts depends on the amount in controversy, and the maximum amount that such courts can handle ranges from $300 to $1000 or $2000. It has been suggested that these amounts may have to be adjusted frequently due to inflation.[10] However, jurisdictional adjustments are rarely made. Some jurisdictions are based on the type of action involved, giving Small Claims Courts jurisdiction over contracts and torts but not over actions that involve complex issues generally viewed as jury questions such as libel or slander actions.[11]

The procedures used in Small Claims Courts are for the plaintiff to file his claim with the court's clerk. This is usually a fill-in-the-blanks form that is obtained from the clerk's office. The clerk may be willing to help the plaintiff, explaining what to do, or provide a written set of instructions that clearly explain how one proceeds.[12] Upon payment of the small filing fee, the action is commenced and the defendant is usually sent a copy of the complaint by registered mail. The service of the complaint on the defendant can be a difficult problem if the state's statutory requirements for service are not adjusted for small claims proceedings.[13] The defendant may be required to answer the complaint, within a short (5 to 20 day) period or no answer may be required at all.[14] At the time the defendant is served with notice of the action against him, he is also notified of when he is to appear in Small Claims Court. Usually the appearance date is within

---

[9] Some small claims courts in New York City are open for night sessions to facilitate working people's access. See "Small Claims Study Group," *supra* footnote 8, at 44 ff; and "Small Claims Court," *supra* footnote 7, at 57.

[10] "Small Claims Court," *supra* footnote 7, at 59, 66-67.

[11] *Ibid.* at 60, 67.

[12] It has also been found that some clerks are extremely uncooperative with claimants. "Small Claims Study Group," *supra* footnote 8.

[13] "Small Claims Court," *supra* footnote 7, at 52-53.

[14] For example, in Illinois it is established, by statute, that all allegations in the complaint are assumed to be denied by the defendant. Thus, joinder of claims is automatic. Michael Minton and Jon Steffanson, *supra* footnote 7, at 324.

three months of service, so the case is presented to the judge and the matter is litigated in a relatively short period of time.

The judge in Small Claims Court is supposed to elicit all the necessary information from both sides.[15] The procedures are summary, the rules of evidence usually do not apply, and the judge can modify procedures in any way he wishes if he feels it will further the end of resolving the dispute fairly and expeditiously.[16] The role of the judge as a passive presider is modified in these courts to permit him to take direct charge of discovering the facts and issues and issuing a decision.[17]

The parties may present witnesses, other than themselves, if they wish. Whether or not witnesses are used depends on the kind of action involved, and how much preparation the litigant can make. The use of an attorney, who often tries to formalize the small claims process, may mean witnesses are used as much as possible.

There is no jury in a Small Claims Court. Since juries generally mean the application of strict rules of evidence, presence of counsel, and witnesses, they would formalize the process and slow it down. This exclusion has been challenged on the ground of violating the Seventh Amendment of the U.S. Constitution. However it is generally agreed that appellate procedures, from Small Claims Courts (discussed below), make that constitutional claim unwarranted. Also some observers would argue that if a plaintiff chooses Small Claims Court, he automatically waives his right to jury trial.

Judgment in a Small Claims Court is usually quick. The judge renders judgment immediately after he has heard the parties' oral statements and has questioned them or their witnesses. Normally, the judge does not deliberate in chambers over his decision. The whole, in-court process may take 5 to 20 minutes. Usually the judge will announce his decision orally and judgment will then be entered by the clerk. The judge writes no opinion explaining his decision, and often he does not even explain his decision orally to the two litigants who are still before him. There is no record or

---

[15] Beatrice Moulton, *supra* footnote 7, at 1867; and "Small Claims Court," *supra* footnote 7, at 48.

[16] "Small Claims Court," *supra* footnote 7, at 54-56, 63.

[17] *Ibid.* at 50.

transcript made of the trial, and no published opinion is entered. Thus, the decision is based on the fill-in-the-blanks complaint, possibly an answer that denies the allegations in the complaint, the plaintiff's and defendant's stories or explanations, and any information a witness may add to this.

Nearly all small claims structures allow for appeal by the losing party.[18] Appeal usually is to the trial court of general jurisdiction where a trial de novo is conducted. That means if the losing party is dissatisfied with the resolution by the Small Claims Court he can get a complete trial, with all the procedural protections, formal rules of evidence, jury, record, and representation by counsel, which he did not get in the truncated, initial proceeding. This may alleviate the constitutional claim regarding a jury trial in these civil cases. It may also meet whatever legal arguments are raised because of the absence or exclusion of legal counsel at the small claims level.

What this procedure and structure show is that there is, in many jurisdictions, an exceedingly simple and quick means of self-help for parties suffering some monetary damage that cannot be settled without some authoritative procedure.[19] Problems do exist with the operation of many Small Claims Courts, as will be discussed in Chapter 5. However, the difficulties should not cloud the essential purposes and procedural outline of these courts. They do provide an open arena in which many claims can be settled, in a quasi-formal arena. Recently, some observers have begun investigating empirical questions relating to Small Claims Court.[20] Examining who uses these courts, and with what results,

---

[18] Either party may appeal in some Small Claims Courts. See, John Steadman and Richard Rosenstein, "Small Claims' Consumer Plaintiffs in the Philadelphia Municipal Court: An Empirical Study," *121 University of Pennsylvania Law Review* 1309, 1324 (1973).

[19] It should be noted that, often, the only remedy Small Claims Court can provide is money damages. Various forms of equitable remedies are excluded because of the costs and difficulties of execution under the simplified structure of Small Claims Courts. "Small Claims Court," *supra* footnote 7, at 58; and John Steadman and Richard Rosenstein, *supra* footnote 18, at 1318.

[20] Barbara Yngvesson and Patricia Hennessey, "Small Claims Complex Disputes: A Review of Small Claims Literature," *9 Law and Society Review* 219 (1975) is a survey of the literature on this subject.

has produced some interesting findings, which disturb some observers. Most plaintiffs are businesses and government agencies. Some studies indicate that the major plaintiff is the independent businessman or local merchant, and his small claims might be exactly what the original small claims advocates sought to facilitate. The primary defendant, however, is poor people, often the debtors on sales contracts. This is distressing to some observers,[21] because a substantial proportion of the judgments obtained in Small Claims Courts are default judgments. For various reasons, the defendants in many small claims cases never appear to contest the case. Furthermore, the likelihood of winning if the defendant shows up to contest is not high. Either because the plaintiff is a regular, represented by counsel, and familiar with the court, or since the defendant is often not represented by counsel, or is unable to present his case adequately, using small claims procedures, the defendant often loses. See Chapter 5 for a more detailed discussion.

There are alternative settlement procedures that have been suggested or adopted for the resolution of small claims. For example, Pennsylvania allows its county courts to establish a compulsory arbitration system for claims of less than $2000.[22] Arbitration of small claims appears relatively successful, and it has provided an alternative, if not a complete solution, to small claims problems.[23] In addition, conciliation can be used as an alternative means for settling such claims. In fact, conciliation procedures are not mutually exclusive with the established small claims court procedures since small claims judges can, if they are so inclined

---

21 See Small Claims Study Group, *supra* note 8; Carl Pagter, Robert McCloskey, and Mitchell Reinis, "The California Small Claims Court," *52 California Law Review* 876 (1964); and Beatrice Moulton, *supra* footnote 7.

22 Maurice Rosenberg and Myra Schubin, "Trial be Lawyer: Compulsory Arbitration of Small Claims in Pennsylvania," *74 Harvard Law Review* 448 (1961) is an examination of how this procedure works in one Pennsylvania system. See, John Steadman and Richard Rosenstein, *supra* footnote 18, for a description of a more traditional small claims procedure in Philadelphia Municipal Court.

23 Small Claims Study Group, *supra* footnote 8, at 91-92; and Maurice Rosenberg and Myra Schubin, *supra* footnote 22. Barbara Yngvesson and Patricia Hennessey, *supra* footnote 20 provides a discussion of these reforms and changes in small claims procedures and what might be expected of them.

and if time permits,[24] seek to conciliate or mediate the dispute if the parties appear to be interested in a compromise.

PROBATE COURT

When a person dies, his property becomes an estate, which requires certain kinds of judicial supervision. The Probate Court is designed to supervise the distribution of the real and personal property in an estate, and to protect certain societal interests in the process. For example, all jurisdictions have some scheme of estate tax, and the Probate Court must insure that estate taxes have been paid. In addition, creditors of the deceased are normally given a period of time during which they can file claims for the debts that the deceased owed, and the Court insures the validity of those claims, if they are challenged, and sees to it that the administrator[25] of the estate pays the valid claims. Finally, the heirs of the estate and the beneficiaries must be provided for either in the written will, or in the common law of inheritance (if there is no will). Any challenges to creditor or heir or beneficiary claims must be examined by the Court and settled by the Court before the estate can be probated. In a few jurisdictions some heirs are given the option of taking under the written will or taking under the common law of inheritance. Where this is possible (usually the wife of a decedent can exercise the option) the court must make certain that the option is exercised intelligently and within the legal time period. Most of these functions can be characterized as clerical in nature, so that judicial or clerical supervision of the probating process is the primary function of the Probate Court. The state has an interest in the transfer of property—whether by sale or inheritance—and that interest is supposedly protected by means of judicial supervision.

The substantive law of probate can vary widely among jurisdic-

---

[24] Small Claims Study Group, *supra* footnote 8, at 88; Beatrice Moulton, *supra* footnote 7, at 1664 ff.

[25] An administrator is a court-appointed person who has the power and the responsibility to administer an estate. He is usually required to post security (bond). An executor is just like an administrator except the executor is appointed by the deceased, in the will, and may not have to post security. An administrator, often a bank, handles all intestate estates.

tions, and most have some combination of the common law and statutory revisions incorporated into a statutory code of probate. As a result, the Probate Court system varies widely among states. Some states have separate Probate Courts that sit only to probate estates, and other states give probate jurisdiction to the trial court of general jurisdiction, which means they devote a small portion of their time to matters of probate. There has been a recent effort to systematize Probate Courts and their procedures in the American Bar Association's Uniform Probate Code.[26] However this model has only gradually been considered or adopted by any jurisdiction. The result is that most states treat probate matters with a patchwork of substantive rules that may be incomprehensible and harsh, and with a somewhat disorganized court structure. However, most states provide some kind of rubber stamp or clerical function for the majority of estates that are neither challenged nor complex.

Often, there is no need for an adversary proceeding in a Probate Court unless the estate is challenged in some fashion. The substantive law of the state provides some guides for establishing the validity of the will and, if someone challenges the written instrument, the court will proceed in an adversary, formal fashion to determine whether the will is valid. Probate Court will also use some kind of adversary procedures if the claim of a creditor is challenged. The executor may claim that the deceased did not owe the claimant anything, and some kind of proceeding must settle that dispute. Furthermore, certain kinds of creditor claims may be given priority, or first opportunity, against the proceeds of the estate, and where the priority of claims becomes an issue, the Probate Court must determine the question. However, most priority questions are determined by the statutory law of inheritance, rather than by an adversary hearing. In the adversary proceeding, the plaintiff is normally the claimant—the party claiming that the will is invalid, the party challenging the creditor's claim, or one of the parties claiming priority. The plaintiff is generally the party who has the burden of attacking the existing situation.

The defendant in most of these cases is the estate, although the

[26] (St. Paul: West Publishing Co., 1969).

creditor whose claim is challenged may also be put to the defense of his position. Because of the nature of the questions that are presented to the Probate Court for determination, juries are not used. The questions are generally determined by the substantive law on the subject, and the judge is supposed to be the knowledgeable expert on such subjects. The validity of the will may present questions of fact that could go to juries, if the Probate Court is given authority to provide jury trials. Testimony and the accompanying rules of evidence may operate in such disputes in court. However, only a small, if notorious, portion of the estates probated actually raise questions that must be resolved by the adversary process.

Much of the Probate Court's function is also clerical in nature.[27] The necessary papers are filed by the executor or his attorney with the clerk of court, and official notice is published by the clerk to any creditors or unknown heirs. There is generally a six week to six month waiting period that allows time for claims to be presented. The administrator officially appointed by the court then prepares to distribute the estate. The court may have to rule on creditor's claims but, once accepted, the creditor must be paid by the administrator. The remainder of the estate, after estate taxes and creditor's claims have been paid, is distributed to the heirs and beneficiaries as provided for by the common or statutory law or by the will. The Court must give its official approval to each step in the transaction,[28] but only rarely must the probate judge perform some function himself in the probate process. This is a clear example of the Court serving an official, rubber stamp function, and rarely settling a dispute by adversary means. The judge of the Court is required to perform these clerical tasks because there is, historically, a suspicion of the transfer of property and the state wishes to tax such transfers. This requires judicial supervision of the administrator's unilateral performance of the tasks. This historical suspicion of the disposition of property is tied especially to the common law where property is

---

[27] Donald Gunn, "St. Louis Speeds the Probate Court," *57 A.B.A. Journal* 1219 (1971).

[28] Richard Wellman, "The Uniform Probate Code: Blueprint for Reform in the 70s," *2 Connecticut Law Review* 453 (1970).

central to the system of wealth, and where many complex and convoluted rules of inheritance govern the taking of property.[29]

One of the major problems of probate is the delay in settlement that is caused by the notice and waiting periods and the interruptive judicial responses to challenged claims. Depending on the jurisdiction and the procedures used, the complete probate process may take from one to three years, and this can be quite detrimental to heirs who have no alternative source of income, and whose material wealth is frozen into the estate until the final disposition can be made. Most estates are small and present no disputes. Yet they must go through the official probate procedure, which means delay and which is probably unnecessary in most of these cases. Unfortunately, there seems to be no easy solution to the problem of delay in probate, largely because the substantive law requires that creditors be given an opportunity to file claims, even though it is the waiting period that creates the delay and hardship under some circumstances.

In recent years a good deal of criticism has been raised about probate procedures and the delay related to probating estates. There have been some efforts to modernize and rationalize the probate process, largely focusing around the American Bar Association's Uniform Probate Code, which is to provide a model for state legislatures in developing their own, streamlined process. The Code would standardize procedures, and provide informal and quick processing of estates where the parties sought such procedures, and where no irregularities appeared on the face of the will.[30] At the option of the parties involved, or where there was a contest, the Code would provide a formal, judicially supervised process for probate. However, the most important part of the process is that informal procedures would not have to be conducted by a judge at all; instead a Registrar, who has official authority to perform all the necessary filing and clerical functions, would process the estates with no contests or where the

---

[29] Ralph Dupont, "The Impact of the Uniform Probate Code on Court Structure," *6 Journal of Law Reform* 375 (1973).

[30] Robert Whitman, "Report to the Probate Administrator on the State of the Probate Courts in Connecticut," *2 Connecticut Law Review* 579 (1970).

parties wished it. Under the Uniform Probate Code, the contested or formal procedures would be handled by a fulltime judge with the necessary jurisdiction and authority to settle any and all disputes completely.

This scheme of dividing probate into a formal and informal procedure would undoubtedly eliminate many of the hurdles or roadblocks that have delayed much of the process. Whether the formal or the informal process is used, the Court or the judicial system would have some control—sufficient to protect creditors and heirs, to give official approval to the transfer of the estate, and to provide whatever state interest exists in control or supervision of the transfer. However, the Code would eliminate any further state or judicial interference with an estate unless it was required either by a dispute or by the parties' wishes.

The Probate Court process shows that courts can perform primarily rubber stamp functions, with little concern for the peculiar needs of individual parties. Probate Courts use a very rigid set of procedures, formalized to insure that certain substantive concerns are protected (taxation and supervision of the property transfer), and there is no interest in providing speedy or simple remedies for the parties who appear before the Court. In fact, Probate Courts have a guaranteed business since every estate must be presented for probate, and there is thus no incentive for the Court to adapt its procedures, or facilitate its operation so that more people will find it easy and available.

FAMILY COURT

Family Courts are generally recent creations, appearing largely during the 1960s.[31] These courts are designed to focus on a particular set of problems—those involving the family—by giving the Court jurisdiction over all of the problems that arise within the family. The general categories of problems involved include divorce and juvenile cases, and often the Family Court simply

[31] Elizabeth Dyson and Richard Dyson, "Family Courts in the United States," Part I *8 Journal of Family Law* 505 (1968) and Part II *9 Journal of Family Law* 1 (1969), at Part 1 508; and Jeffrey Glen, "Developments in Juvenile and Family Court Law," *15 Crime and Delinquency* 295 (1969).

replaces the Domestic Relations Court and the Juvenile Court when a state legislature creates it.

The subject matter jurisdiction that the Family Court could have includes: divorce, separation, support, custody, family offenses, paternity, adoption, juvenile delinquency, supervision, and neglect of children. The general function of Family Courts is to provide assistance, counseling, and guidance to the parties involved, rather than to judge them in light of the law. The Family Court is intended to perform these functions by means of an expert supportive staff of trained psychologists, social workers, physicians, psychiatrists, and probation officers. These are necessary because the problems brought to Family Court generally cannot be solved by the traditional judicial remedies of damages, fines, or imprisonment. The equity powers of a judge are clearly relied on to fashion dispositions that are appropriate for each particular problem. There is a Standard Family Court Act, which is designed to provide an outline of how the jurisdiction, structure, and procedure of Family Courts might be established.[32] The states that have adopted a Family Court, however, have accepted the Standard Act to varying degrees, which creates little uniformity among such courts.

The procedures used by a Family Court are largely dependent upon the problem before it and the judge's interests. A marital problem will require different procedures and remedies than a juvenile case, or a neglect case. The procedures, however, tend to be nonadversary efforts to discover the nature of the problem, what the current position of the parties is, and then to provide appropriate remedies where possible. The procedure can be divided into three stages. The prehearing or Intake Stage, the hearing or Trial Stage, and the Disposition Stage. Only the second stage, the hearing, is directly connected to the courtroom per se, and the first and third stages may involve no judge at all, just social service and clerical people.

The prehearing procedures used by Family Courts are initiated when the police refer a youngster or adult to the Court,

---

[32] Standard Family Court Act, Prepared by the Committee on the Standard Family Court Act of the National Probation and Parole Association, 5 *NPPA Journal* No. 2 (April, 1959).

when the welfare case worker recommends that some member(s) of the welfare family contact a court official, when a neighbor or relative suggests the Court, or when an individual family member seeks assistance for a problem. Generally, the individual is referred to an intake officer, such as social worker, psychologist, or probation officer, who is designated to process cases, or a police officer who is designated as a screening agent for such problems.

The intake process is quite well developed for juveniles, because it has been widely used to divert juvenile cases to "remedies" before they ever reach the court. Probably over half the juvenile cases are diverted to some other social service agency during the intake process. For these juvenile cases, intake involves some investigation by police, probation officer, or case worker to develop background information on the individual and his problem. Usually interviews with relevant people form a major part of the screening process. This investigation may very well raise questions of privacy and constitutional rights, but seldom have these issues been litigated. It is usually done by a set of case workers assigned regularly to perform these tasks. Many of the cases are adjusted and "solved" during the investigation. The investigator may talk with all the parties, may counsel them, may be able to recommend a specific remedy to the intake officer. Investigation takes time, sometimes quite awhile, and questions about the thoroughness of some investigations arise. Courts use varying degrees of in-depth investigation reports—from sketchy to very detailed. The success of screening out juvenile cases at intake varies a good deal from nearly zero to as much as 50 percent. Adult intake, on the other hand, may not be provided at all. However, there is often some effort at investigating and initial adjustment of adult intrafamily differences. This investigation and adjustment may be done by police officers on the scene. However, if adults are presented to the intake procedure, they are probably less likely to be channeled off than are youngsters because of the nature of the disputes.

At the prehearing, Intake Stage a party can be disposed of in several fashions. He can be placed on informal probation (without any court examination of the case), referred to psychiatric guidance, marriage counseling, or detained for mental or physical examination or observation. A person may be released with no "treatment" except a warning or held for judicial proceeding. The Court may formally order any of these results, but it is often never involved in these diversions. The Court's powers in the Intake Stage are important since they can be used to force individuals to undergo special tests or investigations and they can dispose of many disputes informally. The Court can also formally remove a youngster from a home and place him in a temporary shelter, or detention home if it determines the home environment is detrimental to the child's well-being. Some Family Court procedures provide for mandatory marriage conciliation and, it is at the Intake Stage that a couple may have to attend at least one such session. Marriage counseling by the Court itself or by court referral is done in many states.[33] It is also at this intake, prehearing stage that the Family Court may waive its jurisdiction or transfer a party to another Court with concurrent jurisdiction.[34] This Intake Stage permits many cases to be sorted out—some settled by negotiation, some referred to experts, some sent to court for formal dispostion, and many disposed of informally. Either the Family Court judge or social service intake officers operate in formal or informal fashion, respectively, to screen and adjust cases before they reach the second stage of the process.

The hearing is the closest to an adversary trial model that exists in the Family Court setting, but even here the equity powers of the Court to fashion unique remedies are evident. The hearing comes after the intake screening has occurred and the hearing involves the group of cases that need some evidentiary examination by the judge, or involve a nonstandard problem that the intake officer does not know how to handle. The first stage of the hearing is a factual presentation to determine whether the accused individual or the defendant is guilty or should be held responsible for some act. Although some Family Courts have no criminal jurisdiction, others have both civil and criminal, and the Court (without a jury) must make some factual determination regarding whether the defendant committed the alleged acts,

[33] See, for example, N.Y. Family Court Act §911 (McKinney, 1963).
[34] Elizabeth Dyson and Richard Dyson, *supra* footnote 31, Part II at 11-13.

and is therefore in need of direction, rehabilitation, or social ostracism. Here the judge's role may become inquisitorial in nature since he is under some requirements to discover what happened, why it happened, and who did it. Often there is no adversary presentation by two parties even though the state, as prosecutor, may be involved in many of these cases. Thus the judge may be placed in the position of questioning witnesses, family members, and defendants, even when counsel is present, because for these purposes the adversary process may be counterproductive to discovering the "whole story." The reason for getting the entire story and its circumstances is so that the judge can make an informed judgment and disposition of the case.

This hearing often does not involve an adversarial trial, and there is no jury involved under any circumstances. The proceeding is likely to involve a short period of time—one half hour or so—and the end of the hearing will involve either an on-the-spot disposition or the judge will ask for some sort of disposition report or recommendation from the social worker or other expert assigned to the court to assist it in these kinds of dispositional problems. The usual result is the request for dispositional guidance.

The third stage is the Dispositional Hearing, which may be either a completely separate proceeding or a postponed session of the adjudicatory hearing. The Dispositional Hearing is the stage at which the person adjudged liable or guilty, or determined to be in need of assistance is given a formal court directive about the treatment he should receive. The court's decision on treatment may be based on only what was presented at the evidentiary hearing, or it may be based on a great deal of additional material collected by social workers and probation officers at the Court's direction or at intake. Generally, all the evidence and information deemed relevant by the judge will be admitted at this stage even if it is based on hearsay or gossip.[35]

This second hearing may involve the presentation of witnesses and even their cross-examination by counsel. However the purpose of the process is not to determine what happened but to

[35] Monrad Paulsen, "The New York Family Court Act," *12 Buffalo Law Review* 420 (1963).

specify what will happen to the party. The material considered relevant may range widely, depending on the judge's interests and concern and on the problem. One of the major difficulties with Dispositional Hearings involves the judge's basis for decision. The judge has a great deal of discretion about what he does with an individual, and what information he considers. This flexibility causes some concern, and where it exists, it can be abused even if the judge has no such intention. One means of controlling this discretion is that in reality the alternatives available may be severely limited, even if they are quite inadequate for the needs of some people. Although the Family Court has a wide variety of services supposedly available, money, time, and people may limit what the judge may actually be able to do; thus the discretionary choices open to the judge limit the functions of the Family Court. In addition, the basis of decision can become routinized as the judge disposes of a number of cases involving the same kinds of problems; he may develop a clear preference for certain kinds of information and give standard weight to such information. This certainly controls his decisions, even if it does not involve outside or objective control.

In theory, the dispositions that can be made by the Family Court include the traditional remedies of divorce decrees, appointment of legal guardians, and support orders. Depending on whether the Court has any criminal jurisdiction, it may impose criminal penalties. Generally, the Court would have whatever dispositional powers are provided by the substantive law of the jurisdiction in divorce, criminal, or juvenile cases. In addition, however, Family Courts may be given additional powers such as custody orders for neglected children and may require the custodian to observe reasonable behavior as defined in various ways.[36] This kind of authority is really an elaboration of traditional equity powers. Generally misbehaving youngsters can be placed on probation or institutionalized by the Family Court. In addition, powers of temporary custody, or protective institutional supervision have been given to some Family Courts. These wide-ranging alternatives often include a great deal of discretion on the part of the judge as to length of time.

[36] N.Y. Family Court Act §§356, 446, and 842 (McKinney, 1963).

Family Courts are an institution created to deal with unique and difficult human problems. There is no clear solution for many of the problems brought to the attention of these courts. Whether they are appropriate arenas for solving these problems is open to debate. These courts may not be given the necessary remedies and professional assistance resources for solving the problems over which they have jurisdiction. Since the crucial point, however, is that the nature of the problems brought to Family Courts are not amenable to traditional procedures, some adjustments or revisions have been made. These revisions are formal (much as the creation of a Family Court) and informal (such as heavy reliance on social service expert advice before decision). Yet a "court" is given these tasks to perform, using nonadversary procedures.

DOMESTIC RELATIONS COURT

The Domestic Relations Court (or Divorce Court) is not a recent creation, as are Family Courts. The jurisdiction of the Divorce Court tends to be narrower than the integrated jurisdiction of Family Courts. The Court's jurisdiction generally deals with marital problems, and focuses on the process by which divorces are granted, separations permitted, or other marital problems resolved. The marital problems that arise are complex, and difficult to settle, and most Domestic Relations Courts are provided with social service assistance somewhat like that given to Family Courts. In New York, both Divorce Courts and Family Courts exist, which creates substantial overlap and confusion about what jurisdiction each should exercise. However, most states operate with a Domestic Relations Court and no Family Court, and where the Family Court has been created the Divorce Court has usually been abolished.

The first function Domestic Relations Courts perform is giving official scrutiny to marital problems between spouses and is based on the substantive law in most jurisdictions.[37] Historically, the

---

[37] Clayton Rose, Jr., "Non-Fault Divorce in Ohio," *31 Ohio State Law Journal* 52, 52-55 (1970).

marriage was based on the theory of contract[38] with the result that seeking to dissolve the contract required a judicial examination of the grounds for dissolution. Most divorce law is premised on the value of retaining the family unit intact. Thus, obtaining a divorce may be quite difficult. To achieve a divorce, fault must be proven on the part of one of the contractors (spouses).[39] The law usually specifies what the recognized grounds for divorce are and the party seeking the divorce must establish that the spouse is guilty of one of the acts or conditions, for example, mental cruelty or adultery.[40] Usually the plaintiff must also establish that she (or he) has not committed any of these guilty acts, but rather that they have clean hands and that the defending spouse is the person responsible for the marital difficulties.

Such an approach to divorce is quite traditional and the established, adversary processes can handle such efforts well. However, the divorce action, as an adversary confrontation between the two spouses, involves a good deal of strained relations between the parties. The problems that bring a married couple into court may be emotional, and often are characterized by a good deal of tension between the spouses. To force the plaintiff to gather evidence against the defendant and present it in court may add nothing to the marital relationship, but rather encourage the deterioration of the relations. Many divorces are not contested, which means the defendant also is interested in obtaining a divorce; therefore he does not force the use of the adversary process to establish his fault or he may not even show up in court. Then the adversary process of establishing a guilty act as ground for divorce becomes an empty ritual, which serves no purpose except to satisfy the Court and the requirements of the substantive law. The widely used "Reno Divorce" process is an uncontested divorce, available in most states, but easy to obtain in Nevada, which has a very short residency requirement for the plaintiff. Thus the plaintiff can go to Nevada and live for six

---

[38] Donna Zenor, "Untying the Knot: The Course and Patterns of Divorce Reform," *57 Cornell Law Review* 649, 649-650 (1972).

[39] *Ibid.*, at 652-654.

[40] See, for example, Clayton Rose, Jr., *supra* footnote 37, at 55.

weeks, then file for a divorce, and have it granted without the appearance of the defendant spouse.

Some states have begun to modernize their divorce requirements to remove the need to establish fault.[41] In other states, grounds upon which a divorce will be granted have been eased so that if one party can establish that the marriage has "broken down," or that there are "irreconcilable differences" between the parties, the court has legal authority to grant the divorce.[42] However, such modernization is slow, and faces substantial political pressure from various sources.

The second function of Domestic Relations Courts might be termed a social welfare service of the Court. The Court focuses on conciliation of the parties, and mediation of the differences. The process is designed to reconcile the parties so that they can live together in harmony. This is a fairly recent effort on the part of some Domestic Relations Courts.[43] In recent years, legislatures have begun to modify the judicial process in recognition of this social-service function, which they wish the Courts to perform. This has often been done in lieu of changing the substantive law of divorce to a no-fault system. The substantive law and the judicial process are still aimed at maintaining the family unit, but the process seeks to do this by providing the disputants with assistance and counseling. Some states permit the creation of "courts" that are designed only to conciliate marital difficulties, and that have no jurisdiction to deal with the actual divorce process.[44] In most jurisdictions that perform this second judicial function, the courts have been given some procedural means of conducting conciliation sessions either themselves, or by referring the parties to a conciliation service (private or state run).[45]

---

[41] Donna Zenor, *supra* footnote 38; and Clayton Rose, Jr., *supra* footnote 37.

[42] Donna Zenor, *supra* footnote 38, at 658.

[43] Henry Foster, Jr., "Conciliation and Counseling in the Courts in Family Law Cases," *41 New York University Law Review* 352, 352-355 (1966).

[44] Laurens Henderson, "Marriage Counseling in a Court of Conciliation," *52 Judicature* 253 (1969).

[45] David Seidelson, "Systematic Marriage Investigation and Counseling in Divorce Cases: Some Reflections on Its Constitutional Propriety and General Desirability," *36 George Washington Law Review* 60, 65-67 (1967).

In terms of processes, there is initially some sort of intake screening process. This may be handled by a hearing official assigned to conduct all preliminary matters for the court, or a marriage counselor assigned to the Court. Infrequently, a judge may handle intake. Police also serve as a major intake point for the domestic disputes they are called to settle. The officer may have some options for disposition. If he has options, they will include the authority to send the case to the Court to be heard as a divorce action, and the option of sending the case to marriage counseling. The intake decision may be guided by the expert training or experience of the intake officer. It may also be guided by his own discretion and judgment about the people involved, how antagonistic they are toward one another, and what the court can realistically do under the circumstances. In these cases bargaining and mediation processes might be conducted by the intake officer, the judge, or the parties may be referred for counseling to a private individual, such as a clergyman, a private counseling service, or to regular state or local official counseling services.[46]

If the intake officer is more restricted in the options open to him, he may be required to refer the case to conciliation.[47] The parties may be held in contempt of court for not attending at least the first session. The purpose of this procedure is obviously to seek to conciliate the matter and divert the case from the divorce process by formally requiring such effort. In this way the hearing officer can explore the problems and make a formal determination as to whether the case can be reconciled.[48] If the case is hopeless, then the procedure requires that he certify the case for formal proceedings. Thus, this first, required conciliation meeting is a further screening stage since the law may require it as a prelude to formal court action in the divorce proceedings.[49]

The Domestic Relations Judge usually comes into play when a formal petition for divorce is filed by one of the parties. That may

---

[46] Henry Foster, Jr., *supra* footnote 43.

[47] David Seidelson, *supra* footnote 45, at 65-67.

[48] *Ibid.,* at 66-67.

[49] Henry Foster, Jr., *supra* footnote 43, at 363 notes that only about 2 percent of the cases are conciliated successfully by courts.

occur at the outset, or it may arise only after the intake stage, and the officer certifies that the petition should be filed in and accepted by the Court. The procedures used in court will depend on whether the divorce is contested by the other party (defendant) or is uncontested. In the latter case, the procedure is rather summary. The defendant may not be present, and the Court can then enter the equivalent of a default judgment, and no adversary process occurs. In contested divorces, the procedure is adversary in nature since the plaintiff must prove that the defendant is at fault, or that the marriage is irreconcilably lost before the divorce decree will be granted.

The contest is frequently not over the divorce but over custody of the children or the division of property. These issues are usually involved in divorces, but the parties generally agree to a property settlement and custody arrangements, which the court merely incorporates in the divorce decree. When no agreement can be achieved, the Court is requested to make such an arrangement and enter it as part of the divorce decree. The disputes over custody of children and division of the property are usually less along adversary model lines than is the contested divorce. In cases of custody or property, the courtroom battle may be quite vociferous and bitter, but it rarely involves matters of proof, or the introduction of evidence. Usually the parties present briefs and oral argument supporting their claim to the property or showing why the spouse is unfit to have custody of the children. The judge makes a decision on the basis of his judgment and the law or usual practice on such matters.

Marital violence is a large aspect of the business of Domestic Relations Courts, and is an increasing phenomenon in American Society today.[50] Although these crimes are not very visible to society, since many are never reported by the victim, the Courts

[50] Raymond Parnas, "The Response of Some Relevant Community Resources to Intra-Family Violence," 44 *Indiana Law Journal* 159 (1969); Raymond Parnas, "Judicial Response to Intra-Family Violence," 54 *Minnesota Law Review* 586 (1970); Martha Field and Henry Field, "Marital Violence and the Criminal Process: Neither Justice nor Peace," 47 *Social Service Review* 221 (1973); Elizabeth Truninger, "Marital Violence: The Legal Solutions," 23 *The Hastings Law Journal* 259 (1971); and Raymond Parnas, "The Police Response to the Domestic Disturbance," 1967 *Wisconsin Law Review* 914.

are becoming increasingly aware of the acts, and are faced with the difficult task of determining what can be done to remedy such crimes. The basic approach is generally not to punish the perpetrator so much as to remedy the cause of the dispute. This is obviously quite difficult to do since the causes are often emotional, personal, and difficult to discover, let alone remedy, by court processes. However, the Courts have used equity power to attempt to settle the problem and prevent its reoccurrence.

Domestic Relations Courts are given some of the most difficult human problems with which any court deals. Although an adversary procedure may be followed, it may be very counterproductive to a reasonable resolution and settlement of the marital dispute. In the alternative, the process in the courtroom is often far from the adversary process, aimed at conciliating the parties or solving the problems. This occurs either because the legislature has required the process of mediation within the court or because the judges, as humans, realize the futility of formal court proceedings and seek a better alternative to the sterile formality of the court. The result is a quite divergent model of procedure, in which the court serves as a social-service referral mechanism.[51]

Conclusions

Many civil cases are processed in the traditional trial court, following the adversary model. However, a variety of alternative court procedures have evolved or have been created to deal with certain problems for which the adversary model has proven ineffective. Small Claims Court arose because of the cost and delay of the regular process in handling a variety of legal problems. The procedure used in these courts is basically adversary in nature, but modified to permit less rigid procedures that are quicker, cheaper, and understandable to the layman. Probate Court uses an adversary procedure along with a clerical procedure, and these courts arose from the state's need to supervise the transmission of wealth at death, and to tax the transfer of that wealth. Family Courts and Domestic Relations Courts use a social-service

---

[51] Raymond Parnas, *54 Minnesota Law Review, supra* footnote 50, at 634.

model that might best be termed an agency or bureaucratic model of procedure.

The utility of the adversary model varies depending on the court function. Social service welfare functions are in line with agencylike efforts. These suggest that American society has given problems to courts that cannot be handled in the traditional, judicial way, and require, instead, a more bureaucratic, remedial process of providing "assistance" to the parties in the case. Such tasks usually involve difficult problems that cannot be resolved by the allocation of money. In an effort to provide other remedies to courts with agency functions, the decisional process has been altered in various ways, and the purpose of the court has been adjusted.

Table 3.1
Comparison of Characteristics of the Adversary Civil Process and the Nonadversary Civil Process

	Adversary Process	Nonadversary Process
Intake	Lawyer screening decisions Formal pleadings	Social service intake screening Discussion or investigation of problem Disposition or diversion alternatives
Trial	Formal evidence Evidentiary rules Procedural motions for disposition Factual questions Judge–Jury determination	Informal hearing Presentation or discussion of problem Issue is determining problem Judge determination with expert advising
Disposition	Judge enters judgment Remedy: money (jury award)	Judge enters "judgment" Remedy: equity; rehabilitation or correction service Remedy based on advice of social worker or professionals

Table 3.1 sets forth the major characteristics of the adversary process and the other nonadversary (social–service) process used by some courts. The decision maker is effectively different in these two processes. The intake and screening determinations are made in different ways, based on different criteria, and have different effects on subsequent procedures. The disposition of the cases may be called the same thing—a judgment—but they are fashioned for different objectives, reached by different people, using different resources.

As outlined in the Introduction, the specific courts discussed here compose only a part of civil court operation in any jurisdiction. None of these specialized courts can process all of the civil business over which trial courts of general jurisdiction are given authority. Some jurisdictions do not have any of these specialized courts. Some have them, but do not call them by the name used here. In some jurisdictions, the same judge, using the same courtroom, conducts these specialized functions at different times during his work week. Some variations also appear in the criminal court operation, and these will be discussed in the next chapter.

4
Criminal Courts and Procedures

After looking at civil court processes in America, an examination of the criminal process model and the practical operation of these courts will give a wider perspective on the variety of processes in our court system. Alternative bargaining considerations can also be compared to those in the settlement of private disputes. The basic difference between civil and criminal court operations is the parties to the case and the resulting functions that the process serves. The criminal court is designed to provide a governmental arena in which the government as the representative of society, can repress antisocietal behavior and dispense corrective action. The state provides the arena, and is also the prosecuting party (plaintiff) in criminal cases. The defendant can be any person or group within society that is accused of breaking the law. The remedies available in criminal courts include fines, which are similar to the allocation of monetary resources in civil cases, but criminal penalties also include incarceration in an institution, training of one sort or another, designed to rehabilitate or punish the person(s) convicted of the criminal activity, or some probationary remedy. These differences mean that the court is not just available for proceedings to settle disputes, it is usually the mandatory scene of the resolution, and the remedies can be more punitive than in civil cases, where the primary purpose is to restore the injured party to the position he enjoyed before the damage occurred.

In our discussion the model process provides a baseline against which to compare the actual operation of our criminal courts. Then the courts are described according to how they actually proceed. There are many aspects of the criminal justice system that will not be discussed here, not because they are unimportant but because they are not related to the criminal court processes that are the main focus of this book. Thus, the police, a major organization that channels and submits most of the criminal cases to courts, will not be examined in detail. There are several major and difficult questions about the penal systems in this country, but they deserve much greater treatment than we can give them here, since they take what the criminal courts produce —convicted criminals—and process them through their own procedures, designed to achieve a variety of results other than those of the court system. They act as passive receptors of what the courts produce, while the police act as initiators of court business. Neither organization is a direct part of the criminal court process.

There is bound to be some variation among courts in various jurisdictions since all courts do not have the exact same procedural rules to guide them. However, in the area of criminal process, recent Supreme Court decisions involving the constitutional rights of defendants in criminal cases tend to encourage uniformity. The degree of standardization depends on many things, and certainly all courts are not following Supreme Court decisions in lockstep. In fact many of the Court's decisions are general and vague, which does not enhance uniformity. Yet the Supreme Court's efforts to constitutionalize the criminal process undoubtedly has had some standardizing effect.

The Criminal Court Process Model

The model described here is taken in part from the Federal Rules of Criminal Procedure.[1] These apply only to federal courts but they are similar to those followed in many of our states. The variations from this pattern are discussed later in the chapter, when it will become evident that much of the variation is due to

[1] Hereinafter cited as: Fed. R. Crim. P.,

the multiplicity of courts, and an absence of modern, efficient procedure to deal with people accused of crimes.

The initial phase of this process begins when a criminal event or act occurs. Either a private citizen may report it, and swear out a complaint before a magistrate, stating what crime was committed and who committed it or, more likely, the police will file a complaint and obtain a warrant or directly arrest the individual(s) if the crime occurred in the presence of the police. This initial phase actually involves bringing the occurrence of a crime to the attention of the magistrate. This comes in the form of a complaint accompanied by sworn affidavits, and the result of it is the issuance of a warrant for the arrest of individuals suspected of committing the crime. The arrest warrant can be circumvented if the arresting officer is present at the commission of the crime. But if the arrest precedes the warrant, the police must swear out a complaint and obtain an arrest warrant after the suspect has been brought into the station house for questioning or booking. In addition, an arrest warrant can be based on a grand jury investigation and indictment. The complaint and warrant serves as an initial screening device so that before someone is arrested or apprehended, some official (police or magistrate) must evaluate the basis upon which the arrest of the individual is sought.

The magistrate often will rubber stamp the request of the police, as long as the police will attest to the commission of a crime and a belief that the named individual(s) committed the crime. It is also possible that the warrant will be only to apprehend someone for questioning, in which case the police need only specify that the individual is sought for information about a crime, and the warrant allows his detention without a criminal charge for a brief and specified period of time. Usually such a warrant is issued in connection with grand jury investigation and it insures that the grand jury will receive testimony from the people it wants.

The second stage of the process occurs after the suspect is in custody, whether on a warrant or not. This involves the presentment of the suspect before a magistrate and is called the Initial Appearance. This is to occur without "unnecessary delay" and usually occurs within a few hours of apprehension. Before this set of procedures requiring appearance without delay was instituted in 1957, police were able to detain suspects, without charging, and without judicial scrutiny. They could be held *incommunicado* for varying, sometimes long, periods of time. The Supreme Court has ruled specifically that the suspect must be presented to a magistrate shortly after apprehension, apparently because the Court thought that the police would coerce confessions out of unsuspecting persons.[2]

At the Initial Appearance the defendant is given a general set of notices about what rights he has, such as the right to counsel, the right to remain silent, and the right to a Preliminary Examination. In addition to these procedures, the Initial Appearance also involves the scheduling of the Preliminary Examination (Hearing), usually within 10 days, and the appointment of counsel if the defendant requests it. At this stage, the defendant is usually informed of the charges being made against him and, if he was arrested without a warrant, the warrant is obtained from a magistrate; therefore the police must establish probable cause to apprehend the person by satisfying the judge that there is sufficient ground for arresting and holding the suspect on a charge.

Bond is usually set at the Initial Appearance, although it need not be set until later, at the Arraignment. Based on the judge's determination of what amount of money is necessary to insure the accused's return to court for subsequent proceedings, the judge will specify the amount that the accused must post in order to be released until his appearance is necessary. Although bail is not supposed to be used for punishment, it is possible for the judge to set whatever amount he chooses. In some jurisdictions the policy is to release accused persons as frequently as possible, so they are actually required only to post 10 percent of the bond, and will forfeit the remainder only if they fail to appear. In other jurisdictions, as many accused persons as possible are released on their own recognizance (ROR). This means that they are not

[2] *Mallory v. U.S.*, 354 U.S. 449 (1957). The Court held specifically that Rule 5(a) of the Fed. R. Crim. P., which requires appearance "without unnecessary delay," meant that the police had "little more leeway than the interval between arrest and the ordinary administrative steps required to bring a suspect before the nearest available magistrate," at 455.

required to post any bond, if a background investigation indicates that they are unlikely to flee the jurisdiction while awaiting trial. Such practices appear to be successful in terms of getting defendants to reappear at subsequent proceedings.[3] The entire bail system is dependent on the judge and his discretion. The Eighth Amendment of the U.S. Constitution prohibits excessive bail, but does not define what is excessive. In addition, once bail is set, the defendant can move for reduction of bail, and the judge usually holds an extensive hearing on that issue, before changing his original bail.

The defendant has a constitutional right to be represented by counsel at the various stages of the criminal process. The Supreme Court has determined that counsel is necessary during any "critical stage" of the criminal process, or when the criminal investigation has narrowed down from a general search to the investigation of a single individual. There has been a good deal of debate over whether counsel need be present during lineups, whether the police should be allowed to question a suspect, and even obtain a confession from the suspect, without the presence of counsel, or whether counsel should be present at probation revocation hearings. However the court has held the Constitution requires counsel at these stages. The debate involves two questions. First, whether the constitution requires counsel to be present or provided during stages of the process before and after the trial. A narrow interpretation would indicate that the U.S. Constitution requires counsel only at the trial. Second, the question arises of what effect counsel's presence has on the process and the accused. Some observers suggest that the effect is not great;[4]

---

[3] Ronald Goldfarb, *Ransom: A Critique of the American Bail System* (New York: Harper and Row, 1965); Charles Ares, Anne Rankin, and Herbert Sturz, "The Manhattan Bail Project," *38 New York University Law Review* 67 (1963); Note, "A Study of the Administration of Bail in New York City," *106 University of Pennsylvania Law Review 693* (1958); William Landes, "The Bail System: An Economic Approach," *2 Journal of Legal Studies* 79 (1973); and William Landes, "Legality and Reality: Some Evidence on Criminal Procedure," *3 Journal of Legal Studies* 287 (1974).

[4] See *Gideon v. Wainwright*, 372 U.S. 335 (1963) and *Argersinger v. Hamlin*, 407 U.S. 25 (1972) for major Supreme Court opinions on the right to counsel. Robert Stover and Dennis Eckart, "The Indigent's Right to Counsel: How Much Does It Help?" (paper prepared for delivery at the 1973 Annual Meeting of the Midwest Political Science Association, Chicago).

however, much of the Warren Court's activities in the criminal justice area were premised on the protection that counsel would provide the accused in the critical stages of the criminal process.

Counsel is usually selected or appointed after the Initial Appearance. He may choose his own counsel, or may have one appointed for him by the court if he cannot afford to hire his own. Some systems provide a public defender who is the state's attorney for the defendant. The public defender system is a state agency and involves a staff of attorneys and investigators who assist indigent defendants, and present their defense in court. Such agencies operate with varying degrees of success. In some states members of the local bar are appointed in rotation to serve as defense counsel for indigents.

The Preliminary Hearing can be an early but crucial stage in the proceeding because it is at this formal hearing that the prosecution must establish probable cause to hold the defendant and charge him with the crime. The probable cause element of the Preliminary Hearing requires that there must be sufficient evidence submitted by the state to establish that there is probable cause to believe that an offense has been committed and that the defendant committed it. There is a good deal of debate over what is necessary to establish probable cause, but generally the state will present only as much evidence as it feels is necessary to satisfy the judge that there is probable cause. That evidence is usually less than what is required for proof of guilt beyond a reasonable doubt in the actual trial. The rules permit hearsay evidence to be used at the Preliminary Hearing, even if that same evidence is not admissible at the trial on the merits.[5]

The defendant certainly is represented by counsel at this stage, to attack the evidence presented by the prosecution. This proceeding is not a trial to determine guilt or innocence, but rather only to determine whether the defendant should be held and accused. However, the Preliminary Hearing is usually waived by the defendant and his counsel.[6] This may be because the Preliminary Hearing is generally used by the defense to discover how

---

[5] Fed. R. Crim. P., Rule 5.1(s).

[6] Kenneth Graham and Leon Letwin, "The Preliminary Hearing in Los Angeles: Some Field Findings and Legal-Policy Observations," *18 U.C.L.A. Law Review* 635, 916 (1971).

strong a case the state has against the accused, that is, it is used as a discovery mechanism by the defendant. Thus, where the defense knows the prosecution's case, the Preliminary Hearing is of little use to the defense.

The result of the Preliminary Hearing is either that the defendant is bound over to the trial court for trial on the charges, held for the grand jury, or released because the state has failed to establish that it had probable cause. The magistrate who presides over this process is not necessarily the judge who will try the case if it goes to trial. As will be noted later, there are generally two levels of criminal trial courts, an inferior one of limited jurisdiction, which processes the complaints, issues the arrest warrants, and conducts the Initial Appearances and Preliminary Hearings, as well as its own jurisdictional business, and the criminal court of general jurisdiction that tries the major cases going to trial. This will supposedly protect the accused from a judge who has already seen the case or part of it at the Preliminary Hearing. This protection, as well as the other screening devices built into the Preliminary Hearing procedure, are never available where the defendant waives his right to such a hearing.

For some criminal charges there is another stage occurring at about this point that can be viewed as a screen against incorrect criminal charges. That is the grand jury Indictment. Even after apprehension, the accused may be held for a grand jury proceeding, unless he has waived the grand jury. It is required in offenses for which the penalty is death, and it is rarely used for offenses that carry a penalty of imprisonment for less than one year or do not involve hard labor. The grand jury is drawn from the community, as are petit jurors, and the purpose of the grand jury is to examine the evidence presented by the prosecutor, and determine if the accused should be indicted for the crime. The jury can call witnesses, and the proceedings are secret, so that there is little possibility of external, public pressure for or against a particular indictment.

The grand jury is an investigative body, and may very well be called upon to issue indictments for people not yet in custody, if the prosecutor can present enough evidence to convince at least 12 of the minimum of 23 federal grand jurors that a crime has been committed, and there is a reasonable belief that the suspect committed it. Usually if the accused is in custody, and has gone through the Initial Appearance and Preliminary Hearing, the grand jury will be waived, by the defendant. Yet the accused has the constitutional right to a grand jury indictment in federal cases, which he may use if the evidence is weak and if he believes he can persuade the grand jury not to indict him.[7]

Grand juries have been criticized for two kinds of developments, First, they can be used by prosecutors as instruments of political advantage, and can be carefully controlled by the prosecutor to produce indictments exactly as he wants. Second, they have been criticized for just the opposite—they may run-away and issue indictments for crimes that cannot possibly be proven in a criminal trial. Thus, the Grand Jury produces indictments that are either exactly what the prosecutor wants (for his own, political advantage) or precisely what the prosecutor does not want (and he cannot gather sufficient evidence to obtain a guilty finding in a trial on the merits). Some states have all but abolished the Grand Jury because of these problems. The actual use of the Grand Jury in those states that still use it is generally restricted to indictments for felonies or other serious crimes, while the Information is used for misdemeanors.

When the grand jury is waived, or in the case of minor crimes, an Information takes the place of the Indictment. This is a sworn statement filed by the prosecutor indicating to the judge that there is sufficient evidence of the crime and against the individual to proceed with the criminal process. Depending on the jurisdiction, and the styles of prosecutors, most of the criminal cases may be handled by Informations or Indictments. The grand jury Indictment involves a slower process, and it has the risk that the jury will not be persuaded by the prosecutor's evidence; the Information, then, is administratively a much safer means by which the prosecutor may proceed. However, the accused has more protection under the grand jury process. Some would say that grand juries are pliable and controllable by the prosecutor, so it makes no difference which system is used. There has been little empiri-

---

[7] U.S. Constitution, Amendment V.

cal research on the grand jury that would support or discount these suspicions, and until such is presented, the grand jury should be viewed as an investigative "hurdle" that the system places between the power of the state and the freedom of the individual.

After the Preliminary Hearing, and the Indictment or Information, and the apprehension of the accused, there is a formal Arraignment. The Arraignment is the step in the process at which the court formally presents the accused with the charge(s) against him, and the defendant is asked to plead. The defendant is usually given whatever extra time he requests at this stage to secure an attorney, or for the attorney to develop the case so that the best plea can be entered. However, there is probably little need for long delays or postponements at Arraignment since whatever investigations are to be done will have been completed during the earlier stages.

The alternatives open to the defendant here are to plead not guilty, guilty, or *nolo contendere*. The first of these pleas is self-explanatory and it serves notice to the system that it will have to proceed through the formal trial before it can punish the accused in this case. The guilty plea, which will be discussed in greater detail below, is often entered in our criminal court systems, and it is an admission by the defendant that he is guilty of the charges against him. The guilty plea cannot be entered unless the court accepts it, and usually the judge will make various efforts to determine that the plea of guilty is entered voluntarily and with understanding of what it means.[8] The amount of care the judge takes in this process varies, but it is often very little. *Nolo contendere* essentially is a plea of no contest to the charges. It does not admit guilt, but it has the same effect as a guilty plea in that the defendant is indicating that he will not oppose the state in the criminal process, and will accept whatever penalty the court assesses against him. Since the plea of *nolo contendere* must be voluntary and knowingly made, the court has some obligation to insure that the defendant is making this plea intelligently. If, at the Ar-

---

[8] Donald Newman, *Conviction: The Determination of Guilt or Innocence Without Trial* (Boston; Little, Brown, 1966), chs. 2 and 3.

raignment, the defendant refuses to plead, or if the court refuses to accept the plea, because the defendant does not make it with knowledge, the court will automatically enter a plea of not guilty, so that the state will be put to the test of proving guilt before it can punish this individual.[9]

When the criminal process goes beyond the Preliminary Hearing and the grand jury Indictment or Information, there is a period before trial in which the pretrial, discovery processes can operate. The procedures in criminal cases are somewhat different from civil pretrial because the defendant cannot be forced to testify against himself; therefore the prosecution cannot gain evidence by presenting interrogatories to the defendant or taking depositions. However, the rules of criminal procedure usually give the defendant the right to discover what evidence the prosecution has against him. Under this scheme, the defendant may inspect statements, reports of examinations or tests, books, papers, documents, or other evidence. This serves a useful function if the defense does not know the nature and amount of evidence that the prosecution possesses regarding the crime or the defendant. This is important information, especially if the prosecution's case is weak, and the defense can succeed simply by not presenting anything more upon which the prosecution can rely. These discovery privileges are not open to the prosecution unless the defendant takes advantage of them. Then the court may order that the prosecution be given the same privilege with regard to the defendant's papers.[10] However, usually by this time the defendant's counsel has a fairly clear indication of the case against his client, and so discovery is not likely to lead to the revelation of very much new evidence. There is also the provision for a pretrial conference in the Federal Rules of Criminal Procedure.[11] The conference is conducted if one or both parties request it or the court believes it would "promote a fair and expeditious trial." As in civil cases, this conference usually results in a court order setting forth the items agreed upon, and those

[9] Fed. R. Crim. P., Rule 11.
[10] *Ibid.*, Rule 16(c).
[11] *Ibid.*, Rule 17.1.

which are still in dispute. Generally, however, the plea bargaining process (described below) is operating during this stage so that the formal, pretrial processes are rarely used.

The actual criminal trial is based on the adversary scheme. In fact, the criminal trial is generally viewed as more formal, and more rigorous than the civil trial. There are several reasons for this. First, the state, to establish guilt must prove the defendant's guilt beyond a reasonable doubt. This is a heavier burden of proof than exists in civil courts where a party can prevail with a "preponderance of the evidence." The criminal burden of proof requires that the trier of fact resolve all doubts in favor of the defendant. Although there may be some question of whether these differences in words make any empirical difference in the outcome of trials, at least in theory, the reasonable doubt burden makes the model operate differently than does the preponderance of evidence rule.

In addition to this prosecution requirement, the defendant has the right to a trial by jury in all criminal cases.[12] As in civil cases, the jury is supposed to be impartial and composed of members of the local community.[13] The jury trial right can be waived by the defendant, if the prosecutor and the judge approve, and there are some trials for which even the defendant might wish to have a bench trial, in which case the judge is the trier of fact as well as presiding judge. This might occur where the crime is particularly heinous and has wide community visibility.[14] The strategy in selecting a jury is for the defense to choose people who are either in sympathy with the defendant, or who are at least not biased against the defendant. Selection of jurors by attorneys can be a very elaborate process as in political trials.

To some extent the selection is random since the jury panel, from which the 12 jurors to try the case are selected, is to be chosen at random. The exclusion of members from the jury may

---

[12] *Duncan v. Louisiana,* 391 U.S. 145 (1968).

[13] U.S. Constitution, Amendment VI.

[14] See the discussion of Clarence Darrow's decision not to submit the Leopold and Loeb criminal case to a jury and, in fact, plead his clients guilty. Irving Stone, *Clarence Darrow for the Defense* (Garden City, N.Y: Garden City Publishing Co., 1941), pp. 400-401.

be done for cause, in which case the prosecutor or defense attorney has shown, through questioning, that the juror is biased, or is not fit to sit in this case for some reason. There are also some peremptory challenges that each side has. This enables each party to exclude some jurors for no reason. This is the way in which a lawyer's hunches can be useful, since he can exclude someone he does not "feel right about" even though he cannot prove an obvious bias. The parties have a limited number of peremptory challenges, depending on the crime charged, and the party. Although juries are available and used in civil trials, the criminal jury trial is viewed as a very important protection for the defendant, and it is expected that the jury will be harder to convince beyond a reasonable doubt than a judge.

Evidence for this jury role is provided by an extensive study of jury operation.[15] This research indicates that judge and jury would agree on the outcome of criminal trials in nearly 80 percent of the cases tested. Nearly all of the disagreement (20 percent) between judge and jury is in the direction of the jury failing to convict while the judge would convict. This difference would support the proposition that the jury can be viewed as a protection for the defendant, at least in cases where the evidence seems to be somewhat questionable. However, the 80 percent agreement between judge and jury involves 64 percent agreement on convictions. This means that in 64 percent of the cases the jury would convict (just as would the judge). Thus, while juries may acquit where judges would convict, the jury is frequently convinced of the evidence and does convict.

There are safety value motions as in civil cases, which can be used to short-circuit the criminal trial process. In criminal cases, most of these are available *only* to the defendant, since the state, with its power, is not allowed to circumvent the complete process before convicting a person. The defendant's motions fall into two categories. The first is a motion to suppress or exclude evidence. This is usually made before the trial begins, and it is designed to stop the trial by denying the use of certain evidence to the pro-

---

[15] Harry Kalvin, Jr., and Hans Zeisel, *The American Jury* (Chicago: University of Chicago Press, 1971), p. 55-66.

secution, or to reduce the strength of the prosecution's case. It is usable if the prosecution obtained evidence in violation of the constitutional rights of the defendant (particularly the Fourth Amendment). Under the Exclusionary Rule such evidence cannot be used to convict.[16] If the court excludes such materials on the claim of a constitutional violation, then the prosecution may have little or no other evidence, and will have to ask for a dismissal of the charges. This has been used widely in recent years, since the 1961 Supreme Court decision.

The Exclusionary Rule is quite controversial because it seeks to sanction invalid police behavior (illegal searches and seizures) by excluding the tainted evidence from the criminal prosecution.[17] A large minority of the Supreme Court has indicated that the Rule may be abolished in the near future. It is argued that the Rule is not the best way of disciplining police since it may be applied in the criminal prosecution years after the improper police action, it is applied to the prosecutor and his case, rather than to the police, and much police behavior, which might violate constitutional rights, does not result in criminal prosecutions and thus is not sanctioned by the Exclusionary Rule.[18] It appears that the Supreme Court is moving away from reliance on the Exclusionary Rule, but it is unclear what alternative sanctions will be applied to illegally seized evidence in the future.[19]

The motion to suppress is probably the most frequently used safety valve, but the defendant has another one available to him during the trial itself. This is called the Motion for Judgment of

---

[16] *Mapp v. Ohio,* 367 U.S. 643 (1961), applied the Exclusionary Rule to the states. It was initially outlined and applied to the federal courts in *Weeks v. U.S.,* 232 U.S. 383 (1914).

[17] See, for example, Dallin Oaks, "Studying the Exclusionary Rule in Search and Seizure," *37 University of Chicago Law Review* 665 (1970); James Spiotto, "Search and Seizure: An Empirical Study of the Exclusionary Rule and Its Alternatives." *2 Journal of Legal Studies* 243 (1973); and Bradley Canon, "Is the Exclusionary Rule in Failing Health? Some New Data and a Plea Against a Precipitous Conclusion," *62 Kentucky Law Journal* 631 (1974).

[18] *Bivens v. Six Unknown Agents,* 403 U.S. 388 (1971). The dissent was written by Chief Justice Burger.

[19] See, *Schneckloth v. Bustamonte,* 412 U.S. 218 (1973); and *U.S. v. Calandra,* 414 U.S. 338 (1974).

Acquittal. This is very much like the civil motion for directed verdict or judgment n.o.v., except that it is available only to the criminal defendant. It asks the court to enter a judgment of acquittal because the prosecution has failed to present sufficient evidence to sustain a conviction of the defendant. The judge is probably not likely to grant this motion often, since he can present the completed case to the jury, get a verdict, and enter judgment on that verdict with a greater degree of protection from appellate court reversal.

The actual presentation of evidence is similar to that of the civil trial. The prosecution, with the burden of proof, presents its material first. The defense has the opportunity to cross-examine the prosecution's witnesses, to impeach their credibility or reliability, that is, draw into question the truthfulness and accuracy of the testimony. The criminal process involves a set of statutes that define the crimes. When the state charges a person with a crime, the appropriate statute usually specifies the elements of the crime. That is, the statute will define exactly what constitutes armed robbery as opposed to burglary, and first degree murder as opposed to voluntary manslaughter.[20] That means the state, when it presents its evidence, must present sufficient evidence to establish guilt, beyond a reasonable doubt, on each element of the charged offense. This increases the precision with which the state must gather and present its evidence, and the amount of evidence that it must have in order to convict a person. The instructions to the jury usually spell out the elements of the offense, and indicate that if the state has failed to prove one of these elements, the jury must reach a verdict of not guilty.

To prove its own case the defense need not present any evi-

---

[20] For example, robbery may be defined as taking "from the person of another any article of value by violence or by putting in fear, ..." This requires the prosecution to prove several things:

    (1) There was a taking from the victim.
    (2) The items taken were of value.
    (3) The victim was put in fear or violence was used in the taking.
    (4) [By implication] the accused *intended* to take from the victim.

If element 3 is not proven beyond a reasonable doubt by testimony, then conviction may not be had for robbery, but may be obtained for larceny, which does not include element 3.

dence at all, based in part on the privilege against self-incrimination, and in part on the burden that the state has. Usually, the defense will present evidence and, in many jury cases, put the defendant on the witness stand, even though his Constitutional rights do not require it. This will be done largely to present, to the jury, whatever counterevidence is available since the subtleties of the burden of proof may escape most juries. The presentation of evidence by the defense will depend on how strong a case the prosecution has made, the strength of the evidence available to the defense, and the tactical calculations of the defendant and his attorney about the trial and the jurors. If the defendant testifies, he is open to cross-examination by the prosecution, and the defendant must testify about prior criminal convictions. This may reduce the likelihood of second or third offenders testifying in their own behalf. The prosecution is also allowed to submit rebuttal evidence, at the close of the defendant's presentation, if the defense presents an alibi or other new evidence.

After the presentation of the evidence, the attorneys summarize their cases to the jury, and the judge presents the jury instructions. Instructions are suggested by the attorneys, and the judge will choose the ones he feels are appropriate. Since these contain various statements about the burden of proof, the elements of the crime, and so forth, they can be quite crucial to the jury's deliberations. Since the instructions guide the jury on what the law of a subject is, they are crucial to the deliberations of the jury when there are questions about the meaning of the law in the jury room. The instructions can be hotly contested by the attorneys before the judge presents them and they often form the basis of appeal by the defense, after a conviction, claiming that the trial judge erred in the wording of the instructions. There are a variety of forms or standard instructions, and most state jurisdictions have a schedule of instructions to use for various crimes and for various situations, such as when the jury is deadlocked. On appeal, the instructions to the jury are central because the instructions focus on the law and questions of law are the appropriate subjects for appellate courts to decide.

As in civil trials, procedures involving jury deliberations are regularized. However, in criminal trials the procedures are more rigorous, since the parties to a civil trial can agree to any kind of jury decision process they want, and because of general due process requirements in criminal proceedings. The jury is more closely protected from outside information sources—newspapers and television—and from pressures for a particular decision. If there is any possibility of jury tampering, or undue influence from outside pressures, the trial judge will probably sequester the jury—isolate the jury during the trial and deliberations—rather than run the risk of having to declare a mistrial because of some violation of procedures for jury operation.

The jury's verdict normally must be unanimous, although recently the Supreme Court has allowed nonunanimous criminal convictions in certain kinds of cases.[21] In addition, it is constitutionally permissible for the criminal jury to be composed of less than 12 members.[22] In addition to finding the defendant guilty or not guilty, the jury may also find the accused guilty of lesser, included offenses. This means that a person accused of a particular crime, such as first degree murder, may be found guilty of a lesser, included offense such as second degree murder, if the jury finds that the state has failed to prove the elements of first degree murder, but has proved the elements of second degree murder. The lesser, included offense usually involves the same factual crime (in this case, murder) but second degree murder requires different elements be proved, or a lesser number of elements are involved in the second crime. It seems possible that under this situation a conviction of the lesser crime means that the jury could not agree on the original charge, and compromised by convicting of the lesser offense rather than acquitting.

The verdict of the jury may be that the defendant is not guilty, in which case the defendant is permitted to go free, except that he has had the expense of the trial, the limitations on his freedom, and he has a police record. Since police records do not record trial outcomes, an acquitted individual still has the record of having been arrested. Attempts, with increasing success, are being made

[21] *Johnson v. Louisiana,* 406 U.S. 356 (1972); and *Apodoca v. Oregon,* 406 U.S. 404 (1972).
[22] *Williams v. Florida,* 399 U.S. 78 (1970).

to have police expunge their records in such cases. On the other hand, the defendant may be guilty. The judge then must sentence the individual to an appropriate penalty. The penalties available depend on the crime, and the legislature, in defining the crime, will specify the maximum and possibly the minimum sentence for conviction of the crime.

The judge usually has some discretion within these parameters. The supposed reason for this discretion is so the individual penalty can be tailored to the individual and the circumstances of the crime. However, it appears that this discretion is often used by the judge to discriminate against certain groups of people, with no rational or penological basis for the variation.[23]

The variations in sentencing may depend on the race of the convict, his age, his past record, the crime for which he has been convicted, or his attitude toward the judge. Any of these factors may be relevant to the rehabilitation of the criminal, but the state of criminology and penology is such that these sorts of factors still raise some doubt about whether they make sense as reasons for applying particular penalties. There are some recent efforts, informal and formal, to reduce sentencing discrepancies by establishing peer group review of sentences.[24] Also determinant sentences, established by the legislature when it enacts a criminal law, fix the sentence for conviction of the crime, so that the judge has no discretion once the accused has been convicted. Empirical evidence suggests that sentencing procedures do not make any real difference in helping the convicted person and in rehabilitating him into society.[25]

---

[23] See Lawrence Tiffany, Yakov Avichai, and Geoffrey Peters, "A Statistical Analysis of Sentencing in Federal Courts: Defendants Convicted After Trial, 1967-1968," *4 Journal of Legal Studies* 369 (1975); M. Levin, "Urban Politics and Judicial Behavior," *1 Journal of Legal Studies* 193 (1972); Robert Dawson, *Sentencing: The Decision as to Type, Length, and Conditions of Sentence* (Boston: Little, Brown, 1969), and A. Somit, J. Tanenhaus, and W. Wilke, "Aspects of Judicial Sentencing Behavior," *21 University of Pittsburgh Law Review* 613 (1960).

[24] Shari Seidman Diamond and Hans Zeisel, "Sentencing Councils: A Study of Sentence Disparity and its Reduction," *43 University of Chicago Law Review* 109 (1975).

[25] Ronald Goldfarb and Linda Singer, *After Conviction: A Review of the American Correction System* (New York: Simon and Schuster, 1973).

Defendant	Procedural Steps	Prosecutor
	Intake stage	
	Complaint	
	Arrest	
Counsel retained or appointed		
	Initial appearance	
	Preliminary hearing	
		Information or grand jury
		Indictment
	Arraignment	
Plea		
Motion to exclude evidence		
	Trial stage	
	Selection of jury	
		Witnesses and Cross-Examination
Motion for judgment of acquittal		
Witness and cross-examination		
	Concluding arguments	
	Instructions to jury	
	Jury verdict	
	Disposition stage	
	Sentence	

Figure 4-1 Process model of criminal cases.

The model presented here is similar to the civil process, in some respects; in other ways, it is quite different. The criminal process model is outlined in Figure 4.1. The differences are most apparent and include the early stages of formulating the case, which are nearly entirely up to the prosecutor and the grand jury in criminal cases. The pleading stage in the criminal justice system essentially determines what evidence is available, and what charges the evidence will support. The defendant plays a small role in this formulating stage, and his primary relationship to the system is in terms of incarceration or release pending the Indictment or Information. The pretrial discovery stage is also somewhat different since the defendant has the constitutional privilege against self-incrimination in the criminal process. This means that unless the defendant asks for discovery from the prosecution, the prosecutor cannot obtain certain kinds of evidence or information from the defendant. The remainder of the criminal process involves the traditional trial, but with no opportunities for the prosecution to circumvent the trial using various safety-valve motions, as in civil cases. Finally, the criminal process includes a disposition stage that, although it involves only a sentencing process, is not present in the civil trial. In the civil trial, the disposition is established by the fact finder, and there is no need for the court—except in equity cases—to formulate a remedy. Even in equity cases, the plaintiff usually formulates the remedy where the complaint if filed, and the judge will just enforce that remedy, rather than construct his own.

The similarities with the civil process deal with the social service functions that have been given to some civil courts and not the civil process model in Figure 3.1. This relates in part to the dispositional processes of these two kinds of courts. They are similar, partly because they have been given similar functions to perform—social-service and rehabilitation efforts vis-a-vis deviant individuals. Also, both the criminal and social-service processes have a more elaborate intake stage than the civil process model (Figure 3.1), since the handling of particular cases by either of these processes involves determining what the particular problem is in each case. Although the criminal intake stage is tied to the specification of charges and due process protections for the individual, it does result in an outline of what the alleged crime was and how the defendant relates to that crime according to the evidence against him. The similarities in these judicial processes will be even more apparent after a discussion of particular criminal court procedures.

VARIATIONS OF THE MODEL

In recent years a good deal of scholarly research and writing has explored how the criminal justice process actually works. As a result, there have been some additional models presented that attempt to provide a theoretical structure for the empirical findings in the literature. These models differ not only in terms of procedures, which is the focus above, but also in the purposes and functions for which the system operates. Probably the most widely known model was outlined by Herbert Packer.[26] Packer posits two models of the criminal justice system, based on quite different assumptions, and which produce quite different outcomes.

The model outlined in the preceding section is probably closest to Packer's Due Process model. This model, according to Packer, is based on values and assumptions that focus on a|suspicion of the fact-finding processes that are used by courts. The model is designed as an obstacle course for the state, with each stage presenting increasingly more difficult impediments to convicting the accused. The early stages of the process, the investigation stages, are suspect because they are unreliable, and the later, formal procedures of adversary adjudication are more reliable because they are formal and uniform. This is all designed to prevent and eliminate mistakes of fact-finding, which would result in the conviction of innocent people. The basic Due Process view is that the procedures offer safety from convicting innocent people. The doctrine of legal guilt is important to this model. The guilt of a person is established not by the probability of guilt but the procedural certainty of it. The integrity of the process is protected by its formalized nature.

---

[26] Herbert Packer, *The Limits of the Criminal Sanction* (Stanford, California: Stanford University Press, 1968), pp. 149-173.

In contrast to this, Packer's Crime Control model has as its objective the repression of criminal conduct in the most efficient manner possible with the use of only limited resources. Packer suggests that this model can best be analogized to the production assembly line in which people at various stages, perform specific tasks on the line of criminal cases that pass them. The Crime Control model is structured in terms of system apprehension, trial, conviction, and disposition of criminals, in large numbers, and with a minimum of disruption to the routine operation of the process. It is important for the process to be speedy and final; that means there is a premium placed on not allowing any case to be held up by procedural problems or by the tactics of the accused. The assembly line does not necessarily process all the cases that are initially placed on it. The early, investigatory stages screen out innocent people, and then begin the processing of only those not selected out—those who are *probably* guilty. In fact, Packer suggests that the Crime Control model treats suspects, once they have been placed in the process, as probably guilty (or they would have been selected out), and the probability of guilt increases as the case gets further into the process. The emphasis on efficiency of operation leaves little room for procedural obstacles or individual protections. Once the suspect is beyond the early screen, and the probability of his guilt increases, the Crime Control model does not emphasize the adversary trial process at all. One of the major characteristics of the later stages is the plea bargain, which can resolve the case, in a "successful" fashion by a conviction without the need for an adversary trial and ritual; the trial, according to the model, adds nothing to the reliability of the process and is likely to be cumbersome and inefficient.

These two models may have some common elements,[27] but they also point up some marked differences in the values that the system furthers. Any criminal justice system (whether national, state, or local) contains various elements of each of these models, and probably thus contains a number of conflicting and contradicting values and procedures. Recent Supreme Court decisions regarding the rights of persons accused of crime may be an effort to bring reality more in line with the Due Process model, yet

[27] *Ibid.*, pp. 154-157.

even with these decisions, there are elements of the Crime Control model present in most criminal court systems. The original model of the procedures outlined above is oriented toward the Due Process model, and the material that follows examines mostly the procedures of courts, rather than the administrative, investigative, factfinding stages of the process. However, within particular courts, the reality of the system's operation shows elements of the administrative, efficiency model at work.

PLEA BARGAINING

A very widespread phenomenon in the criminal process has raised a great deal of controversy in recent years. Bargaining between the prosecutor and the defense attorney over a plea of guilty is responsible for a great deal of the time and effort of most prosecuting and many defense attorneys, and it results in many of the convictions that are reported each year in various court statistics.[28] Since a large proportion of criminal cases are settled by a guilty plea (bargained or not), few convictions involve the criminal trial of the Due Process model. Plea bargaining is probably used most frequently in urban criminal courts where there is a large backlog of criminal cases awaiting trial. Probably most bargained guilty pleas involve more serious crimes that constitute felonies but that become misdemeanor convictions. The reasons why plea bargaining is used so widely are not clear. It may be because it is quicker than a full trial and it is more certain. It might reduce the backlog and delay in trial that many urban criminal courts face. It may also be due to the values of the Crime Control model, which suggest that participants see it as more efficient to negotiate a plea; thus it is better for the system. Whatever the reason, the fact of its existence cannot be denied, and its expansion seems likely to continue despite various challenges and arguments against it.

---

[28] The President's Commission on Law Enforcement and Administration of Justice, *Task Force Report: The Courts* (Washington, D.C: U.S.G.P.O., 1967) uses 1964 statistics to estimate approximately 87 percent of the total convictions are the result of guilty pleas. p. 9. Of guilty pleas, various percentages are the result of plea bargains. Probably 60 to 75 percent of guilty pleas result from a bargain. See p. 9.

The bargain involves the agreement by the defendant to plead guilty to the charge rather than contest the charge and put the state to the task of trying the case. In return for this, the prosecutor agrees to one or more of several items. The prosecutor can agree to reduce the charge against the defendant. This often means that the defendant will receive a lesser sentence for the lesser crime. For a reduced charge, or the elimination of several charges, or for a promise of a particular sentence recommendation on the part of the prosecutor, the defendant pleads guilty to whatever the resulting charge. These sentence considerations —reducing the potential sentence—are a major consideration from the defendant's point of view, since that is one tangible benefit he receives from such an arrangement. Second, the prosecutor can agree to make a particular recommendation to the judge about what sentence would be appropriate for the particular defendant involved.[29] Thus the judge, who often takes sentencing cues, if not formal recommendations, from the prosecutor, will assess a lighter penalty because of the prosecutor's recommendation. Third and quite frequently, the prosecutor can change one offense even though there may be four or five included offenses in the case. Fourth, the prosecutor may drop or dismiss all the charges against an individual, in return for the defendant's cooperation and information about other criminal activity that the prosecutor feels are more important than the activity of the defendant.

The defendant's calculus in the bargaining process involves the likelihood of being convicted if he goes to trial, the resulting criminal record he would have, and the amount of penalty he might receive if convicted at trial. He reduces the uncertainty by agreeing to the bargain. He can be fairly certain of what he faces when he goes into the courtroom to plead guilty.[30] The defen-

---

[29] See *Santobello v. New York,* 404 U.S. 257 (1971) in which the Supreme Court held that the state was bound to abide by its part of such a bargain, involving a sentence recommendation—or allow the defendant to withdraw his guilty plea.

[30] Lynn Mather, "To Plead Guilty or Go To Trial," (paper prepared for delivery at the 1972 meeting of the American Political Science Association, Washington, D.C.); and Lynn Mather, "Some Determinants of the Method of Case Disposition: Decision-Making by Public Defenders in Los Angeles," *8 Law and Society Review* 187 (1973).

dant must accept the final arrangements before it becomes effective. It is interesting to note, however, that the defendant himself rarely participates in the bargaining at all, so he may not make any careful calculation of the costs and benefits himself. His counsel does the bargaining, sometimes without even telling the defendant what he is doing or why.[31] In fact, the defense attorney's role may end when he has convinced the defendant to accept the bargain and plead guilty, as the best alternative open to him.[32] Whether this is a proper role for the defense attorney to play, especially a court-appointed attorney, is quite debatable, but it appears that this is often what the defense lawyer does in his role of defending the person accused of a crime.

An example of this bargaining process might illustrate some of the factors and characteristics that relate to the plea bargain. If we have a case in which someone is accosted on a dark street and asked to give the assailant his money, or his life, this generally constitutes the crime of robbery. Let us assume the victim did not clearly see the face of his adversary or a weapon. If there was a weapon, or a possibility of a weapon involved, the assailant may be subject to an additional, felony charge. However, these facts may also involve a lesser included offense, such as grand larceny or petit larceny (depending on the amount of money taken in the encounter). The prosecutor may begin by charging the defendant with the maximum, robbery and the associated felony of using a deadly weapon. However, in return for a plea of guilty on the robbery charge, the prosecutor might be persuaded to drop the deadly weapon charge because the facts are not clear that a weapon was involved. The prosecutor might be bargained down to larceny, if the victim could not make a positive identification of the defendant, so that the probability of conviction was reduced. If the defendant agreed to cooperate and testify against a ring of

---

[31] Jonathan Casper, *American Criminal Justice: The Defendant's Perspective* (Englewood Cliffs, N.J: Prentice-Hall, 1972); Abraham Blumberg, "The Practice of Law as a Confidence Game: Organizational Cooptation of a Profession," *1 Law and Society Review* 15 (1967); and Jackson Battle, "In Search of the Adversary System—The Cooperative Practices of Private Criminal Defense Attorneys," *20 Texas Law Review* 60 (1971).

[32] Abraham Blumberg, *supra* footnote 31.

thieves, the prosecutor could reduce the robbery charge to larceny.

Each of these possibilities involve some consideration obtained by the prosecutor, in return for the defendant's plea of guilty. Each of the potential charges involved in this case involve different possible sentences, and the defendant may find that pleading guilty to larceny (e.g., 1 to 10 years and $500 fine) is much more attractive to pleading guilty to robbery (e.g., 10 to 25 years). In addition, the prosecutor may agree to recommend leniency, (the minimum sentence) in any of these charges, in return for a plea, if the defendant is a first offender, or is cooperative in testifying in another case where the prosecutor needs evidence to increase the likelihood of conviction. The original charges may be more nearly accurate, but the subsequent reduced charges are not totally inaccurate, although they do not reflect the maximum charge possible. The strength of the prosecutor's evidence will influence how easily he bargains. If the victim could not clearly see the defendant's face, then it might be difficult to prove the defendant committed any crime at trial. If the prosecutor can get a plea to larceny, without a trial with tenuous identification, he has obtained as much, if not more, than he could out of the full, due-process trial.

The prosecutor gets a great deal from the plea bargain. He gets a conviction without a trial and the work that a full trial requires of him and his staff. The conviction is important for most elected prosecutors since his general conviction rate (batting average) may be an important part of his record in office, upon which he would run for reelection. Prosecutors who seek reelection would be happy to have as many quick and easy convictions as possible. The prosecutor is not really interested in the crime for which the conviction is gained, since the difference between an assault and battery conviction and a disorderly conduct conviction probably escapes the grasp of most observers, especially the electorate. This process has a great deal of payoff, and little cost for the prosecutor. He has wide discretion about setting bargaining policy, and he can determine which cases not to bargain. Thus, a widely noted crime or a gruesome crime would not be bargained because of the publicity, while the unnoticed crimes can be disposed of quite rapidly.[33]

From the defendant's point of view the bargain has advantages and disadvantages, depending on his situation and past record. If the defendant did not commit the crime of which he is charged, then he may strongly wish to go to trial and be acquitted. However, there is always some uncertainty about whether he would win at trial. If he has a prior criminal record, he may be very hard pressed to go to trial where that record might be disclosed and his innocence jeopardized by past convictions. Thus, he may find it "cheaper" to plead guilty to this charge even when he is innocent. As an advantage, if the accused is guilty, the bargain may result in a lesser penalty than he could expect after a trial conviction. His calculations are based on the strength of the case against him, not his actual guilt. The bargaining process never addresses the issue of guilt. This suggests the basis of some of the strong criticism of plea bargaining, since it can be used to obtain a guilty plea from an innocent person.

The judge is not a participant, generally, in the bargaining process.[34] Yet the judge has a particular role to play. Judges know that bargaining occurs and they probably know when a case before them is a bargain. The judge has a constitutional obligation to ascertain that the defendant's plea (whatever it results from) is made knowingly and voluntarily.[35] This the judge may do in a perfunctory, ritualistic fashion, or with some care so that the defendant is informed of what is happening and what conse-

[33] Note, "Discretion Exercised by Montana County Attorneys in Criminal Prosecutions," *28 Montana Law Review* 41 (1966); and John Kaplan, "The Prosecutorial Discretion—A Comment," *60 Northwestern University Law Review* 174 (1965).

[34] James Klonoski, Charles Mitchell, and Edward Gallagher, "Plea Bargaining in Oregon: An Exploratory Study," *50 Oregon Law Review* 114, at 128-131 (1971); but see Abraham Blumberg, *Criminal Justice* (New York: Quadrangle Books, 1967).

[35] In *Boykin v. Alabama,* 395 U.S. 238 (1969) and *McCarthy v. U.S.,* 394 U.S. 495 (1969) the Supreme Court held that plea bargaining could be constitutional if the trial court establishes that the plea is intelligent and voluntary.

quences will arise from his plea.[36] It is probable that in most bargained cases, the judge's role is simply to place the courts' official stamp on the bargain, although in a few others, the judge insures the defendant's knowledge of what is happening.

There are several questions about the propriety of plea bargaining that are quite fundamental to our system of justice. There are constitutional questions about due process of law, and whether the defendant's plea is voluntary or induced by some promise made by an official.[37] Supposedly, a plea cannot be induced by a promise and, although it appears that many pleas are so induced, this problem is circumvented when the trial court "establishes" that the plea is completely voluntary. This is often done in perfunctory fashion by the defendant stating there has been no promise, even when one has been made. In addition, is it appropriate for a defendant to plead guilty to crimes that he did not commit? In some cases, there is the likelihood that the plea bargain results in just this plea, and it is a questionable outcome. There are questions about pleading guilty to a crime when there is a good chance that trial would result in an acquittal. Yet because of counsel's advice or because of the long delay before a trial, the defendant may choose to plead guilty and "get it over with." These are major problems for the accurate operation of the criminal court system. These show a major difference between the Crime Control model and the Due Process model. The former finds nothing wrong with bargaining for a guilty plea to charges because it is efficient and administratively appropriate. The latter model raises strong objections to such bargained pleas because the defendant may not be guilty of the charge and the system should not be allowed to achieve conviction.

Specialized Court Procedures

In a pattern like that presented in the last chapter, this section contains a description and discussion of various criminal courts. Although all of these courts may not exist in some jurisdictions,

[36] See Lynn Mather, *supra* footnote 30 for a description of "taking the waivers" in guilty plea cases in one jurisdiction. Donald Newman; *supra* footnote 8.

[37] Note, "The Unconstitutionality of Plea Bargaining," *83 Harvard Law Review* 1387 (1970).

and all specialized criminal courts are not discussed here, it is possible to present some of the variations in procedures and functions in criminal courts by examining these particular courts.

Most criminal judicial systems have a tier of courts that might best be termed criminal courts of inferior or limited jurisdiction, like those described in Chapter 3 relating to civil courts. These courts serve a set of criminal functions in the criminal process, but their name varies widely and includes misdemeanor courts, police courts, magistrate's court, or justice of the peace courts. Whatever the name, this court is the one that serves as the point of contact between most citizens and the judicial system.[38] This court has jurisdiction over a number of minor criminal offenses that "net" most of the people who become criminal defendants. These offenses include violation of traffic ordinances, housing codes, or misdemeanors (minor crimes involving minimal penalties such as no more than six months in jail and/or $1000 fine). This court obviously deals with large numbers of people and offenses even if they are minor. Some have characterized these courts as very undignified and unpleasant mills that leave a very negative impression with most people who come in contact with them.[39] However, these courts perform quite essential functions in the criminal process. These functions are performed in all criminal justice systems. Specialized courts are most likely to exist in urban or metropolitan areas where the caseload in the criminal courts is quite high, and where there is the greatest need for an administrative arena in the criminal courts to handle much of the routine business presented to the courts.

MISDEMEANOR COURTS

The functions and jurisdiction of these courts are one of their unique characteristics. Such courts may have jurisdiction over the

---

[38] Note, "Metropolitan Criminal Courts of First Instance," *70 Harvard Law Review* 320 (1956); Wallace Buck, Jr., "A New Procedure for Municipal Courts," *42 Journal of the Bar Association of Kansas* 7, 8 (1973); and Robert Oliphant, "Reflections on the Lower Court System; The Development of a Unique Clinical Misdemeanor and a Public Defender Program," *57 Minnesota Law Review* 545 (1973).

[39] Lewis Katz, "Municipal Courts—Another Urban Ill," *20 Case Western Reserve Law Review* 87, 90-91 (1968).

trial of some misdemeanor criminal offenses, although some of
the lower criminal courts in metropolitan areas do not have this
jurisdiction.[40] Such courts usually have jurisdiction over summary ordinance offenses, such as vagrancy and disorderly conduct, charges that violate local ordinances and are handled without full-fledged criminal trials. Much of the court's time may be
devoted to the handling of such matters.[41] These courts may
handle ordinance violations such as traffic offenses or housing
code violations, although these may either be handled by a special
branch of the misdemeanor court or as part of the court's general
business. A second important function of these courts, where
they exist, is to conduct the arraignment and preliminary hearing
stages of the regular criminal process.[42] In areas where there are
many criminal cases, a major part of this court's time is devoted to
screening the criminal cases that are brought into the system, and
conducting the preliminary hearings in order to determine what
cases should be tried and which ones have insufficient evidence to
warrant further judicial scrutiny. These courts may also have
some civil jurisdiction, especially where the system involves a
justice of the peace.[43] In rural states, the justice of the peace is
both the civil and criminal court of first instance for some cases,
However, in more populous areas, where the judicial workload is
quite large, there is no civil jurisdiction lodged in these criminal
courts, since all their time is devoted to handling the criminal
matters.

The procedures used by these courts in the conduct of their
business depend on what function is being performed,[44] and the
particular judge who is conducting the proceeding.[45] Generally,

[40] Note, *supra* footnote 38.
[41] *Ibid.*
[42] *Ibid.*, and Kenneth Graham and Leon Letwin, *supra* footnote 6.
[43] Kenneth Vanlandingham, "The Decline of the Justice of the Peace," *12 Kansas
Law Review* 389 (1964); and George Partain, "The Justice of the Peace: Constitutional Questions," *69 West Virginia Law Review* 314, 318 (1967).
[44] Note, *supra* footnote 38.
[45] David Atkinson and Dale Neuman, "Judicial Attitudes and Defendant Attributes: Some Consequences for Municipal Court Decision-Making," *19 Journal
of Public Law* 69 (1970).

there is not a very rigorous effort to follow the criminal process from a Due Process model orientation.[46] In addition, whereas recent judicial decisions have focused on aspects of the early stages of the criminal process (which are tied to this court), there may very well exist a sliding scale of due process that assigns a relatively low priority to procedural niceties at this level of the criminal process. This may not be a conscious policy of the system or the judges in the courts. However, the kinds of business these courts handle and their jurisdictional limits do produce an orientation in this court that differs from the Due Process model. As an early study of the procedures of these courts indicated,[47] the role of defense counsel and the treatment of the accused in preliminary hearings before these courts are quite disparate from a Due Process Model of criminal procedures.

The quality of the process in this court is also only as high as the judges who conduct the procedures. Thus, if a judge is untrained or poorly trained in the law and does not know the substantive law, the preliminary hearing will be a rubber stamp of the prosecutor's request since the judge is incapable of making his own, independent determinations of the issues. How the judge conducts Housing Court or Traffic court will largely depend on what he knows about the law and his powers, and how he feels about the people who appear before him as defendants.

A primary set of functions conducted by this level of court involves the trial of a variety of summary ordinance offenses. The sorts of offenses involved include vagrancy, disorderly conduct, and public intoxication. These categories are very broad, and the definitions of the crimes are so vague that many types of behavior can be prosecuted under these rubrics. The procedures used here are usually quite summary. There is no jury and, if a jury trial is requested, as is rarely the case, the case is transferred to the trial court of general jurisdiction. In the past, there was usually no regular prosecuting attorney assigned to these cases, and the

---

[46] Lucinda Long, "Innovation in Urban Criminal Misdemeanor Courts," (paper prepared for delivery at the 1973 Meeting of the Midwest Political Science Association, Chicago).

[47] Note, *supra* footnote 38.

arresting police officer served as the complaining witness and the representative of the state. In addition, since the defendant rarely had counsel, the process involved the judge, the defendant, and the police officer.[48] It appears that often under these circumstances the defendant was found guilty even if the elements of the crime were not proved.[49] However, these trials today may involve more procedural due process and more attention to the rights of defendants, although it is likely to be more casual than a felony trial.

TRAFFIC COURTS

Traffic Court handles a tremendous number of cases (650,000 per week according to one source).[50] Such courts, which operate fulltime, are found in major urban areas where the number of automobiles and people generate large numbers of offenses. In rural areas, traffic violations are handled by Justices of the Peace (often as a major part of their business).[51] The criminal orientation is the traditional function of criminal courts; in regard to traffic ordinances this means that due process of law considerations should operate. However, in most traffic courts defense counsel is not present[52] and the jury is a very rare phenomenon, although where it is used in Traffic Court it may be used by the defendant for delay purposes or in an effort to get a more sympathetic trier of fact than the stereotyped traffic court judge.[53] The prosecutor may be an administrative official from the police department or from the prosecutor's office, and he is not always a lawyer. What usually happens is the ticketing police officer presents his story, and the defendant is then called upon to tell his story, and the judge will then determine the case on the spot. One of the problems with this informal process is that the

---

[48] *Ibid.*

[49] *Ibid.,* at 331.

[50] Ronald Schiller, "No Traffic-Court Jam," *59 National Civic Review* 141 (1970).

[51] George Warren, *Traffic Courts* (Boston: Little, Brown, 1942), p. 21.

[52] "Traffic Court Reform," *4 Columbia Journal of Law and Social Problems* 255, 256 (1968).

[53] George Warren, *supra* footnote 51, pp. 75-76.

judge tends to believe the policeman's story because of his repeated appearances in this court, and the judge is inclined to find
the defendant guilty so that the case does not take any more time
than is absolutely necessary.[54] This sort of traffic court operates
with what might be called administrative efficiency such as
Packer's Crime Control model suggests.[55] These court procedures usually involve courts with the authority to fine or imprison
defendants convicted of violations, and that is one of the major
reasons for this criminal procedure even if it is not very due
process oriented.

Some jurisdictions have developed highly efficient and administrative means of dealing with traffic offenses. For example,
when the driver does not want to contest the ticket, he is sometimes permitted to appear simply at the police station, within a
specific period of time (for example, within 10 days of the issuance of the ticket) and pay the scheduled fine for the offense. In
other situations, especially for nonmoving violations (parking
tickets), the offender may be able to place the scheduled fine in
the traffic ticket itself, which is actually a self-addressed envelope,
and mail it in. These kinds of administrative processes exist for
the less serious traffic offenses, and for those drivers who do not
want to contest the offenses—they admit their errors. It is far
removed from the criminal process model, and it completely
circumvents any of the would-be protections available to the
accused in the criminal process.

Traffic court remedies have been expanded to include more
than fines or license suspensions, such as education and protection of the population. Thus, the Court can serve as a means of
training poor drivers, improving the skills of others, and removing the incompetent drivers from the highways altogether. This
function can be performed by control over the license of the
drivers or the licensing function itself.[56] Also, courts can provide
schools or training sessions for offenders under this scheme in

---

[54] Ronald Schiller, *supra* footnote 50.

[55] "Traffic Court Reform," *supra* footnote 52, at 256.

[56] James Economos, *Traffic Court Procedure and Administration* (Chicago: American
Bar Association Standing Committee on the Traffic Court Program, 1961).

order to improve driving and to reduce the chances for accidents in the future. This is based on a public interest function, which allows the state to regulate the use of highways, and on the privilege of driving in an administrative manner.

HOUSING COURTS

The Housing Court is a misdemeanor court, and the usual procedures it follows are summary in nature. There is usually not a jury, and the judge conducts a supervised "hearing" in which he asks the questions. The defendant may have an attorney, but the prosecution is usually done by a housing code enforcement official rather than the city's prosecutor's office.[57] The purpose of the defendant landlord's attorney may be to obtain a minimal sanction rather than to establish his client's innocence. The code enforcement proceeding is usually a routine procedure in which the city (prosecution) has already verified violations and is seeking the application of sanctions only because of the aggregious nature of the violations or because the defendant is unwilling to make necessary repairs. Where the Housing Court has been given general jurisdiction over all landlord–tenant problems, in addition to code enforcements, and where the Court has been given social-service functions, such as supervising housing repairs, the civil procedures involving landlord–tenant disputes may be very informal and ad hoc. In such proceedings, the parties (city, tenant, or landlord) may be able to tell the "whole story," which may involve charges and counter-charges and representation of a very complicated situation. The court's resolution of issues is often based on its equity powers.

The procedures used by traffic courts and housing courts illustrate that these kinds of "crimes" are generally treated in a bureaucratic or administrative fashion by the courts. That is, these cases are processed rapidly, without great attention to procedure or the rights of defendants, and they generally result in standard and uniform fines or peculiar equitable remedies. Al-

---

[57] Sholom Comay, "The City of Pittsburgh House Court," *30 University of Pittsburgh Law Review* 459 (1969).

though there are defendants who are able to argue their way out of a traffic ticket and some landlords who are not punished for code violations, the general result of these criminal court proceedings is to hold the defendant guilty and assess some penalty.

Housing code enforcement is aimed at correcting violations when they are discovered, but enforcement tends to be haphazard and not very effective in terms of criminal sanctions.[58] Code enforcement usually requires action by housing officials in the form of inspections and notice procedures, as well as in the actual prosecution of violators. However, there are some instances in which the tenant himself, can initiate the enforcement of code provisions.[59] Housing Courts are designed to centralize the code enforcement process and add some civil remedies for the disputants, especially the tenants. In addition, some of these courts have been created with the idea of providing social-service functions for the parties, as well as providing a criminal or civil arena for the settling of disputes.[60] Such social-service functions may be similar to some of those performed by Domestic Relations or Family Courts, except that in Housing Courts, the function relates to the landlord and the tenant and usually serves educative ends. Since the problems may be only partially emotional and largely economic, education may be ineffective as a solution. Yet some feel that the court can perform social services in relation to these housing problems. For example, the Court can provide clinics at which landlords may learn what is required of them and tenants may discover what recourses they have.[61] Such clinics may serve educative functions and be connected with the Court only because the Court refers people to the clinics or requires attendance by offenders. In addition, the judge may participate in the

---

[58] Note, "Enforcement of Municipal Housing Codes," *78 Harvard Law Review* 801, 801-804 (1965); and Tova Indritz, "The Tenant's Rights Movement," *1 New Mexico Law Review* 1, 50-51 (1971).

[59] Alvin Jaffe, "Recent Developments in Illinois Landlord-Tenant Law," 1972 *University of Illinois Law Forum* 589, 593.

[60] Judah Gribetz and Frank Grad, "Housing Code Enforcement: Sanctions and Remdies," *66 Columbia Law Review* 1254, 1287 (1966).

[61] Sholom Comay, *supra* footnote 57.

clinics, although the judge's involvement is likely to be constrained by his role perceptions.

Civil remedies may be available to Housing Courts, and they illustrate how the Court might deal with these kinds of problems. One recent essay has suggested that slumlordism be made a tort that would provide the tenant with a civil legal remedy, in damages, for the difficulties the tenant experiences in such housing.[62] This is a tenous proposition, and it has not been utilized by most jurisdictions. The most widely used civil remedies are those equitable ones developed by the courts, or provided by state statute. For example, the Court can issue a repair order that requires the landlord to make specified repairs, at the risk of a contempt citation for ignoring the order. In addition, the tenant may be given the right to self-help. That is, the tenant makes whatever repairs are necessary to his apartment. The tenant may then be able to deduct the cost of the repairs from his rent.[63] Some jurisdictions permit various sorts of rent withholding by the tenant. In some states, only when the rent is in the form of welfare payments can the state withhold the rent.[64] In other states, the tenant may, on his own, withhold the rent under certain circumstances, and use it to make repairs.[65] Housing in the worst condition may be demolished by court order. If the Court determines that the building is hazardous and threatening to the occupants and neighborhood, the statutes of some states permit the Court to order the building either vacated or demolished. This emergency power has drastic results for the landlord and for the tenants who must find some other place to live.

SUMMARY

The standard procedures and sanctions in criminal courts of limited jurisdiction have been described above. There are some variations in their procedures, especially from the criminal process model, which are largely because these courts perform func-

---

[62] Joseph Saxe and Fred Hiestand, "Slumlordism as a Tort," *65 Michigan Law Review* 869 (1967).

[63] Note, "Landlord v. Tenant: An Appraisal of the Habitability and Repair Problem," *22 Case Western Reserve Law Review* 739, 748 (1971).

[64] *Ibid.,* at 757-760.

[65] *Ibid.,* at 748.

tions that differ from the traditional, felony criminal court, and that parallel the social-service functions of some civil courts. Many of the criminal charges involve skid-row inhabitants, drunken drivers, landlords interested in making a profit, or others for whom the traditional criminal penalities would make no sense. Since these criminal remedies are often inadequate to solving the "problem" presented to the court, the judge resorts to his powers of equity and his own imagination to devise some solution that would aid the defendant and the plaintiff—whether the state or a tenant.

For example, in the case of convictions for some misdemeanors, penalties appear to rest on the judge's discretion such as requiring a contribution to the judge's favorite charity, or barring that, the defendant must spend the day cleaning up the stationhouse and is free to go when his chore is completed. In some localities, a person convicted of driving under the influence of intoxicating beverages may be ordered to donate two pints of blood to a local hospital. Judges sometimes utilize institutionalization or referrals to private agencies that might assist the defendant, such as church groups and Alcoholics Anonymous. The court may be able to utilize the social services of the local government that are frequently available for various civil problems. Also, the judge can order 24-hour detention, which is sufficient time to get the defendant's clothes cleaned, provide him with a shower, and give him a chance to "dry out."

These illustrate some of the variations in outcomes in these courts. The processes by which these are determined and applied vary widely from the Due Process model or the other criminal process models. They border on an administrative agency model of processing "cases' or a social-service model somewhat like the civil courts discussed in Chapter 3. These emphasize the disposition stage of the process, and the intake processes that accompany civil courts performing these functions, rather than the adversary, trial stage of the model.

JUVENILE COURTS
Juvenile Courts could be treated as civil in nature, and distinguished from the criminal courts in America. However, in recent

years the criminal or quasi-criminal nature of these courts has been emphasized, and it is clear that the impact of these courts on the youngsters who appear in them can include incarceration as well as other "penalties." In addition, recent Supreme Court decisions have emphasized the criminal nature of some of the proceedings of these courts. So, although there are many aspects of these courts that parallel civil courts, and although some civil courts, such as Family Courts, do deal with juvenile problems, this general discussion of Juvenile Courts is included as part of the criminal court system.

The specialized treatment of juveniles by the legal system was initially based on separate juvenile detention centers that segregated youngsters from hardened criminals,[66] the development of probation as a sentence alternative to incarceration, and the emerging emphasis on social sciences and psychiatry as a diagnostic and treatment tool. There is a strong element of humanitarianism in this orientation toward children in our society who run afoul of the law,[67] and the specialized court treatment of children is based on the state's role as *parens patriae*.[68] This is the idea that the state acts as the parent in the absence of adequate parental guidance; it treats the child with a firm but enlightened hand as a parent ought to. The process outlined in Juvenile Courts was to be nonadversary and informal since there was to be no punishment of a child. There was a strong emphasis on remedies that were rehabilitative so that the child would become a productive and responsible member of society after his treatment. The treatment was to be individualized so that each youngster received special treatment, designed particularly for him, rather than a standardized sentence for whatever criminal activity he was found guilty of. This Juvenile Court outlook is

[66] The President's Commission on Law Enforcement and Administration of Justice, *Task Force Report: Juvenile Delinquency and Youth Crime* (Washington, D.C: U.S.G.P.O., 1967), p. 3.

[67] Margaret Rosenheim, "Perennial Problems in the Juvenile Court," in Margaret Rosenheim, ed., *Justice for the Child* (New York: Glencoe Press, 1962), pp. 1-4.

[68] Orman Ketcham, "The Unfulfilled Promise of the American Juvenile Child," in Margaret Rosenheim, ed., *Justice for the Child* (New York: Glencoe Press, 1962), pp. 25-26.

probably the basis for much of the recent judicial work in social-service programs discussed in relation to Family Courts and Domestic Relations Courts. The court, at most, could find a child "delinquent," and this would then give the court authority to give guiding and rehabilitative help to correct the causes of the delinquency.

Juvenile Court jurisdiction is a very unique feature of the court. Jurisdiction is based on several factors. First, the age of the accused is important. Most states do not provide for a minimum age, although some provide that no one under seven years of age can be brought before the court. All states specify some maximum age of people under Juvenile Court jurisdiction. The arbitrary age line may be 16, 18, or 20 years, but usually the court has jurisdiction over anyone for alleged misconduct occurring before the maximum age limit. Most Juvenile Court jurisdiction ends completely when a person reaches 21 years of age, although some courts have jurisdiction over adults for certain kinds of offenses such as contributing to the delinquency of a minor, or neglect of a minor. In addition to age, the Juvenile Court's jurisdiction is based on substantive areas of the law.[69] Generally, jurisdictional matters include juvenile delinquents, persons in need of supervision (PINS),[70] and neglected children.[71] There are some offenses, unique to youngsters, over which most Juvenile Courts have jurisdiction, such as truancy, incorrigibility, and moral deprivation. Some of these categories, such as persons in need of supervision, are quite vague, and they can be used by the Juvenile Court to exert jurisdiction over a large number of youngsters who are marginally in need of supervision. Certainly the juvenile judge can limit his discretion in these areas of jurisdiction, but if he does not do that, the Juvenile Court has a wide range of jurisdiction. The juvenile delinquency jurisdiction involves acts

---

[69] Monrad Paulsen, "The Delinquency, Neglect, and Dependency Jurisdiction of the Juvenile Court," in Margaret Rosenheim, ed., *Justice for the Child* (New York: Glencoe Press, 1962), pp. 44-45, 49.

[70] "Nondelinquent Children in New York: The Need for Alternatives to Institutional Treatment," 8 *Columbia Journal of Law and Social Problems* 251, 254-255 (1972).

[71] *Ibid.*, at 256-257.

that would be criminal if committed by an adult. However, because of the age of the alleged perpetrator (less than 16, 18, or 20), the Juvenile Court has jurisdiction in order to examine the entire situation—including the reasons for the action—and apply a remedy where it thinks it is appropriate.

Juvenile Court jurisdiction may be exclusive or concurrent. Concurrent jurisdiction is shared with another court, and usually involves criminal acts. Which court will exercise jurisdiction depends on which court gets its hands on the accused first.[72] In addition, the Juvenile Court usually has the discretion to waive its jurisdiction over some crimes. Thus a person who is at the upper age limit of the Juvenile Court's jurisdiction (usually a specified age category) may be turned over to the adult, criminal court for trial, usually because the offense he is charged with is a felony or a capital offense.[73] Thus, depending on a state's statute, a youth charged with certain crimes and of a certain age may be quite vulnerable to the "adult" criminal trial by the exercise of waiver.[74]

The processes involved in the handling of juveniles vary somewhat, although parallel those of Family Court or of the social-service courts—intake, hearing, and disposition. Recent Supreme Court decisions may standardize certain portions of the procedure. The initial, and often crucial stage, of intake involves a variety of screening procedures designed to channel juvenile cases to the "appropriate" kind of assistance. The function of intake is to determine if the court has jurisdiction over the case, determine the sufficiency of the evidence in the case, and screen out cases in which the offense is too minor to justify the formal procedure.[75] If it is determined that the evidence is insufficient, the court does not have jurisdiction, or some other assistance is more appropriate, the case is diverted from the juvenile justice system. The intake screening can be done by one of several

---

[72] Monrad Paulsen, *supra* footnote 69, p.61.

[73] Samuel Davis, "The Jurisdictional Dilemma of the Juvenile Court," *51 North Carolina Law Review* 195, 197 (1972).

[74] See *Kent v. U.S.*, 383 U.S. 541 (1966) for a discussion of the rights of a juvenile in a waiver hearing.

[75] Elyce Zenoff Ferster and Thomas Courtless, "The Intake Process in the Affluent County Juvenile Court," *22 The Hastings Law Journal* 1127 (1971).

agencies. First, there are a number of informal screening opportunities in police systems, and police officers often choose not to take a youth in at all.[76] In metropolitan areas, the police department usually has youth officers who will screen out a number of cases because of the insufficiency of the evidence obtained, or the minor nature of the offense. Second, welfare and social work agencies also have intake officers who perform such tasks. The Juvenile Court judge sometimes participates in the intake screening; however, this appears to be rare.

The intake officer, whether in the police department or the welfare agency, has a working knowledge of the variety of agency and informal means of assistance that siphon off over half the potential juvenile cases.[77] As with other intake procedures discussed in Chapter 3, intake decisions are based on interviews and investigations. The usual result of this intake hearing is the use of a nonjudicial remedy such as counseling, psychiatric analysis, or informal probation, and the Juvenile Court never even knows of the existence of this case. However, if the intake officer feels that no informal remedy would work, he will begin the formal process by filing a petition in Juvenile Court. This petition is equivalent to a formal criminal complaint. In some jurisdictions, the prosecuting attorney has final control over the filing of a petition.[78] However, usually the intake officer has discretion to determine whether the petition will be filed.

There is another crucial matter that occurs at the intake stage; this is whether the juvenile is detained until he appears before the judge. There is no right to bail in juvenile proceedings, yet there is a general inclination to release the youngster in the custody of his parents, or guardian, or a friend pending the formal hearing on the case.[79] Incarceration or detention depends on the judgment of the intake officer, and his decision usually depends on his

[76] Charles Clayton, "Emerging Patterns in the Administration of Juvenile Justice," *49 Journal of Urban Law* 377, 378 (1971).

[77] Richard Chused, "The Juvenile Court Process: A Study of Three New Jersey Counties," *26 Rutgers Law Review* 488, 505 (1973).

[78] Monrad Paulsen, *supra* footnote 65, at p.61.

[79] Alan Burns, "Juvenile Detention: An Eyewitness Account," *4 Columbia Human Rights Law Review* 303 (1972).

assessment of the likelihood that the youngster will appear on the date scheduled for the court hearing. Although this is somewhat like the calculation the judge makes in setting bail, the matter here also involves whether the youngster is in danger from his current surroundings, such as threats of violence from his parents or his friends, and whether he may be a danger to the community into which he would be released.

If a juvenile is detained pending the filing of the petition and the hearing, he is usually entitled by statute to a speedy appearance before the judge within a short (one to five day) period after the intake officer decides to file the petition and detain. If he is not detained, his appearance may be delayed much longer. This initial appearance may operate like an Arraignment in the adult criminal process—just a notice of the charges filed, a statement of the youth's rights, and a plea or response to the charges by the youngster. It can include also a speedy, substantive hearing on the merits. Part of this depends on the amount of work facing the Juvenile Court and partly on how well prepared the social workers are to present the case.

The Juvenile Court hearing is the most formal portion of its procedure. It is the equivalent of a trial on the issue charged against the juvenile, and it is the initial stage in which the Court itself plays the major role. The actual hearing process, when it involves a delinquency hearing with the possibility of institutionalization, is probably the most formal of Juvenile Court proceedings, largely because of the requirements of *In re Gault*.[80] The Supreme Court held in *In re Gault*[81] that in a juvenile proceeding, which involved the determination of delinquency possibly resulting in the youth's institutionalization, certain constitutional protections must be afforded him. Thus, the youth has a right to a notice of the charge(s) against him, a right to be represented by counsel, a right to confront his accusers and cross-examine the witnesses against him, and a privilege against self-incrimination. The Court has also held that the state has the same burden of

---

[80] Monrad Paulsen, "Juvenile Courts and the Legacy of '67," *43 Indiana Law Journal* 527 (1968).

[81] 387 U.S. 1 (1967).

proof in juvenile proceedings that it has in adult criminal proceedings—proof beyond a reasonable doubt.[82]

Empirically a number of Juvenile Courts still conduct many hearings in informal fashion without the sorts of procedural rituals that are expected in a criminal trial.[83] In fact, some Juvenile Courts have divided their hearing procedures explicitly into formal and informal categories and they give the youth the option of choosing one or the other.[84] The procedures used will depend on what the issues are and who the participants are. When a youth is charged with a delinquent act, the court may be concerned with whether the act occurred and the youth committed it. However, the court is usually concerned with whether it should exert its jurisdiction over neglected children or other youngsters that have been brought to it. Most of the time the facts are secondary to the court,[85] and the court assumes anyone before it needs court assistance. In a fashion like other social-service agencies, the courts are primarily concerned about the most appropriate remedy for this individual.

The prosecutor may be the complaining police officer, or the intake officer who has decided to file the petition. However, the appearance of a lawyer from the prosecutor's office is becoming more frequent, in part because of the *Gault* requirements and accompanying formalization of the proceeding.[86] This tends to make the proceeding more adversary in nature.[87] In some jurisdictions the Juvenile Court judge still conducts an inquisitorial proceeding in which he asks the questions of the accused and the witnesses, and requests defense counsel to participate only as an

---

[82] *In re Winship,* 397 U.S. 358 (1970).

[83] Bradley Canon and Kenneth Kolson, "Rural Compliance with *Gault*: Kentucky a Case Study," *10 Journal of Family Law* 300 (1971).

[84] Richard Chused, *supra* footnote 77.

[85] Robert Emerson, *Judging Delinquents: Context and Process in Juvenile Court* (Chicago: Aldine Publishing, 1969), chs. 4 to 7.

[86] Sanford Fox, "Prosecutors in the Juvenile Court: A Statutory Proposal," *8 Harvard Journal on Legislation* 33 (1970).

[87] See, Bradley Canon and Kenneth Kolson, *supra* footnote 83; and Richard Chused, *supra* footnote 77 for examples of procedures with defense attorneys absent.

afterthought or to insure that the defense has an opportunity to bring out matters the judge has overlooked.[88] There is no jury present at this hearing, although this is the stage of an adult, criminal trial at which the jury would be the trier of fact.[89] The judge seems to be willing to accept any evidence that he thinks is important or that is offered by either side in the proceeding.[90]

The third stage of the Juvenile Court proceeding is probably the most unique aspect of any criminal court. The disposition hearing is the heart of the social-service function of the court because of the effort to fashion a disposition for the individual. The disposition proceeding may be bifurcated and separate from the adjudicatory hearing or it may be a continuation of it. Usually the disposition proceeding takes place some time after the hearing, although it can occur immediately after the court has made its adjudicatory decision. The evidence used in disposition is part of the unique quality of this proceeding, and the evidence differs from that used at the hearing.[91] The disposition is based largely on a "social study," which is prepared by the intake officer, a social worker, or the probation officer either at the time of intake or later after the hearing on the issues. Depending on when it is prepared it can also form the basis for the adjudication hearing outcome.[92]

The social study may be in depth or it may be superficial, depending on the time available, the information obtained, and the training and interests of the person who prepares it. The

---

[88] Robert Emerson, *supra* footnote 85.

[89] In *McKeiver v. Pennsylvania,* 403 U.S. 528 (1971) the United States Supreme Court held that a jury was not constitutionally required in juvenile hearings.

[90] Robert Emerson, *supra* footnote 85, chs. 4 and 5.

[91] Theodore McMillian and Dorthy Lear McMurtry, "The Role of the Defense Lawyer in the Juvenile Court—Advocate or Social Worker," *14 St. Louis University Law Journal* 561, 582 (1970); and Sanford Fox, *The Law of Juvenile Courts in a Nutshell* (St. Paul: West Publishing, 1971), p. 39.

[92] Elyce Zenoff Ferster and Thomas Courtless, "Pre-Dispositional Data, Role of Counsel and Decisions in a Juvenile Court," *7 Law and Society Review* 195 (1972); and see, Martin Frey and Charles Bubany, "Pre-Adjudication Review of the Social Record in Juvenile Court: A Low Visibility Obstacle to a Fair Process," *12 Journal of Family Law* 391 (1972-73) for a discussion of the problem of bias in the hearing stage caused by the social report.

study contains all the background material that the preparer thinks is relevant to fashioning the disposition for the youngster. It generally includes a good deal of hearsay evidence, and other material that would not be admitted in a trial, but such information is used to discover enough about the child so that the best remedy can be provided and not to determine guilt. The presence of defense counsel at this dispositional hearing can be quite important, especially if the social study has some gaps or does not contain all the information that is relevant or important for disposition.[93]

The alternatives available to the judge for disposing of a juvenile vary a good deal depending on the jurisdiction, the organization of the court, and the resources available to the court.[94] In theory, the following alternatives might be used by a juvenile judge in dealing with a youngster. The case might be dismissed if the offense is minor and the judge convinced that it will not happen again. The judge might include a lecture ot the youth. Second, the judge might release the youngster in the custody of his parents and prescribe certain conditions or rehabilitative efforts that must be pursued, such as attending counseling sessions, or reporting to the judge regularly. Third, protective custody can be given to a legal guardian or a parent. This requires that the guardian be legally responsible for the deeds of the youth. Fourth, an agency or an individual could be given legal custody of the youngster, especially if the judge does not think the parents are capable of taking care of the child. Usually such custody means the child will receive specified correction or institutional help. The child could be committed to a state institution for medical or psychiatric treatment. This is usually done for a limited time period (such as 30 to 90 days) and then the court must reexamine the child and his progress with the treatment. Of

---

[93] Sanford Fox, *supra* footnote 91, at 38; see Elyce Zenoff Ferster and Thomas Courtless, *supra* footnote 92, for a contrary view of defense counsel's role at the disposition hearing.

[94] See Mary Lawton, "Juvenile Proceedings—The New Look," *20 American University Law Review* 342 (1970-71); and Stanton Darling, II, "Youthful Offenders and Neglected Children Under the D.C. Crime Act," *20 American University Law Review* 373 (1970-71) for one statutory scheme of dispositional alternatives.

course the child could be placed on formal probation, which differs from informal probation in that the court can supervise the probation and the probation officer will make more explicit efforts to see the youngster. Finally the most severe remedy is to incarcerate the youngster in some state or county-maintained youth facility such as a training school or reform school.

The actual remedies available to the judge may be more limited than this list, given limited resources and limited social services available.[95] Thus, most Juvenile Courts either dismiss the case, place the youngster on probation, or incarcerate the child. There may be some gradations in incarceration if the locality maintains a part-time camp or school, and probation may vary depending on the judge's and probation officer's assessment of what is needed for the individual. However, these are often the only alternatives given to the court. Certainly the amount of attention that is given to a youth once he has received a disposition depends on the provision of social services, the caseload of probation officers, and those officers' committment to treating the child.[96]

The right to an appeal from the Juvenile Court proceedings presents some complications. Normally, the Juvenile Court hearings are conducted in private and without a transcript. This may make it difficult to appeal to a state appellate court in the usual fashion. One of the arguments presented to the Supreme Court in *In re Gault* was that the juvenile had a right to an appeal. Since the Supreme Court, however, did not reach that question, there is no recognized constitutional right of appeal for the juvenile. There is always a habeas corpus petition available to a youngster who has been incarcerated. However, to the child placed on informal probation, or sentenced to attend a special training school for afternoons during a summer, there is no clear avenue for review of the disposition by a higher court. Some statutes provide for either a trial de novo or an appeal to the trial court of

---

[95] Howard Fradkin, "Disposition Dilemmas of American Juvenile Courts," in Margaret Rosenheim, ed., *Justice for the Child* (New York: Glencoe Press, 1962), p. 126

[96] Note, "A Right to Treatment for Juveniles," 1973 *Washington University Law Quarterly* 157 presents a discussion of the legal arguments relating to the youth's *right* to adequate treatment.

general jurisdiction. However, the unique approach of the Juvenile Court to rehabilitation and treatment make appeal after disposition very difficult.

The Juvenile Court is the prototype of the social-service courts that have begun to proliferate in certain civil areas of the law. However, recent empirical evidence suggests strongly that the Juvenile Court is a failure at what it is supposed to do, or at least it is not a complete success. The criticisms of the court revolve around its rehabilitative remedies, which may be very inadequate, and its procedures, which deny the offender his basic rights under the United States Constitution. In addition, it will be interesting to see what success the civil social-service courts, which have recently been created, have with similar, complex human problems. The civil courts do not have to defend their procedures against strict constitutional parameters as the Juvenile Court must do, yet the basic functions of these courts may be the reason for their difficulties, and their lack of success.

Conclusions

Criminal courts appear to vary in procedures and forms, but they may not be as diverse as the civil processes that were examined in the preceding chapter. There are several reasons for this narrower range of criminal court operation. First, there are constitutional requirements that apply to the criminal process, but not the civil courts. These increase the uniformity that is likely to exist in criminal courts. The general rubric of "due process of law" standardizes some protections for the defendant, and the more specific procedural requirements of the Fourth, Fifth, Sixth, Eighth, and Fourteenth Amendments of the U.S. Constitution increase the uniformity of procedures.

In addition, there is less diversity in functions in the criminal courts. These courts function largely on the basis of statutorily defined behavior. The state is always the prosecutor (plaintiff). The court is to examine the charges and see if some sanction should be applied to the accused for his behavior if he is convicted. Although these courts are presented with some unique and diverse questions from time to time, the general business of these courts remains markedly uniform when compared with civil proceedings in American courts.

There are, of course, variations in the operations of criminal courts. Some of this variation is due to the functions given some criminal courts. These may parallel or be identical to the social-service functions some civil courts perform. The Juvenile Court processes and remedies clearly resemble those in the civil courts that perform social-service functions. Although it can be debated whether Juvenile Courts are "criminal" rather than "civil," it is clear that many of the criminal courts of limited jurisdiction also use procedures that are less formal and more oriented toward fashioning specific remedies for individuals, based on equity powers. Thus, driver education programs, landlord-tenant schools, and other peculiar remedies for particular people charged with minor violations such as disorderly conduct, parallel some of the social-service remedies used in civil courts. Whereas the other criminal courts discussed here are not identical in process or remedy to the civil courts, they do indicate some isomorphism with civil process. Thus, it could be argued that the distinction between the two kinds of courts, in actual process and remedies, may be decreasing. It is not at all likely that the two courts will merge entirely. In fact, the constitutional requirements of due process probably will prevent that from happening. However, at the edges, the two processes may be merging.

The variations in criminal courts may be due to several factors. Since there are a number of "minor" crimes that the police and court officials do not feel are very important, full constitutional protections may be ignored. Traffic tickets are an example of this and many ordinance violations such as disorderly conduct are treated summarily by the court. On the other hand, a felony is considered important and receives more careful attention by the court. There is no likelihood that felony cases—even with plea bargaining—will become a social-service function.

Variations in the criminal court process may also be due to social and organizational pressures. The entire phenomenon of plea bargaining, which is so widespread, is partly due to the press of time, politics, and the reality of the criminal justice system. The practices of law enforcement officials also impinge on the court's process. Police perspectives on the apprehension and treatment of persons accused of crimes may not coincide with the due process elements of court procedure, and these differences are sometimes reflected in variations from the model in court procedures. The lack of adequate resources—money, judges, courtrooms, and other personnel—can definitely affect the criminal process. It may be that the judge has every intention of giving the accused "due process" but, because of a lack of lawyers for indigents accused of crimes or a lack of money to pay them, the judge may be hard pressed to give the accused this fundamental protection.

Some of the difficulties that courts encounter in performing their various functions have been mentioned in this and the preceding chapter. The next chapter deals directly with some of the problems of local courts. This should provide a clear understanding of the context in which some of these specialized, unique courts must operate.

5
Some Problems of Local Courts

Courts of limited jurisdiction face certain unique problems, which are discussed in this chapter. Sometimes only certain courts have these problems. In other jurisdictions the problems can generally pervade the environment and create difficulties for all the courts operating. Such problems might relate to the politics of the locality, and the particular judiciary and bar composing the local legal system. On the other hand, problems can arise within a particular court as a result of particular and unique functions that the court performs, the particular procedures that the court must follow, or the particular clientele that the court is designed to serve. The problems may impact differentially on different courts because of variations in the setting and the powers that each court of limited jurisdiction enjoys. These relationships between particular court structures and procedures, and the problems that arise from the court's various functions are the focus of this chapter.

Staffing Courts

The process by which judges are selected has long been a subject of debate and controversy.[1] Selection can be by appointment by

[1] Richard Watson and Rondal Downing, *The Politics of the Bench and the Bar* (New York: Wiley, 1969); Bradley Canon, "The Impact of Formal Selection Processes on the Characteristics of Judges—Reconsidered," *6 Law and Society Review* 579 (1972); and Stuart Nagel, *Comparing Elected and Appointed Judicial Systems* (Sage Professional Papers, American Politics Series, I, 1973).

the executive, through election to office on a partisan or non-partisan ballot, or by some combination of these procedures designed to eliminate "politics" from the process. Any of these judicial selection processes may produce unqualified judges.

Whereas most trial court judges are required to be trained in the law, the inferior courts that have been described above may be staffed with untrained people. These courts are not prestigious and, except for local "politicos," many lawyers probably would rather not serve in these courts.[2] More important, the specialized courts would benefit from a judge who has specialized training or unique training in areas related to juveniles or domestic relations. No such training or experience is ever required for judicial selection to such positions. Although some observers would argue that such specialized experience or training provides no particular assistance for these judges, most would agree that legal training alone, even if required, is of little value in dealing with the cases presented to these courts.

For example, Justices of the Peace are frequently local politicans not even trained in the law.[3] Many Justices of the Peace use the office as a base of operation and, when their remuneration is based on a fee system, there are basic constitutional questions about the validity of the judgments of such courts.[4] Even where this court is part of the regular criminal justice system, the judges are often selected for overt partisan reasons, and many view the position as a political reward.[5] These inferior courts may be viewed as more amenable to political influences than the rest of the judicial system, so that selection of these judges may be the last process to be reformed within the judiciary of a state.

Similarly, probate judges, in some jurisdictions, are laymen, untrained in the law, who use the office as a base of political

---

[2] Lyle Truax, "Courts of Limited Jurisdiction Are Passé," *53 Judicature* 326. 327-328 (1970); and Lewis Katz, "Municipal Courts—Another Urban Ill," *20 Case Western Reserve Law Review* 87, 91 (1968).

[3] George Partain, "The Justice of the Peace: Constitutional Questions," *69 West Virginia Law Review* 314, 322 (1967); Kenneth Vanlandingham, "The Decline of the Justice of Peace," *12 Kansas Law Review* 389, 391 (1964); and Lyle Truax, *supra* footnote 2, at 326.

[4] George Partain, *supra* footnote 3.

[5] Note, "Metropolitan Criminal Courts of First Instance," *70 Harvard Law Review* 320, 323 (1956).

operation within the community. The judges in probate courts like the established process and have fought to retain it.[6] In Connecticut, for example, where a major effort has been made to implement the Uniform Probate Code, the Probate judges formed an effective interest group that lobbied before the state legislature, and litigated several cases in an effort to prevent the change, modify it, or at least insure the established judges' positions in the new process.[7] Whether one views this as healthy political activity or conservative reaction to needed reform, it illustrates a political dimension of the problems of changing our legal system or improving the quality of judges that staff it.

Another very important problem in these courts, which relates to staffing, is that in many of these courts judges are rotated into and out of the court on a short-term basis. Where there is no permanent, judicial staff for an inferior court, or where there is no effort to provide these minor courts with trained, competent judges, the entire trial judiciary may serve a period in each court. On the average, rotations involve six months to a year in a specialized court. The problem with this kind of staffing is the temporary nature of each judge. If a judge is temporarily rotated into the Family Court for a three to six month term, he may have no interest in the problems before him, and he may not have any experience with or specific knowledge about the problems that come to the Family Court for solution. Neither the substantive law nor the procedures of the court are familiar to the newcomer. The result of this is that the people who bring cases to these courts may have a lawyer who "knows the ropes" better than the judge or may suffer from a judge who does not yet know how to conduct the court, what authority he has, or what assistance he can provide to the disputants. All judges, even if they have uniform

---

[6] I. Ridgeway Davis, "Connecticut Probate Courts are Slow to Change," *60 National Civic Review* 204 (1971); Ralph Dupont, "The Impact of the Uniform Probate Code on Connecticut Court Structure," *2 Connecticut Law Review* 563 (1970); and Ralph Dupont, "The Impact of the Uniform Probate Code on Court Structure," *6 Journal of Law Reform* 375, 382 (1973).

[7] I. Ridgeway Davis, *supra* footnote 6.

training, are not equally interested in or capable of handling various kinds of courts cases with equal dispatch. Judges may not be interchangeable among these various courts.

An associated problem involves the role perceptions of judges. There are fixed-role expectations that most lawyers have about judges in the adversary process. That is, judges are to sit, passively and respond to the points made by lawyers during the proceedings. Most trial court judges probably share these passive role expectations. However, in a number of these specialized courts the judge is presented with the opportunity, if not the obligation, to take an active role in questioning witnesses and talking with the parties in order to develop the case and reach a satisfactory solution. Judges, having been trained as lawyers, may find such role expectations impossible to adopt or perform successfully.

For example, the traditional role of the judge in an adversary proceeding is not generally appropriate in the Family Court because of the nature of the problems presented. The judge may have to talk with the parties to get them to agree to a settlement; he may have to question parties himself until he is confident that he understands the "whole story"; he generally must make his decision on the spot. This nontraditional role is not always possible for judges to accept, and many apparently do not find it at all comfortable.

These problems of judicial selection and judicial political activity complicate the effective operation of courts of limited jurisdiction. Solutions to some of these problems might be to require legal training for all judicial personnel. However, that creates its own problems. First, since well-trained lawyers might not want to take such positions, the "judges" are those least qualified and most interested in other, nonjudicial careers. Second, legal training may not be an adequate preparation for some of the functions these officials are required to perform, such as marriage counseling. Third, legal training for judges—already a widespread phenomenon—does not prevent political pressures from influencing judges and courts. Finally, no amount of training is likely to engender a spirit or enthusiasm for certain kinds of cases or problems which courts must consider.

NonJudicial Staff

There is a set of problems that relate to nonjudicial staffing for courts. These involve the professional counselors, intake officers, and therapeutic personnel who are essential to the functioning of some of the social-service courts such as Family, Domestic Relations, and Juvenile Courts, in addition to the clerks in Probate Courts and Small Claims Courts, who often perform important quasi-judicial functions. The performance of clerical functions is often done by low level civil servants who have no legal training, and need none. However, for the operation of some courts, such as Small Claims Courts, the clerk by his attitude can help people or make it difficult for them to complete the necessary forms. In Probate Courts, clerks may be given authority by the judge to sign certain forms and actually to transact the business of the Court. Such clerks can be helpful and efficient, or obstreperous. This depends on the clerk's personality and the judge's orientation toward helping people.

The staffs provided courts with social-service functions are often inadequate. The kinds of assistance that need to be provided to the people who come to these courts is very labor intensive in that one professional must often spend numerous hours with one client before any improvement in that person's situation can be seen. Yet, case workers and probation officers are often strapped with huge workloads because there are more people in need of assistance than there are people to provide it. In addition, some clients may need costly specialized guidance that the court does not have and cannot provide.

This problem is basically a question of money. State legislatures are reluctant to pay the price that must be paid to get the kind of experts and assistance that these courts need. Under the normal budgetary constraints, these kinds of services appear to be frills. They rarely get the priority which may be necessary, given the problems they deal with. Without sufficient funds, it is impossible to hire enough assistants to provide the right kinds of expert advisers. It is also impossible to hire good experts for low salaries, when they can command very high prices for their services in private practice. Thus, without the resources, these courts are at a great disadvantage in acquiring and keeping competent people to perform essential services that the court has been given responsibility for.

As an example of this set of problems, Juvenile Courts often lack resources to assist in the treatment and rehabilitation of juveniles.[8] The social service staffs assigned to courts—the Probation Officers and Psychiatrists—are often overworked, underpaid, poorly trained or, in some cases, nonexistent.[9] State and local governmental units do not provide much money for such services. There has been a good deal of debate about what sort of services should be provided to these courts. However, citizens are not willing to tax themselves enough to pay for the cost of any such services.[10]

There are also organizational problems that arise in this context and that inhibit the court's performance of its duties. In any bureaucracy there are staff jurisdictional disputes and jealousies. A wide variety of these kinds of disputes can arise. They all inhibit the performance of the functions that have been assigned to these courts. For example, the probation officer who is responsible to the court for a juvenile may refuse to take the expert advise of a court psychiatrist about the youngster in question. In some instances the professionals are not assigned to the court, but rather are part of a state agency that provides service to any and all state agencies, such as the court, that need it. Under these circumstances, the expert assistance may be less useful to the court, since the expert is not familiar with the unique kinds of problems that

---

[8] The President's Commission on Law Enforcement and Administration of Justice, *Task Force Report: Juvenile Delinquency and Youth Crime* (Washington, D.C.: U.S.G.P.O., 1967), p. 7; William Burnett, "The Volunteer Probation Counselor," *52 Judicature* 285 (1969); and J. A. Seymour, "Youth Services Bureaus," *7 Law and Society Review* 247 (1972).

[9] Alex Elson, "Juvenile Courts and Due Process," in Margaret Rosenheim, ed., *Justice for the Child* (New York: Glencoe Press, 1962), p. 96; and President's Commission on Law Enforcement and Administration of Justice, *supra* footnote 8, p. 6.

[10] Paul Alexander, "Constitutional Rights in Juvenile Court," in Margaret Rosenheim, ed., *Justice for the Child* (New York: Glencoe Press, 1962), p. 85; and Margaret Rosenheim, "Perenial Problems in the Juvenile Court," *Ibid.,* p. 15.

the court must treat. Furthermore, the court must compete with other agencies for the professional's time and attention, and may end up at the bottom of the priority scale.

Court Jurisdiction

One frequent problem that inferior courts encounter is that their jurisdiction does not reach to the people and problems that are essential to solving the problems and disputes they are assigned to deal with. The limited jurisdiction of these courts may prevent them from exercising complete jurisdiction over a problem to achieve a "solution" to the case.

For example, Family Courts in New York do not have jurisdiction over divorce, annulment, separation, and dissolution cases.[11] These cases compose a very large segment of the disputes that arise within the family. In other states, the Family Court has concurrent jurisdiction with another Court. There are not a great number of Family Court jurisdictions in the country. Where they have been created, as in New York, Rhode Island, Hawaii, Ohio, and South Carolina, they have not been created on a clean slate. Rather, the Court has been superimposed upon the existing Court system, and sometimes the established Courts have not been reshaped to make room for the Family Court.

One very interesting area over which some Family Courts have jurisdiction involves criminal violence. The kinds of violence involved are usually between spouses or between parent and child. The Family Court has jurisdiction only over minor kinds of violence, or over all types of violence as long as they involve only members of one family. These disputes might be referred to the criminal courts if reported to the police. However, many of these violent acts are reported by the injured party or by a relative, and they are reported to the social worker or an intake officer rather than to the police. The question initially arises whether these actions should be treated as crimes, and it appears that one of the

---

[11] Monrad Paulsen, "The New York Family Court Act," *12 Buffalo Law Review* 420, 423 (1963).

determinations that the judicial system is allowed to make, where there are Family Courts, is that these should not be crimes, but rather should be treated as the occasion for some remedial social-service actions rather than as an incident for the penal systems. The nonadversary procedures used in Family Courts might be the best means of dealing with these kinds of violence since they involve heated emotions and tensions that would be magnified by a formal, adversary treatment by the court.

There seems to be a continuing problem involving juvenile cases, where the judge can waive jurisdiction and bind the juvenile over to be tried in the adult, criminal court. In some states, the Juvenile Court does not have clear jurisdiction over these cases, and the court that gets jurisdiction first (i.e., where the youngster is first presented) exercises it. It is quite important to the outcome in the case whether the juvenile is handled in a Juvenile Court where the social-service function is understood and attempted, or in a felony criminal court where the criminal process operates without regard to the age of the accused.

Probate Court presents another problem of jurisdiction. Where there is a problem with a will or the probating of it, the Probate Court may have to relinquish jurisdiction to the trial court of record that conducts a traditional trial to settle the dispute. This delays the settling of the estate, and may cause unnecessary hardship on the heirs. It also illustrates that Probate Court may be incapable of performing its duties. In some Probate Courts the probate functions are decentralized so that no single court has the authority and jurisdiction to handle the entire matter.[12] Thus, in some Probate Courts the judge cannot assign guardians for minors who need supervision with their share of the estate. This problem is the opposite from those states in which jurisdiction over probate matters is given to a court that also must perform a large number of other, unrelated duties in the locality. These other duties divert attention, and require a second level of court to decide contested estate issues, because the Probate Judge is too busy with the other duties.

---

[12] Ralph Dupont, "The Impact of the Uniform Probate Code on Court Structure," 6 *Journal of Law Reform* 375, 381 (1973).

Court Clientele

One of the major characteristics of the courts of limited jurisdiction is that they illustrate efforts at expanding the court's functions and making the arena available and helpful to more people. However, one of the problems these courts face is reaching the target clientele.

One example of this effort to expand court clientele is the Small Claims Court. This court was designed to permit people with very limited resources to use an official arena to right a wrong that they had suffered but that they could not afford to litigate in the traditional, expensive manner. However, there appears to be a surprisingly low level of knowledge about the existence of Small Claims Courts, and in some jurisdictions these courts are very difficult to locate, even when one is consciously looking for them.[13] Some people appear to be intimidated about using such courts—especially poor or low income and minority group members.[14] And further, if a person does find the court and seeks to file a complaint he may be faced with an uncooperative clerk who will not help him by providing even basic information about how to begin the process.[15]

Lawyers and Courts of Limited Jurisdiction

There has been a wide, and long-standing debate about the provision of legal counsel for litigants. In criminal cases, the case law has established that counsel must be provided, if the accused cannot afford to hire a lawyer, in order that his rights be fully protected during the criminal proceeding. On the civil side,

---

[13] The Small Claims Study Group, *Little Injustices: Small Claims and the American Consumer: A Preliminary Report to the Center for Auto Safety* (Washington, D.C.: Center for Auto Safety, 1972); "Small Claims Court: Reform Revisited," *5 Columbia Journal of Law and Social Problems* 47, 67 (1969); and Beatrice Moulton, "The Persecution and Intimidation of the Low-Income Litigant as Performed by the Small Claims Court in California," *21 Stanford Law Review* 1657, 1669 (1969).

[14] *Ibid.*, at 1664.

[15] The Small Claims Study Group, *supra* footnote 13.

lawyers are a necessity in most cases but must be hired by the litigants. However, in Small Claims Courts particularly, lawyers may not be required or may even be excluded. Lawyers are not necessary because the procedures are simple enough for the layman to understand, the cost of lawyers can be too great, and the judge will uncover all the facts without the assistance of counsel. In terms of actual use, most plaintiff creditors use an attorney to file and prosecute all their claims in Small Claims Court. Defendants (individual debtors) usually appear to defend without attorney because of cost or because they don't realize the disadvantage they face.[16] From the studies made, the presence of a lawyer tends to formalize the small claims process a great deal, even if the judge is inclined to be informal.[17]

One study found that the likelihood of defendant winning is much greater when the defendant has counsel, because counsel can raise legal defenses that are good but that a layman would never recognize.[18] It is interesting that in California, where lawyers are excluded from small claims proceedings the result is not greatly different. A businessman or executive of a corporation may repeatedly appear as plaintiff, and eventually develop an expertise for handling the claims and a rapport or credibility with the small claims judge. Eventually the judge will implicitly give a de facto presumption in favor of that plaintiff's case even if the procedure is relatively informal because of the absence of lawyer.[19] It has been advocated by several students of small claims processes that the court should provide a small claims advisor,[20] or some less specific in-court assistance,[21] so that defendants will not be placed at a disadvantage whether opposed by legal counsel

---

[16] See, Beatrice Moulton, *supra* footnote 13.

[17] For example, "Small Claims Court: Reform Revisited," *supra* footnote 13, at 55-57, 64; Michael Minton and Jon Steffanson, "Small Claims Courts: A survey and Analysis," *55 Judicature* 324, 326-327 (1972); and The Small Claims Study Group, *supra* footnote 13, at 109-110.

[18] Michael Minton and Jon Steffanson, *supra* footnote 17, at 327; see generally Beatrice Moulton, *supra* footnote 13, at 1664-1667 for a discussion of laymen representing themselves and raising their own defenses.

[19] Beatrice Moulton, *supra* footnote 13, at 1662-1668.

[20] The Small Claims Study Group, *supra* footnote 13, at 7.

[21] Beatrice Moulton, *supra* footnote 13, at 1665.

or just an experienced layman. Another study indicates, however, that consumer plaintiffs can win their claims without lawyers even if the likelihood of winning is greater with a lawyer.[22]

The suggestion that paraprofessionals be made available on a continuing basis to all defendants might produce a more balanced, adversary process where attorneys or experienced laymen operate for plaintiffs. However, such a solution does not facilitate the simple, cheap, and expeditious processes that Small Claims Courts were initially designed to provide.

Small Claims Courts are not the only ones where the presence or absence of a lawyer can make a substantial difference in the atmosphere, and possibly the outcome of the court proceeding. The Juvenile Courts in this country often operated without the youngster being represented by an attorney before the *Gault* decision in 1967. In fact, many proceedings probably still do not involve attorneys because *Gault* applies only to those instances in which the juvenile may be subject to institutionalization, and many jurisdictions are able to disregard the explicit requirements of the decision. Without an attorney, the proceeding is likely to be more informal than in the cases where a lawyer represents the juvenile. This informality was a major point the Supreme Court wanted to eliminate in its *Gault* decision. Such informality may or may not be beneficial to the juvenile, and his due process rights.

Conclusions

The kinds of limitations that courts face can be categorized, in terms of the conditions creating them. One set of problems relates to limited resources that do not provide the court with adequate facilities, supportive personnel, and judges. The scarce resources available in any political system—local, state, or national—do not tend to be channeled into judicial arenas beyond a minimal amount. One of the reasons for this difficulty with money is that there are no organized lobbies in the state

---

[22] John Steadman and Richard Rosenstein, " 'Small Claims' Consumer Plaintiffs in the Philadelphia Municipal Court: An Empirical Study," *112 University of Pennsylvania Law Review* 1309, 1332-1333 (1973).

legislatures, or at any other level of government, that support and seek legislative support for courts. It is unrealistic to expect courts to perform new social-service functions well, if at all, without the supports needed for an adequate job.

Money limitations can affect the training and experience of the personnel who staff these courts, but there are several personnel problems not connected directly to money. Many of the judges who serve in the social-service courts, such as Domestic Relations Courts and Family Courts, do not enjoy the functions they must perform. They do not feel competent to handle the kinds of problems brought to them, and the nonadversary judicial roles that they may be called upon to perform are foreign or at best uncomfortable to them. This tends to decrease the success of these courts. The performance of the nonjudicial people who serve these courts is affected by overwork, lack of certain kinds of expertise, and bureaucratization of their functions. All these problems contribute to a failure, in many cases, to provide much assistance and service to the courts or the clientele.

A basic problem involves the functions that some courts must perform. The creation of social-service courts, and the grafting of social-service functions onto established courts places substantial strain on judicial processes. The usual result is the modification of processes and remedies to deal with these complex, human problems. Yet the solutions available to courts for these problems depend on the viability of judicial treatment. Courts may not be appropriate means of handling many of these problems. However, that essential question is rarely examined by legislatures or other political actors, which see the courts as an arena available to handle such tasks. If society is going to continue to request courts to deal with these kinds of problems, then the necessary changes in money allocations and training must be achieved before any basis exists for expecting these courts to "succeed."

6
Appellate Courts

So far, the procedures and context of trial courts in America have been examined in this book. The variety of procedures that exist in various courts, have been indicated and it has been suggested that trial courts perform a number of functions, depending on the kinds of problems over which they have jurisdiction. This chapter examines the appellate courts that operate in our legal system.

Appellate courts may not be as important to individual litigants as the trial courts that handle and dispose of most of the cases litigated in America. However, appellate courts do play several very important roles in our political system. Appellate courts have been much more widely studied than have most trial courts.[1] These courts are much more visible than most trial courts, and the decisions of appellate courts are much easier to find and analyze than are the decisions of trial courts. In addition, appellate courts do play a more important role in the formulation of policy than do trial courts. Whereas trial courts handle many cases and resolve those conflicts on an individual basis, appellate courts perform the tasks of reviewing trial court decisions and reversing them if errors of law have been committed. This means that appellate courts, through their functions and procedures, as well as the institutional setting in which they operate, play a major

[1] See Charles Sheldon, *The American Judicial Process: Models and Approaches* (New York: Dodd, Mead, 1974) for a survey of the literature on appellate courts.

role in judicial policymaking and supervision of the judicial system. Other arenas may perform similar policymaking tasks, but none operates with the same limitations and opportunities as the appellate court.

Appellate courts probably have less procedural and structural variation than do the trial courts examined above. The variations are few in number, and the impact of these differences does not appear to be very great. The model procedures will not be compared with actual procedures because there is little difference between the two in the operation of these courts. Several things should be kept in mind about these courts. First, most cases that are decided by trial courts are not appealed. Most litigants accept even an adverse trial court outcome rather than appeal it. This can be for a variety of reasons such as costs in time and money, the merits of their case may be too weak to win on appeal, or they litigated in the first place only to save face and, once an adverse court decision has been rendered, they accept it and appealing does not enter their minds.

Table 6.1 presents data on the number of cases filed in Federal District Court, and the number of cases appealed to Federal Courts of Appeals for a six-year period. The comparable figures for any state court system would vary, but these give some indication of the numbers and proportions of cases reaching the appellate level. These figures suggest that approximately 90 percent of the cases treated by the trial court are not appealed.

Second, different kinds of cases are appealed at different rates.[2] The kinds of cases appealed vary with the subject matter of the case or the questions involved. Thus, certain kinds of cases may be appealed more than others.[3] Whereas traffic court convictions are seldom if ever appealed, cases involving civil rights are

---

[2] Richard Richardson and Kenneth Vines, *The Politics of Federal Courts: Lower Courts in the United States* (Boston: Little, Brown, 1970); Kenneth Dolbeare, "The Federal District Courts and Urban Public Policy: An Exploratory Study (1960-1967)," in Joel Grossman and Joseph Tanenhaus, eds.,*Frontiers of Judicial Research* (New York: Wiley, 1969), pp. 390-395.

[3] See, J. Woodford Howard, "Litigation Flow in Three United States Courts of Appeals," *8 Law and Society Review* 33 (1973).

Table 6.1
Cases and Appeals Filed in Federal District Courts and Courts of Appeals For Fiscal Years*

	1969	1970	1971	1972	1973	1974	Average
Courts of appeals	10,248	11,662	12,788	14,535	15,629	16,436	13,550
District courts	112,606	127,280	136,553	145,227	140,994	143,284	134,324
Percent of cases in district that are appealed	9.1	9.1	9.3	10.0	11.0	11.4	10.0

*Source. Director of the Administrative Office of the United States Courts, *Management Statistics For United States Courts 1974* (Washington D.C., U.S.G.P.O., 1974). It is not completely accurate to rely on the percentages in the bottom row of this table, since the cases appealed during a year do not come from the cases filed in the trial court during that same year. This proportion may be somewhat reduced because cases filed include many cases that the District Court dismisses without any litigation or final court resolution, while the cases appealed are generally not likely to be rejected or not considered by the appellate court.

probably appealed quite frequently.[4] It appears that the appellate courts may consider procedural questions at a rate higher than some substantive areas.[5] Questions involving some substantive areas of the law such as labor law are appealed more frequently than other topics. Variations appear not only because different kinds of questions require different sorts of final settlement by courts, but also because some courts can pick and choose the cases they will decide on appeal. Thus, a court with discretionary jurisdiction, such as the U.S. Supreme Court, will exercise its jurisdiction differently in terms of the kinds of cases it wishes to decide,[6] than will an appellate court with mandatory jurisdiction.

Appellate Court Structure

The general purpose of appellate courts is to review questions of law raised by trial court proceedings. A question of law involves the interpretation of law or the procedures used by the court to reach the decision in a case. What the words of a statute mean is an example of a question of law. The primary purpose of reviewing such questions is to correct errors of law that the trial court has allegedly made in settling the dispute brought to it. This is based on the principle that a person has a right to a trial free from legal error and, thus, everyone must have the chance to appeal a trial court error and have it corrected by the reviewing court. This corrective function is the essential reason for the existence of appellate courts, and the trial court will be corrected if the reviewing court can be convinced that the error occurred and that it prejudiced the trial outcome. Under this framework, the trial

[4] See, Richard Richardson and Kenneth Vines, *supra* footnote 2, at ch. 6 for an interesting discussion that indicates that appellate courts may change the subject of appeal into a civil rights issue when they hear and decide appeals, pp. 127-129. The issues may not remain the same today, but this illustrates that appellate courts can decide the kinds of issue they wish to deal with.

[5] William McLauchlan, "An Empirical Study of Civil Procedure: Directed Verdicts and Judgments Notwithstanding Verdict," 2 *Journal of Legal Studies* 459 (1973).

[6] Gerhard Casper and Richard Posner, "A Study of the Supreme Court's Caseload," 3 *Journal of Legal Studies* 339 (1974).

court makes all determinations as to the facts in the case, and the appellate court can make final determinations as to legal questions. However, the law–fact distinction upon which this theory is based is hazy, and oftentimes appellate courts are able to reverse factual findings under the guise of correcting errors of law.[7] Mixed questions involving both facts and interpretations of law are presented to the appellate court, and decided if the lawyer is skillful in phrasing questions so that the appellate court views them as questions of law.

The function of correcting errors of law in appellate courts creates the need for different kinds of court structure and procedure than is followed in the trial court. The first major characteristic of appellate courts is that they are always composed of a group of judges. Although the trial court is presided over by a single judge, appellate courts are composed of a collegial body of judges, who must reach a decision as a group, rather than individually. For example, the Federal Courts of Appeals have anywhere from three judges (the First Circuit) to 15 judges (the Fifth Circuit). The court may sit *en banc,* which means together, or the court hears cases in panels, which are smaller groups of judges who decide the case in place of the full court. The multijudge arrangement is designed to give the appellant (party seeking reversal of the trial court decision) an opportunity to convince a majority of judges on the court that a legal error was made below. This means that the reversal of a trial judge can only be done by a group of judges who have been convinced that serious legal error was committed in the trial.

A second, structural difference with trial courts is that appellate courts never use juries to find the facts in a case. Since supposedly no questions of fact are resolved by appellate courts,

---

[7] For example, various administrative agency statutes require the agency to decide what is in "the public interest." A reviewing court may be asked to define what the term "public interest" means—a question of law. In addition, the appellant may argue that a particular agency decision of what is in "the public interest" is unsupported by evidence in the record—a question of fact. These two questions can be merged, and often are, by the reviewing court in determining an appeal from an agency decision.

there is no need for a fact finder at this level. The facts are fixed by the trial, and the appellate court deals only with legal questions. Thus the facts come to the court for review, fixed in the record. This does not permit a direct question about their validity. This functional and structural difference from trial courts also alters the kinds of material presented to the appellate court upon which it can make its decision. This will be discussed below.

The primary structural characteristic of appellate courts is determined by the jurisdiction and operation they have been given. The appellate court structure in a state involves either a single court that reviews all appeals taken from trial courts, or two tiers of appellate courts, with the intermediate tier handling the great bulk of cases, and the second tier considering only those cases the court chooses to consider in a discretionary fashion.[8] Most states that use intermediate appellate courts have given them general jurisdiction to handle all kinds of cases that arise from trial courts. However, there are some states that have given this level of court only limited jurisdiction, such as over civil or criminal cases.[9] The reason for creating the intermediate tier of courts is not clear. One source suggests that the reason was to reduce the workload on the high court in the jurisdiction.[10] However, additional research suggests that this is not clearly the reason for intermediate courts.[11] It has been suggested that the likelihood of intermediate appellate courts is greater as a state's urban population increases. However, there is no precise correlation between intermediate courts and urbanization since some states with low population and no urban centers have this level of appellate court.

The court of last resort, often called the "supreme court," is the pinnacle of the appellate court structure in any jurisdiction. This court, if operating with intermediate appellate courts, has a wide

---

[8] See Daryl Fair, "State Intermediate Appellate Courts: An Introduction," *24 Western Political Quarterly* 415, 423 (1971); and Henry Glick and Kenneth Vines, *State Court Systems* (Englewood Cliffs, N.J.: Prentice-Hall, 1973).

[9] Daryl Fair, *supra* footnote 8, at 419-420.

[10] *Ibid.,* at 415-416.

[11] Henry Glick and Kenneth Vines, *supra* footnote 8, at p. 35.

degree of discretion in choosing the cases it hears. If there is no intermediate tier, the supreme court will hear all cases that are appealed from the trial court. The supreme court in a jurisdiction plays several very important roles in the political system. First, as the court of last resort, it is final arbiter of legal disputes. These courts also supervise the procedures used by the jurisdiction's judiciary. That is, the supreme court will make various procedural adjustments in the criminal and civil processes used by trial courts in the jurisdiction, either by just adopting new procedural codes, or by initiating legislative changes by means of proposals to the legislature. Furthermore, it is the final interpreter of the jurisdiction's statutes and constitution. Although state courts of last resort may have their decisions appealed to the United States Supreme Court, that can only occur on a question of federal law, and then the state court's interpretation of the state law is binding on the U.S. Supreme Court. This court clearly plays a major role in making, interpreting, and settling policy within its jurisdiction. The legislature can always change the statute after the court's interpretation. However, in most situations, the court's interpretation remains controlling and operative for some time even if the legislature wishes to change it, therefore generally the court's decision controls the parties, and the general population with regard to the matters it has decided.

At least as important as appellate court interpretation of statutes and constitutional questions is the court's interpretation and development of common law. This has long been an established appellate court function, and in many states it is the primary means by which courts adjust the substantive law.[12] Although statutory law is increasing in volume and comprehensiveness in most states, the judicial interpretation and creation of common law doctrines still may have a profound effect on the operation of the judiciary as well as the commercial and private transactions that occur in a state. For example, the court may interpret the "holder in due course" doctrine in the established manner to protect a subsequent buyer from a flaw in an initial sales con-

---

[12] Karl Llewellyn, *The Common Law Tradition: Deciding Appeals* (Boston: Little, Brown, 1960).

tract. However, recently, courts have begun to change this doctrine to require a third party purchaser to be responsible for the defects in the original contract and transaction to which the holder in due course was not a party.[13] This will substantially adjust commercial transactions that occur within a state for many years.

The discretion of the supreme court to choose which cases it hears depends on the court structure. The most studied example of this discretion and its exercise is the U.S. Supreme Court's *certiorari* procedure.[14] The writ of certiorari is granted in most cases that the Supreme Court decides to hear. By statute, the writ can be granted in only certain instances but, in fact, these are so general as to permit very flexible use.[15] Even where there are precise statements as to when certiorari may be granted, the Court seems to follow its own preferences about policy areas and kinds of cases. The discretion permits the court to avoid issues that it does not want to decide for whatever reason. It also gives the court more opportunities to choose the occasions upon which to make policy decisions. Thus, the court can become a more overt policymaker, if it has the discretion to choose among possible cases for review. This does not mean that all courts with such discretionary jurisdiction calculate all their decisions very carefully in terms of policymaking. Yet some courts publicly state that their choice of cases is for the purpose of deciding the legal questions that are most important to the operation of the courts or other political arenas in the jurisdiction. This clearly is a policy decision and will produce policies in the direction of the court's interests.

[13] See for example, Grant Gilmore, *The Death of Contract* (Columbus, Ohio: Ohio State University Press, 1974). See, also, Charles Bunn, Harry Sneed, and Richard Speidel, *An Introduction to the Uniform Commercial Code* (Charlottesville: Mitchie Co., 1964).

[14] Joseph Tanenhaus, *et al.*, "The Supreme Court's Certiorari Jurisdiction: Cue Theory," in Glendon Schubert, ed., *Judicial Decision-Making* (New York: The Free Press of Glencoe, 1963); S. Sidney Ulmer, *et al.*, "The Decision to Grant or Deny Certiorari: Further Consideration of Cue Theory," *6 Law and Society Review* 637 (1972); and S. Sidney Ulmer, "The Decision to Grant Certiorari as an Indication of Decision 'On the Merits,' " *4 Polity* 429 (1972).

[15] 28 U.S.C. Supreme Court Rules 19.

Appellate Court Procedures

The procedures used by appellate courts differ a good deal from those involved in trial courts. This is the result of the different functions that appellate courts perform. First, since there is no evidence presented to the appellate court, and no need for finding of fact, the major material submitted to the reviewing court is legal argument by the parties (appellants and appellees) that focuses on the questions of law the court is supposed to decide in reviewing the trial court. These legal materials can be presented in a variety of forms. The written brief or petition is the most frequently used medium. The brief is a statement of the questions presented for appellate review, the factual basis upon which the appeal of these questions is founded, the legal precedents that should govern the determination of these questions, and the remedy the party is seeking (reversal or affirmance of the trial court's result). The brief can be highly stylized and written in a sort of jargon for the appellate judges. It is usually printed and presented in a formal, "polished" fashion.

In addition to the written brief, the reviewing court may wish to hear oral argument on the issues presented by the case. Although parties request oral argument as a matter of course, the appellate court has discretion to hear oral argument if it chooses. Oral argument provides the parties with the opportunity to present and emphasize particular points in the case that each feels should be controlling. Oral argument also gives the court the chance to clarify the case and the problems by posing questions to the attorneys. Oral argument, historically, was viewed as a very important part of appeals, and some of the major U.S. Supreme Court cases in the nineteenth century required weeks of oral argument to hear all parties in great detail. Nowadays, most attorneys do not see oral argument as very important in persuading the court in a case.

Finally, appellate decisions may be based on a copy of the trial transcript, which is a verbatim record of the testimony and oral presentations at the trial, or relevant portions of it. Usually the parties will excerpt the relevant portions of the trial transcript so as to highlight it for the appellate judges. However, some reviewing courts wish to have the complete transcript before them at the time of judgment. The appellant (the party appealing) is charged with the costs of the transcript preparation.[16]

The process of appealing a trial court judgment involves a substantial amount of formal ritual. It is different from that involved in the adversary model, although it does involve some parallel items. The Federal Rules of Appellate Procedure will be used as an example. The initial stage of an appeal is for the appellant, usually the losing party below, to file a Notice of Appeal with the trial court within a short period of time after the entry of judgment (in the federal system, 30 days for civil appeals and 10 days in criminal cases). The clerk of court then serves the notice on the other parties. Appellant may be required to post a bond for costs pending appeal as specified by the trial court (e.g., $250). The civil appellant usually petitions the trial court for a stay of the judgment pending appeal. In criminal appeals the defendant would petition for release. However, both release of the defendant pending criminal appeal and the stay of judgment in civil cases depends on the trial court's discretion, or in some instances, the appellate court's stay order.

The major portion of the appeals process involves getting the record on appeal ready and that burden usually falls on the appellant's shoulders. The original papers and exhibits in the trial case, certified copies of the trial court docket entries, and the transcript all are part of the record, and the appellant must prepare that record and usually pay for it, unless the appellant is an indigent criminal defendant. The briefs for the parties must contain specific items, such as a statement of the issue, a statement of the case, the argument supporting the contentions of the appellant, and a conclusion. Page limits (50 pages), the style of printing (printed, right-hand justified), and number of copies

---

[16] The Supreme Court has held that the cost of a trial transcript in criminal appeals cannot be used to bar an indigent from having his case heard on appeal. *Griffin v. Illinois,* 351 U.S. 12 (1956). In *Douglas v. California,* 372 U.S. 353 (1963) the Supreme Court held that an indigent would be denied equal protection of the law, if his appeal was considered without the benefit of appointed counsel to represent him on appeal.

may also be specified. Amicus briefs, briefs from nonparties who are interested in the case, may be filed upon written consent of both parties or by leave of the court.

The appellate court may provide for a Prehearing Conference, which operates somewhat like the Pretrial Conference. The court can simplify the issues and specify the particular questions or issues which it will consider. However, it is generally not used by appellate courts, since the briefs and other written documents are narrowly phrased and specific enough to indicate exactly what the issue is. There are substantial sanctions that the appellate court can apply to "frivilous" appeals, such as throwing the appeal out, summarily without consideration on the merits, or granting the appellee damages and costs after full consideration of the appeal. Thus, the appellant is not likely to bring frivolous appeals that are vague, peripheral, or a waste of the court's and appellee's time.

Oral Argument is often sought, and can be granted or denied by the court. It is generally limited to a short period of time (30 minutes per side). This limit, as most others, can be waived if the appellate court agrees to grant an exception. As noted above, the effect of Oral Argument on the decision may be doubted. However, most parties seek to have oral argument in the hopes that they will be able to convince the judges, or will be able to clear up even a single point that will swing the case in their favor.

The result of the appellate court's consideration of a case is a decision that is usually announced by a written opinion. Being a collegial body, an appellate court reaches decisions by some sort of deliberation involving all the members of the court who participate in the particular case. That may mean that the judges meet in conference, discuss the merits, and reach a decision. It may also mean that one judge is assigned the decision and prepares an opinion that he circulates to his colleagues, and then announces as the decision if the other members of the court raise no objections.[17] The opinion is the written justification for the

[17] Walter Murphy, "Marshalling the Court: Leadership, Bargaining, and the Judicial Process," 29 *University of Chicago Law Review* 640 (1962); and Walter Murphy, *Elements of Judicial Strategy* (Chicago: University of Chicago Press, 1964) presents interesting and illustrative outlines of the bargaining processes

decision, and it seeks to rationalize the outcome in terms of the law and the judgment of the appellate court on the meaning of the law under review in the case. The publication of opinion is the final, public announcement of the appellate court's review process except for possibly some additional administrative decisions on the case by the court.

The opinion becomes part of the common law in the jurisdiction, and thus, it is part of the public policy of the jurisdiction as formulated by the court. The degree to which the court and subsequent courts are bound by a decision and opinion vary, since courts and judges have different ideas about how binding precedent should be on subsequent decisions. The norm is to follow precedent, and many appellate courts do just that. However, the U.S. Supreme Court has always maintained that it is not so tightly bound by past court decisions as many other courts feel they are. This decrease in adherence to precedent is largely related to the Court's duty of constitutional interpretation.

The decision by the court results in the entry of a Judgment. The Judgment is based on the opinion of the court that is prepared after the judges participating in the case reach their decision. The Judgment is a reversal or affirmance of the trial court's judgment. It results in an order to the lower court to proceed in the fashion that carries out the judgment of the appellate court. As will be noted below, this remand process gives the trial court substantial flexibility for complying with the appellate decision. The motion for a rehearing of the case is always available to the losing party on appeal. It must be made within a short period of time of the entry of Judgment (14 days) and may be limited in length (10 pages). The effort here is to raise the possibility that the appellate court erred in its decision or failed to consider the material sufficiently. Rehearings are rarely granted, but they are always available to the losing party, just as the motion for a new trial is available at the trial level for the losing side.

The appellate process is displayed in Figure 6-1. It shows that

---

involved in U.S. Supreme Court decision making. For an example of state court decisional processes see, Thomas Morris, *The Virginia Supreme Court: An Institutional and Political Analysis* (Charlottesville: University Press of Virginia, 1975), ch. III.

Appellee	Procedural Steps	Appellant
	Brief stage	
		Notice of appeal (bond)
		Stay of execution of judgment
		Preparation of appeal record
Brief		Brief
	Amicus brief	
	Prehearing	
	Presentation stage	
	Conference	
	Oral argument	
	Court	
	Decision stage	
	Decision	
	Opinion	
	Entry of judgment	
	Petition for rehearing	
	Remand	

Figure 6-1 Model of appellate court.

the various stages of the processes are tailored to provide an adversarial presentation of the case, and to facilitate the court's deliberation on the questions presented. There is no test of the truth of facts at the appellate level. There are no safety-value motions that permit the circumvention of the process by one of the parties. Furthermore, there is a much more removed or abstract presentation process based on logic, inference, and interpretation. At trial the evidence is presented to convince the trier of what factually happened in the case. At the appellate level the questions presented are determined in an abstract context relating to interpretation of the law to the facts.

It should be emphasized here that the discrepancy between the model in Figure 6.1 and the actual appellate process is very slight. Because of the absence of various kinds of motions to circumvent the process, and because the decisions of appellate courts are based on few, highly stylized documents, the likelihood of variations is low. Furthermore, the functions that appellate courts serve have not been expanded to include social-service functions and other functions that are not amenable to the modular process. Although, as will be discussed below, appellate courts may "make policy," that function does not require them to deviate from the traditional procedures discussed here.

Appellate Court Decision Making

The processes of reaching decisions in appellate courts is a very widely studied aspect of the judicial process, largely because statistical methods of inference permit great sophistication where there are data of decisional outcomes. The studies have not produced a clear, single explanation for how decisions are reached by these groups of political actors. In fact, the most that can be said is that there are a number of schools of thought about how decisions are reached by appellate court judges.[18]

One approach to explaining judicial decision making is that the decision is the result of bargaining among the judges.[19] This small-group approach suggests that judges have certain goals or objectives in reaching a decision and that they seek to achieve those through persuading, threatening, bargaining, and compromising with their fellow judges. This process can be intensely political in terms of process, even though it may have nothing to

---

[18] Charles Sheldon, *supra* footnote 1, and Richard Richardson and Kenneth Vines, *supra* footnote 2, are examples of various schools of thought.

[19] Walter Murphy, "Marshalling the Court," *supra* footnote 17, is one of the major proponents of this approach. Others are cited in Charles Sheldon, *supra* footnote 1, at ch. 2.

do with partisanship among the judges. A judge, to obtain the support of another, might be willing to modify his opinion a great deal.[20] Thus, the resulting opinion in a case is not the reflection of an absolute legal doctrine that dictates the decision so much as a product of compromise and give-and-take among the judges as to the doctrine and other legal bases for the decision.

The kinds of bargaining that can arise in decision making include persuasion on the merits, appeals to loyalty, threats to dissent, and log-rolling. This approach may explain particular case outcomes, and it may suggest the context in which all the decisions of an appellate court are made. However, it is difficult to prove that these activities are causal in the production of any particular judicial decision. Thus, whether a particular decision will be controlled by such bargaining efforts is impossible to predict beforehand. After the fact, various sorts of evidence —such as judicial papers, and comments in opinions—may suggest that compromise and bargaining were determinative in the case. Unfortunately, this does not greatly assist our general understanding of future decisions by a court, since bargaining is very closely tied to the personalities on a court and issues before the court. Different judges will bargain or compromise in different ways, in different kinds of cases.

Another, widely researched approach to explaining judicial decision making is based on the idea that the vote of a judge is the result of his attitudes toward a variety of factors such as the issue in the case, the parties in the case, or his general political philosophy.[21] This approach would suggest that the vote is the judge's response to a variety of stimuli, and that scaling the votes of judges, relating to a single attitudinal dimension, will indicate

[20] Alexander Bickel, *The Unpublished Opinions of Mr. Justice Brandeis* (Chicago: University of Chicago Press, 1967) is a classic study of the use of opinion preparation to achieve particular results by a justice on the U.S. Supreme Court.

[21] See Charles Sheldon, *supra* footnote 1, pp. 34-48, for a general treatment of this material and various sources. Undoubtedly, Glendon Schubert is the leading proponent of this approach. Two of his major works are: *The Judicial Mind Revisited* (New York: Oxford University Press, 1974) and *The Judicial Mind* (Evanston: Northwestern University Press, 1965).

each judge's position vis-a-vis the other judges on the court. It will also suggest the strength, if not the intensity, of each judge's attitude. There have been a number of methodological and substantive criticisms of this approach to explaining decisions. Yet it does provide an additional perspective on the factors that influence a judge to vote the way he does. This approach does specify that the vote of a judge, in a particular case, may be predictable. Furthermore, other research suggests that the prediction can be done in terms of isolating the facts of a case that will trigger a certain voting response in a judge.[22] Isolating precisely which facts will cause which response may be difficult methodologically, but the orientation of this approach to judicial decision making suggests the weight that facts in a case may play for a deciding judge.

There are several suggestions that the decision of a judge is the product of a variety of social or external pressures and factors to which judges, just as other decision makers, are sensitive. For example, the partisan orientation of judges has been suggested as determinative or at least predictive of the way they will vote.[23] More generally, social backgrounds have been suggested as causative of judicial decisions, but there is a great deal of dispute about the causal conection and how strong it is, empirically.[24] It is safe to state that judges, like any other decision makers, are the product of their backgrounds, but these general, environmental

---

[22] Fred Kort, "Simultaneous Equations and Boolean Algebra in the Analysis of Judicial Decisions," *28 Law and Contemporary Problems* 143 (1963); and Fred Kort, "Content Analysis of Judicial Opinions and Rules of Law," in Glendon Schubert, ed., *Judicial Decision-Making* (Glencoe: The Free Press, 1963) are examples.

[23] See, for example, Stuart Nagel, "Political Party Affiliation and Judge's Decisions," *55 American Political Science Review* 843 (1961); and David Adamany, "The Party Variable in Judge's Voting: Conceptual Notes and a Case Study," *63 American Political Science Review* 57 (1969).

[24] For example, John Schmidhauser, "The Justices of the Supreme Court: A Collective Portrait," *3 Midwest Journal of Political Science* 49 (1959); Joel Grossman, "Social Backgrounds and Judicial Decisions: Notes for a Theory," *29 Journal of Politics* 336 (1967); and S. Sidney Ulmer, "Social Background as an Indicator of the Votes of Supreme Court Justices in Criminal Cases: 1947-1956 Terms," *17 American Journal of Political Science* 622 (1973).

factors are not likely to be directly causal of their votes in a particular case. Social background may create a general disposition on the part of the judge, but whether the background causes a particular vote is very difficult to determine.[25] The characteristics of the parties appearing before an appellate court may influence the decision in the case. However, it is not likely that sympathy for a particular party will influence more than the decision in that particular case, if it influences the judicial response at all.

The factors that seem to influence judicial decision making can be classified in two categories. The first might be termed internal, and these relate to the psychological and other, internal pressures to which an individual judge may respond. These factors include his attitudes toward the parties, his role orientations, his attitude toward the type of case presented, and his preferences, whether partisan or personal. The second set is external to the judge and emphasizes the social, judicial, and political context in which the judge decides cases. Thus, his partisanship, his social origins, the public notoriety of the case, and the collegial climate in which his colleagues and he must decide the case, all influence the decision for the individual judge and the outcome in the case. Probably the most conclusive statement that can be made about these factors and their impact of the judicial decision is that they all contribute to *decision making,* but seldom, if ever, is one of them determinative of the *outcome.*

This sort of analysis of decision making among judges should not be surprising, since all political decision makers are in fact influenced by these kinds of factors. The shock may be that judges are "supposed" to be immune from certain kinds of outside pressure,, which we expect the other, elected officials in our government will be concerned about. However, judges are not isolated from all these factors, even if their roles supposedly

---

[25] Kenneth Vines, "Federal District Judges and Race Relation Cases in the South," *26 Journal of Politics* 337 (1964); and Kenneth Vines, "The Role of Circuit Courts of Appeals in the Federal Judicial Process: A Case Study," 7 *Midwest Journal of Political Science* 305 (1963), suggests the general setting in which judges may operate and that influence their decisions.

preclude consideration of some of the factors mentioned here. Judges, in fact, are human, and they cannot possibly be completely removed from the pressures that other humans face in policymaking positions. Judges may be able to divorce themselves from some of the partisan pressures others acknowledge—or at least eliminate those pressures—but a judge cannot make himself objective simply by wearing a black robe.

Appellate Court Policymaking

Traditionally, courts have been thought of as much more limited in policymaking than other political institutions. Courts cannot initiate the cases they decide; courts are limited in decisions by precedent and other rules that proscribe the kinds of decisions and actions they can produce. Furthermore, traditionally, courts have been viewed as apolitical and, therefore, not involved in the formulation of policy. Courts decide individual cases, which are directly connected to particular questions of law and, thus, they cannot range far into a policy area unless the case permits. Courts lack affirmative powers to enforce their decisions in many situations, and often they lack the ability to fashion appropriate, affirmative remedies to correct a problem or to forge a particular policy objective. Courts, in sum, generally have negative powers of policymaking, permitting them to block inappropriate (unconstitutional) policies formulated by other branches of government.

Other forms of policymaking include the interpretation of statutes. Interpretation of a statute can be either positive in nature, as when a court sees the written law as requiring the political system to do something it had not been doing previously, or negative, as when a court declares a law null and void as unconstitutional. The statutes or written laws that appellate courts devote much effort to interpreting permit the courts to structure and reshape legislative policies to reach particular cases the legislature never thought of, or to achieve ends that are quite different from the intention of some legislators.

Recent studies of court policymaking have taken the view that courts are only slightly more limited than other political institutions in formulating and enforcing policies.[26] This perspective, however, is not revolutionary. It reflects only a realization that courts have unique characteristics and powers for policymaking. Courts can formulate very general policy statements that clearly apply far beyond the particular case they are deciding.[27] The real question is whether the court will take the opportunities that are available to it to exercise these kinds of decision alternatives. Most courts probably do not contain policy-active personnel; judges are generally noted for being conservative (politically) or restrained in their exercise of judicial power. However, even a conservative, restraint-oriented court makes policy by deciding in favor of the status quo, rather than change to a new policy. Such decisions are still policy decisions.

Courts can be viewed as one of several policymaking arenas that are available to people who seek to achieve particular policy outcomes. In fact, courts have certain characteristics that make them quite amenable to certain kinds of policies, and to certain kinds of policy interests that seek a resolution to a question. Courts permit a single litigant—individual or group—to present significant policy questions. Thus, while legislatures are sensitive to pressure group efforts only when the interests are large enough to present either electoral threats to incumbent legislators or where the interested parties can provide substantial payoffs for considering legislation (such as campaign contributions), courts consider policy matters of just as significant import, although they are raised by a single individual.

Some observers view courts as an arena open to those interests that have failed to attract legislative attention. An interest that is unpopular with the majority, or an interest that cannot mobilize a majority of policymakers in another arena, may be able to present an appellate court with an important opportunity to change or

---

[26] Kenneth Dolbeare, *supra* footnote 2; and Richard Wells and Joel Grossman, "The Concept of Judicial Policy-Making: A Critique," *15 Journal of Public Law* 286 (1966).

[27] See, for example, *Brown v. Board of Education,* 347 U.S. 483 (1954). This case clearly applied to the Topeka, Kansas, Board of Education, and the other named Boards. However, it also applied to any school system that pursued an intentional policy of racially segregating facilities.

create policy. Whether a court will take such an opportunity depends on the judges on the court and their view of the appropriateness of policymaking as a judicial functions. Certainly the U.S. Supreme Court did make significant policy changes favoring electoral minorities in *Reynolds v. Sims*.[28]

In terms of the kinds of minorities that may benefit most from the judicial policy arena, unpopular minorities such as religious groups[29] or racial minorities[30] may be the most notable. However, the Supreme Court, generally part of the national policymaking majority,[31] is not always likely to be disposed toward such minority requests. That is, the Court often reflects the same policy dispositions as the executive and legislative branches, and so would not provide an arena for some alternative set of policy preferences, or alternative policy demands.

Conclusions

Appeal depends on a variety of factors that have been alluded to earlier. The cost of an appeal may exclude some people from taking an appeal, even a meritorious one. Although the Supreme Court has tried to lower certain cost barriers such as trial transcripts and counsel for criminal appeals,[32] there are still appellants who cannot afford the cost, especially civil litigants. The time involved in appealing may also deter some people. Since the delay in having a case heard by an appellate court may range from six months to two or three years, it may not be possible for some people to take an appeal and wait for a decision. There are psychological costs to appealing as well. The party who lost in the trial court would be the person who would appeal, and if appeal-

[28] 377 U.S. 533 (1964).
[29] Martin Shapiro, *Freedom of Speech: The Supreme Court and Judicial Review* (Englewood Cliffs, N.J.: Prentice-Hall, 1966).
[30] Clement Vose, *Caucasians Only* (Berkely: University of California Press, 1959).
[31] Robert Dahl, "Decision-Making in a Democracy: The Supreme Court as a National Policy-Maker," *6 Journal of Public Law* 279 (1957); and Richard Funston, "The Supreme Court and Critical Elections," *69 American Political Science Review* 795 (1975).
[32] *Supra* footnote 16.

ing raises the potential of another loss, this time before a higher court with more visibility, the potential appellant may prefer simply to cease litigating rather than be embarassed again. There is the factor of how strong a case the appellant has. Appellate courts do not reverse all the trial court decisions that are appealed to them. In fact there is a legal doctrine suggesting that all legal errors in a trial may not be reversible, but only significant or important errors, which might have influenced the outcome, warrant a reversal. Thus, it may be quite possible that the losing party below has a very weak case, at best, upon which to take an appeal. Whether this is the controlling factor in a decision to appeal probably depends on the litigant and the accuracy of the advice his lawyer is providing.

Appellate courts are quite different from the trial courts in our judicial system. They operate for different purposes, and they proceed differently from the trial court because of those purposes. The decisions of appellate courts are widely studied, because of the nature of their decision-making processes, and because the decision (on questions of law rather than the facts of the particular case) is more generalizable than trial court decisions, which are fact-specific to the individual case and largely dependent on the fact finder's evaluation of the evidence. The appellate courts in any jurisdiction are more visible than trial courts, and they are presented with more opportunities to make major decisions than are trial courts. Thus, appellate courts may play a larger policymaking role than do the trial courts. This role may depend on the interests of the judges on the court and their policy preferences, as much as on the visibility of the courts themselves.

The next chapter will examine the effects or the impact of court decisions. This topic is important because different courts—trial and appellate—have differing impacts, and the treatment of court decisions depends on the court that issues the decisions. It should be apparent that the effect of judicial decisions is crucial to the policy impact of courts, and the effects on behavior and attitudes that these decisions have suggest the role of courts in society and as policymakers.

7
The Effects of Court Decisions

The discussion so far has focused on the processes followed by courts in resolving disputes between parties. This chapter deals with the consequences of court decisions. The effects of a court decision are examined in order that the potentialities of court decisions can be explored. There has been a good deal of recent interest in the impact of court decisions and compliance with them.[1] However, despite the growth in literature, there are no coherent or comprehensive theories explaining the varieties of impact and compliance that case studies have uncovered. Most of the completed case studies focus on highly visible cases involving controversial issues such as the Supreme Court's decisions regarding school prayers or released time,[2] school desegrega-

---

[1] See Charles Sheldon, *The American Judicial Process: Models and Approaches* (New York: Dodd, Mead, 1974), ch. 5 for a survey of the literature. Also Steven Wasby, *The Impact of the United States Supreme Court* (Homewood, Illinois: Dorsey Press, 1970); and Theodore Becker and Malcolm Feeley, eds., *The Impact of Supreme Court Decisions* 2d ed. (New York: Oxford University Press, 1973) contains a good deal of the literature.

[2] Kenneth Dolbeare and Phillip Hammond, *The School Prayer Decisions: From Court Policy to Local Politics* (Chicago: University of Chicago Press, 1971); Richard Johnson, *The Dynamics of Compliance: Supreme Court Decision-Making from a New Perspective* (Evanston: Northwestern University Press, 1967); Frank Sorauf, "Zorach v. Clauson: The Impact of a Supreme Court Decision," *53 American Political Science Review* 777 (1959); and Richard Birkby, "The Supreme Court and the Bible Belt: Tennessee Reaction to the 'Schempp' Decision," *10 Midwest Journal of Political Science* 304 (1966).

tion,[3] or criminal procedures.[4] Since these include constitutional issues and are controversial, some noncompliance or variation in compliance can be expected. However, trial court decisions should also be examined. These kinds of decisions far outnumber those visible ones issued by appellate courts, and they affect a large number of individual litigants each of whom is concerned with the decision in his case. The effects of such cases may not be spectacular and they are difficult to measure empirically, beyond the several factors that can be described below in general terms. Yet in most instances these court decisions are the only ones that most litigants face and these usually control the behavior of most litigants.

Several variables affect the impact of a decision and, although none may be causal, individual studies suggest that some have great influence in particular kinds of decisions. More broadly, it is possible to examine what happens after a court reaches a judgment and announces its decision.

Impact and Compliance

The discussion of the effects of court decisions implies that someone or something is required to change behavior patterns as a result of the court decision in a particular case. In fact there are a number of dimensions to the term "impact," and those should be

[3] For example, Jack Peltason, *Fifty-Eight Lonely Men: Southern Federal Judges and School Desegregation* (New York: Harcourt, Brace and World, 1961); Note, "Implementation of Desegregation by the Lower Courts," *71 Harvard Law Review* 486 (1957); and Kenneth Vines, "Federal District Judges and Race Relation Cases in the South," *26 Journal of Politics* 337 (1964).

[4] Neal Milner, *The Court and Local Law Enforcement: The Political Impact of Miranda* (Beverly Hills: Sage, 1971); Neal Milner, "Comparative Analysis of Patterns of Compliance with Supreme Court Decisions: Miranda and the Police in Four Communities," *5 Law and Society Review* 119 (1970); Richard Medalie, Leonard Zeitz and Paul Alexander, "Custodial Police Interrogation in Our Nation's Capitol: The Attempt to Implement Miranda," *66 Michigan Law Review* 1347 (1968); Michael Wald, Richard Ayres, David Hess, Mark Schantz, and Charles Whitebread II, "Interrogations in New Haven: The Impact of Miranda," *76 Yale Law Journal* 1519 (1967).

explored at the outset.[5] The impact of a decision can be focused narrowly on the parties to the litigation. At this narrow point, impact actually relates to compliance, and whether the parties comply with the court order—transfering money, ceasing to pollute the air, or going to prison. Impact, however, certainly can have a broader reach that would extend beyond the two parties to the case and the specific order of the court. This chapter explores some of the aspects that determine the impact, in both the narrow sense and the broader social and political context.

Compliance can be viewed largely as behavioral compliance with the decision. This may be achieved easily, especially when a person is sentenced to prison and has little alternative but to follow the jailer to prison. However, impact may reach into attitudinal and psychological aspects of the parties and broader communities. The school desegregation cases involved elaborate compliance requirements, but they also reflected efforts by the courts to change attitudes of school children, if not their parents, about racial equality. Where such attitudes must change to achieve compliance, and the occasions of this are not frequent, complaince is more difficult.

Impact of Appellate Court Decisions

Most of the studies of impact have been studies of single, appellate court decisions. Thus our knowledge of impact derives primarily from appellate court cases. A good deal of the impact of judicial decisions does relate to appellate courts since they are more visible, have jurisdiction over larger groups of people, and have more authority in terms of interpreting the law than do trial courts. The primary factors that shape the impact of these courts are discussed below. Some of these features might be considered in examining trial court impact such as parties and communication; however they are placed here for completeness.

[5] See Steven Wasby, *supra* footnote 1, at ch. 2; Malcolm Feeley, "Coercion and Compliance," *4 Law and Society Review* 505 (1970); and James Levine, "Methodological Concerns and Studying Supreme Court Efficacy," *4 Law and Society Review* 583 (1970).

THE DECISION

One of the major distinctions between appellate courts and trial courts is that appellate courts decide questions of law rather than of fact, and justify their decision with reasoned opinions. Certainly the clarity of the rationale presented in the appellate court's opinion affects the impact of the case. The reasoned analysis that justifies an appellate court decision is an effort to convince the legal community, as well as the parties, of the correctness of the decision. However, courts and individual judges vary in their ability to present convincing justifications. The more controversial the issue before the court, the more difficulty it will have in presenting a convincing argument for its decision. Some courts seem purposely to avoid a clear opinion, or a clear direction in the written opinion. However, assuming the appellate court seeks to provide clear and convincing guidelines and justification for its decision, the opinion may be confused or unclear on particular points. As a result, the impact and the degree of understanding of the court decision may be clouded.

One of the major factors that determines the effect of the appellate court's decision is the specific case—the kind of question involved, the clarity with which the court disposes of the question(s) presented, and the legal basis of the decision. A decision relating to a technical area of contract law may draw little attention from anyone other than the parties involved and the business community. There may be little disagreement, and the decision is simply a clarification of an unclear point of law. As a result, the effect is probably easy to predict, and it is rapid. However, if the decision involves a controversial issue regarding the rights of persons accused of crimes, or a question relating to a local community's school operation, the social and political issues in the case may submerge the technical question decided. The result is that the pressures in the community will dictate a reaction that may exceed the import of the case. The appellate court is faced with interesting variations in the kinds of legal questions it decides, and the reaction to its decisions depends on the kinds of questions presented. During the Warren Court era, the kinds of cases decided by the Supreme Court tended to involve controversial areas of civil liberties, criminal procedure, and political questions. Although the technical questions of antitrust or patent law were not ignored, they did not receive much visibility and did not provoke opposition from large portions of the population. To the extent that the Court refrains from deciding such controversial issues, compliance will probably be relatively quick and complete.

The legal basis of a decision may shape its impact. A decision based on the Constitution may carry more prestige and weight than a decision based on other sources. Although constitutional decision may generally be among the more controversial, reference to the basic governing document of the country cannot help but give the decision some credence among some people, which it would not have otherwise. The judge-made common law may also be a strong basis for a decision, since there is no outside standard against which to compare the decision. The common law has always been viewed as the appropriate province of the courts and, although the legislature can amend or revoke the common law by statutory enactment, until that occurs, the common law is what the judges say it is. This is a strong basis for claiming a decision has legitimacy.

LOWER COURTS

In the judicial hierarchy appellate courts do not order the parties once a decision is made. Rather the case is remanded to the lower court—eventually to the trial court that made the original decision—for that court's order to the parties. As a result, the judicial bureaucracy can provide a substantial filtering process for the appellate court decision. This can reach the point of nearly completely circumventing the higher court's intent.[6] This involves problems of the appellate court's clarity in the opinion. However, it also involves lower court judges' perceptions and values, and their understanding and agreement with the appellate court decision. Since the remand from the appellate court, ordering the lower court to take action "not inconsistent with this opinion," is a vague order that provides a good deal of flexibility,

[6] Walter Murphy, "Lower Court Checks on Supreme Court Power," 53 *American Political Science Review* 1017 (1959) is the classic study of this subject.

the lower court can adjust the order it gives to fit its own interpretation and policy objectives. A classic example of filtering is associated with the "all deliberate speed" directive that the Supreme Court provided for implementation of the *Brown* decision.[7] Judges had to take the decision, with which many of them personally and professionally disagreed, and translate it into specific desegregation orders in subsequent cases. The *Brown* decision was not popular with most Southern communities, and the unclear order of the Supreme Court gave a good deal of latitude to those judges.

In addition to applying the remand to the particular parties involved in the case, the appellate court decision also serves as precedent for future decisions by lower courts in cases raising the same question. Thus, the clarity of the appellate decision and opinion, and the lower court judge's understanding of and agreement with the decision, are probably very crucial to subsequent decisions he will render in that subject matter area. How the appellate decision is interpreted and applied depends on the lower courts.

THE PARTIES

One of the major factors that influences the impact of a decision relates to the parties involved in the litigation, or the breadth of the clientele that is affected by the court ruling. At the appellate level, a party is quite likely to have some organized backing either in terms of financial and legal assistance or in terms of organizational support. Cases that are appealed often seek particular policy objectives through court rulings. Although a victory at the trial court for the interest is beneficial to that interest, it is not as useful as a favorable decision by the appellate court. Thus, the parties and interests that appear at the appellate level differ somewhat from trial court parties who do not seek appellate review.

Some interest groups litigate to enhance or gain certain rights for all members of their group. The NAACP, the American Civil Liberties Union, and various groups emphasizing environmental

---

[7] *Supra* footnote 3.

policy concerns illustrate that such clientele use litigation when other avenues are closed, or when they seek to utilize existing laws as a means of enhancing a particular policy view. If such a group loses in court, they are probably likely to express emotional concern, since they have a commitment to an objective that the court has failed to support. Depending on the degree of commitment, the reaction will be vociferous outrage, or restrained disappointment, or they may seek a decision in an alternative arena. Rarely will such a group "storm the barricades" if they lose in court, but they may seek legislative resolution as an alternative. Certainly such a group is most likely to have the necessary resources to seek other arenas where a win might be achieved. However, such interest groups may not be able to find a favorably disposed arena beyond the judiciary.

Class actions permit a number of people, "similarly situated," to litigate a single case on behalf of all the members of the class. For example, the telephone company customers might bring a class action against the company for a return of an overcharge that the company allegedly assessed. The individual user would not sue because the amount of return to each might be very small (like $1 or $2). However, together, in one action, the suit would get all the overcharge from the defendant, and that could be distributed to the individual members of the class. These actions involve a larger number of plaintiffs than do most litigation. However, it means that more parties (plaintiffs not defendant) are affected by a single decision.[8] There are a number of mechanical problems with identifying the class, notifying its members, and distributing the judgment, if one is awarded. Yet the class action permits an ad hoc group to litigate a particular matter.

There have been occasions when the Supreme Court has made decisions which relate to particular groups of people such as racial minorities,[9] economic groups,[10] genders,[11] or age groups.[12]

---

[8] See the discussion in Chapter 2, *supra* regarding class actions.

[9] For example, *Brown v. Board of Education,* 347 U.S. 483 (1954).

[10] For example, *Shapiro v. Thompson,* 394 U.S. 618 (1969); *Goldberg v. Kelly,* 397 U.S. 254 (1970); and *Dandridge v. Williams,* 397 U.S. 471 (1970).

[11] For example, *Reed v. Reed,* 404 U.S. 71 (1971); *Frontiero v. Richardson,* 411 U.S. 677 (1973); and *Stanton v. Stanton,* 95 S. Ct. 1373 (1975).

[12] For example, *In re Gault,* 387 U.S. 1 (1967); and *In re Winship,* 397 U.S. 358 (1970).

As these kinds of categories suggest, the beneficiary group may be well organized or poorly organized politically. The impact of such decisions may depend on the degree of organization and support which can influence the degree of compliance and the kind of impact the decision will have on opponent groups. The beneficiaries here are more clearly identifiable, and their identity is stronger and more permanent, than the ad hoc class action. The likelihood of compliance will depend on how such a group can mobilize itself to take advantage of the decision.

While most groups that litigate are identifiable and have specific interests, some cases really involve a community such as the school prayer or school desegregation cases. The impact of a court decision on the community may involve either the behavior of particular officials within the community, or the attitude of the entire community, in the face of a court decision. Here peer pressure or community norms may be important in determining how the decision will affect the operation of the community's institutions (i.e., compliance by officials) or its members.

As just mentioned, one major target of court decisions is governmental institutions, which are ordered to refrain from some action or to proceed in a particular fashion in order to comply with the court decision. The most frequent agencies to litigate in recent years include school systems and school boards, and local police departments. These two sets of institutions reflect local norms and particular organizational structures that filter and adjust court decisions to fit peculiar requirements. The degree of compliance with *Miranda*[13] by police departments depends on a number of factors relating to community pressures, as well as organizational and professional structures within police departments.[14] School boards ordered to devise a busing scheme that complies with particular attendance requirements outlined by the court may be placed in a difficult position, not only in terms of community opposition, but also because of budget constraints within the school system that prevent the purchase and operation of the transportation system required. The difficulties in such

[13] *Miranda v. Arizona,* 384 U.S. 436 (1966).
[14] See Neal Milner, *supra* footnote 4.

cases relate both to the organizational pressures of the agency, and to community spirit or pressure that provide support for noncompliance under these circumstances.

In the preceding two paragraphs two separate groups of actors were mentioned; each may be party to a case or be affected by the court decision. These two groups—the community and the community's institutions—derive support from each other regarding compliance with a decision. It would be difficult for a school superintendent, no matter what his personal and professional feelings, to comply with a decision that was completely rejected by the community. The more likely case arises where there is no clear opposition to the decision, but where the official gets informal indication of disapproval or approval for his actions from some members of the community.[15] In the case of technical decisions, such as law enforcement procedures, where the community is less directly concerned or knowledgeable about the decision, the administrative organization may have more flexibility in how it responds, and may thus fashion its response in light of professional or organizational pressures.

Some court decisions are directed at particular government institutions such as legislatures,[16] the executive,[17] or the government generally.[18] How such institutions react to decision depends on the issue. For example, court decisions stating that the institution does not have the power to accomplish something in a particular fashion may result in a constitutional amendment, or a retreat by the institution involved.[19] Many of the decisions of the Warren Court in the late 1950s relating to congressional investig-

---

[15] See Kenneth Dolbeare and Phillip Hammond, *supra* footnote 2; and Richard Johnson, *supra* footnote 2.

[16] For example, *Reynolds v. Sims,* 377 U.S. 533 (1964).

[17] For example, *U.S. v. Nixon,* 418 U.S. 683 (1974).

[18] For example, *Schechter Poultry Corp. v. U.S.,* 295 U.S. 495 (1935).

[19] These two reactions are exemplified by the Sixteenth Amendment to the U.S. Constitution that resulted from the Supreme Court's decision declaring the income tax unconstitutional,*Pollack v. Farmers' Loan and Trust Co.,* 157 U.S. 429 (1895), and 158 U.S. 601 (1895); and President Truman's acceptance of the Supreme Court's decision in *Youngstown Sheet and Tube v. Sawyer,* 343 U.S. 579 (1952), which held the President did not have constitutional authority to seize and operate the steel mills.

ations of communist activity in government agencies resulted in specific legislative proposals to curb the court's power or to change its jurisdiction.[20] Part of this reaction depends on the mood of the institution and the country. In the case of the Nixon tapes and the request by the Watergate Special Prosecutor that the President release those tapes for purposes of criminal prosecution of several of Nixon's advisors,[21] the Supreme Court could have been faced with a constitutional crisis of the first order if the President had not been willing to comply with its order to release the tapes. However, the mood of the country, and President Nixon's previous statements to the effect that he would comply with whatever decision the Court reached, averted that particular crisis.

The effects of such decisions as these tend to be diffused, but they can still raise substantial concern among the general population. The interest may be more political than legal in the sense of political preferences and dislikes. However, these societal pressures can be reflected in the action of the institutions involved. On this broadest scale, *Brown v. Board of Education* might be a general principle with which nearly everyone can agree. However, when that principle is applied to one's own community, as is currently being done in various Northern communities and suburbs, the compliance with court orders in these areas may drop off sharply, and result in violent opposition regardless of the agreement many people have with the abstract principle involved.

COMMUNICATION

The communication of court decisions is quite important in terms of their effects. There has been some research on court communication specifically.[22] However, the research relating to

---

[20] See Walter Murphy, *Congress and the Court* (Chicago: University of Chicago Press, 1962): John Schmidhauser and Larry Berg, *The Supreme Court and Congress: Conflict and Interaction, 1945-1968* (New York: The Free Press, 1972); and C. Herman Pritchett, *Congress Versus the Supreme Court* (Minneapolis: University of Minnesota Press, 1961).

[21] *Supra* footnote 17.

[22] See Steven Wasby, "The Communication of the Supreme Court's Criminal Procedure Decisions: A Preliminary Mapping," *18 Villanova Law Review* 1086 (1973) for a fine example.

communication of Supreme Court decisions suggests that the process is not efficient, involves a good deal of inexpert reporting that modifies and alters the point of the decision and the opinion, and generally does a poor job of reaching people.

The communication of appellate court decisions occurs in several ways. First, the written opinion of the court transmits the decision to the lower court that is ordered to apply it, and probably that information is also transmitted to the parties. As noted above, this transmission can be less than completely accurate or immediate, depending on the clarity of the opinion, the lower court personnel, and what they are required to do. Second, the decision of an appellate court may be transmitted to the parties and to the public by means of the news media.

The accuracy and kinds of transmission done by the media depend greatly on the particular newspaper or broadcaster and the sources they use for their information. Few media can afford the expense of an expert reporter who clearly understands court decisions and other complicated legal matters. The *New York Times* and CBS and NBC television networks do use their own, expert reporters with legal educations, and the transmission here is likely to be more accurate than otherwise, although copy editors and other technicians can still modify and confuse a knowledgeable reporter's work. Most media, however, do not use expert reporters, and instead rely on wire-service stories that are not prepared by a legal expert. The likely result is a superficial story, covering over the subtleties and the complexities of the decision. Furthermore, the newspaper coverage is likely to be devoted to highly visible and controversial cases that people are interested in reading. Thus, the determination of what is "newsworthy" is very important to newspaper coverage, and this decision may bear no relation to cases of "legal" importance. Certainly, local newspapers, and other mass media will cover local trials only when they are particularly unique, rather than on a regular basis, for the intrinsic legal value of court coverage. Although the clarity and meaning of a court decision may be obfuscated through translation by the media, any communication to the mass population is better than none. To whatever extent possible, it is desirable to inform the public about what courts are deciding and outline the importance of their decisions.

Communication can inform the public or the target community of a specific decision and its general meaning. The same communications lines may inform the public about what the courts are doing generally, and thus set the stage for public perceptions of the legal process and courts, as well as expectations about what the court decision in a particular case means for the public or the community.

Impact of Trial Court Decisions

There is a general lack of understanding about what effect the trial court judgment has on the parties or the target population. This is a substantial weakness since examining impact and compliance has ignored most of the judicial process and most of the final judgments rendered by courts in this country. There are several important characteristics of trial courts that make the impact of trial court decision different from that in the appellate court. The first difference is that trial courts do not issue reasoned opinions justifying findings of fact in a case. The jury or judge merely states the findings, orally in court, or in a written one or two line order, and a judgment is entered on the record for the decision. The judgment finds the defendant guilty of the charges and sentences him to prison, or finds the defendant negligent and thus liable for the plaintiff's damages in the amount of $10,000. This is a much clearer statement of what is to be done than an appellate court opinion. Once the judgment has been entered, the party, if ordered to act—to pay damages or to go to prison—has only a short period of time either to appeal or satisfy judgment. The execution of the judgment can be suspended pending appeal at the judge's discretion. However, if the loser chooses not to appeal, he must either comply with the judgment or be declared in contempt of court upon the initiative of the winning party and the court.

The fact that there is no written opinion issued by the trial court also places the party's lawyer in the central position of communicating the court's decision to the party. Without the alternative means of communication that exist at the appellate level, the lawyer may be the sole interpreter of what the court decided and why, at the trial level. Although any party who is interested in and who knows something about his case will have a general idea of what the decision means to him, his lawyer may be called upon to explain the court's judgment and to outline what alternatives the party has after the decision. Lawyers certainly vary in competence to explain, although most generally know what is required. Some poor translation by lawyers is probably because of their own reluctance to admit defeat, or explain particularly harsh decisions. The accuracy with which a lawyer will communicate a decision for a client may depend on whether the case was won or lost, and on a variety of factors relating to the complexity of the case and what the party is required to do by the decision. However, it should be clear that the lawyer occupies a crucial role position in this set of processes. Lawyer explanation of a decision will also affect whether the losing party decides to appeal the trial court decision.

A second difference from appellate courts is that most trial court decisions reach only the parties to the case. This is particularly true of civil cases where the two parties redefine their relationship based on the court's decision, and in criminal cases where the defendant is the only individual concerned, and society is only generally affected by each case. In civil cases, the decision will order the transfer of money damages or order that the plaintiff takes nothing. The behavioral patterns involved here are fairly straightforward and do not require much explanation or interpretation before the aarty can understand what is required. These kinds of decisions do not reach the community or the population generally, but only the named parties that are ordered by the judgment to act in a certain way.

In criminal cases the state and the accused may be the most directly affected. However, the criminal judgment supposedly affects society since the penalization of the guilty person improves society, and the individual involved. When the defendant is acquitted, the effects of the case may be more limited than when a conviction occurs. The defendant goes free, but sometimes with the costs imposed by a long trial, temporary incarceration awaiting trial, and the stigma of having been accused of a crime. Since the prosecution may learn that the evidence it had in the case was insufficient to obtain a conviction, in future cases it may be more careful to gather more evidence before going to trial. However, in an acquittal the effects of the court decision reach the accused more emphatically than in a civil case in which the defendant is not subject to physical incarceration. In both civil and criminal situations the defendant may have had the cost of defending, but in the criminal situation the psychological effects of the trial remain with the acquitted defendant much longer than with the civil defendant who won. When a conviction is achieved, the repressive power of the state insures that the criminal serves the sentence that has been given to him, whether it is formal incarceration in a penal institution, suspended sentence, probation, or some other institutional arrangement. It is clear that the alternatives to compliance with a criminal conviction are very narrow, since the judicial system is provided with institutions that insure compliance of the convicted person.

A third difference from appellate courts is that trial court decisions are not precedents for future trials. Since each case is peculiar on the facts, and the trial finds the facts in the case, a later trial, even in a similar kind of case will not be governed by the earlier trial. However, there are two ways in which trial court decisions can be a sort of precedent. First, the trial judge may use an earlier interpretation of the law if he has had the same legal question arise in an earlier trial. Thus he may establish his own precedent that he follows in later cases. Second, a large number of cases relating to a particular topic can build up public awareness of a problem or a situation. Thus the repeated acquittal of defendants in felony cases because the judge excludes evidence may create pressure on the judge and the police department to change their procedures and their rulings. Certainly, even a few trial court decisions that substantially alter the landlord-tenant law or the grounds for divorce may change litigation patterns in a community. Although these trial decisions may be altered on appeal, they serve notice on potential parties and on other community members that the court will treat certain problems in a certain fashion.

Fourth, the impact of trial court decisions may be different in criminal and civil cases. The civil cases presume that the winning party will insure that the loser satisfies the judgment. As a result, if the winner does not receive the award ordered in the judgment, he will reappear in court to invoke the court's procedures to insure compliance. This initiative is assumed on the part of civil trial courts. In criminal cases, however, the defendant, if convicted, may have no option but to comply. The trial court is provided with several institutions that translate or enforce the judgment for the court. These translation mechanisms may have effects similar to the impact lower courts have with respect to appellate court decisions. However, the institutions that enforce trial court criminal judgments are designed only to do that, not to exercise judicial power on their own.

The penal system incarcerates the individual, in compliance with the sentence imposed by the court. The purpose of incarceration may be to punish the criminal, to rehabilitate him so that he is a useful member of society, or to isolate him so that society is protected from him. There is a good deal of debate over which objective and function should be the focus of penal systems, and there have been frequent and recent debates over whether the penal system is performing any useful objective—let alone the intended one.[23] Whatever the merits of these arguments, it should be noted that this institution focuses on individual parties to criminal cases, and the prison system is directly related to the court decision, and societal power to deal with antisocial behavior.

Most convicted criminals are not incarcerated. Either because the penal system is overloaded, or more likely because the sentence considered appropriate for the individual criminal does not include incarceration, the person is placed on probation or sentenced to some other rehabilitative program. This process involves a court-assigned bureaucrat—probation officer or case worker—to supervise and counsel the criminal during his period of rehabilitation. He may be released into the community, with the provision that he must report to the probation officer periodi-

---

[23] Ronald Goldfarb and Linda Singer, *After Conviction: A Review of the American Correction System* (New York: Simon and Schuster, 1973); and John Conrad, "The Future of Corrections," *381 The Annals* 1 (1969).

cally, or report for periodic treatment, and other restrictions on his behavior, short of incarceration, can be imposed if the judge deems it necessary. The judge's sentence is supposedly fashioned to help the criminal and to utilize those translating mechanisms that will implement the judge's wishes.

In addition to penal and probation systems, criminal courts use some professional assistance such as psychiatrists and psychologists, as well as medical doctors, to deal with certain kinds of persons. These cases, again quite individualized, involve people with mental or physical difficulties that prevent them from being treated by regular criminal translators. Thus, the court may remand some defendants to institutions for the "criminally insane" either for an indefinite period or until the expert professional determines that the defendant is "cured" of his illness. Such translation is remedial in that the efforts are not to punish but to help or cure the individual. Most criminals do not receive this sort of treatment, but it is considered part of the available mechanisms for enforcement of court orders.

Although these translation mechanisms are generally prevalent in criminal cases, there are more translation systems appearing in civil, private litigation areas. While civil cases involve the private utilization of courts and most outputs are directly felt only by the litigants, the social-service functions of some civil courts require translation and enforcement by various agencies. These functions are most frequently involved with counseling functions such as arise in Family, Domestic Relations, or Juvenile Courts. There is a rapidly expanding set of counseling services, rehabilitative systems, and other institutions for such civil filtering. This trend has developed to the point that some courts use private citizen volunteers to help some civil litigants by acting as advisers, counselors, or providing employment-agency functions for some civil litigants. The reason for these translators is the need to service various problems that come to the attention of courts as cases, which are not criminal problems but which are considered of social concern to the entire community rather than just the private litigants.

As the social-service functions of trial courts increase, it is likely that the distinctions between the impact of civil and criminal cases

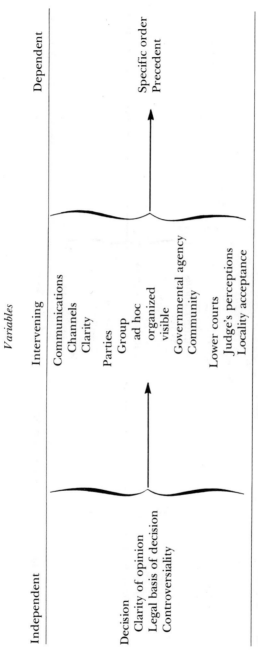

Figure 7-1 Components of an impact model for appellate court decisions.

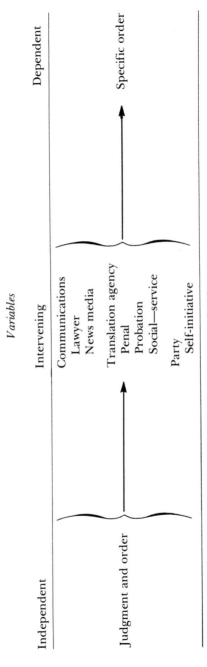

Variables

Independent	Intervening	Dependent
Judgment and order	Communications Lawyer News media Translation agency Penal Probation Social—service Party Self-initiative	Specific order

Figure 7-2 Components of an impact model for trial court decisions.

may decline or disappear. The increasing need for civil as well as criminal judgments to be translated and applied by some agency or service suggests that the courts may merge some of their civil and criminal functions in order to carry out the social-service duties imposed on them by legislatures. The strict civil case in which the two parties make their own transfer of resources depending on the court's judgment may be declining in frequency. While it is unclear that all civil cases require some agency translation, the social-service areas of civil cases do, and these may increase. At least in the area of impact or application of trial court judgments, the civil–criminal distinctions may be unimportant.

Conclusions

Figure 7.1 presents the major factors which seem to operate to determine or affect impact of appellate court decisions.[24] The independent variable is the court's decision itself, and the characteristics of this decision and opinion have a major role in structuring impact. The most important determinants of impact, however, are the intervening variables that intercede between the decision and the parties. It is rare that the appellate court decision is not complied with in some fashion by the parties. The filters outlined in the figure, however, indicate that the actual manner of compliance and the impact of a decision can vary a good deal depending on these numerous factors.

The impact of trial court decisions is much less developed in the literature, but Figure 7.2 seeks to provide some scheme for examining these aspects of decisions by courts. There are some important differences from the appellate scheme. The independent variable is less flexible and much less difficult to understand at the outset. The intervening variables, however, are rather numerous, and clearly can have a substantial effect on impact. More important, these factors seem to be increasing in importance in civil as well as in criminal cases at the trial level.

---

[24] See for example, Steven Wasby, *supra* footnote 1, at pp. 44-56.

8
Courts and Procedures

This book has presented a picture of the legal organization and processes operating in America. Several major points can be made as a result of this examination that raise some fundamental questions for those who are interested in judicial processes and the treatment of disputes by judicial institutions.

The presence of the bargaining model suggests the context in which litigation occurs in our society, and it indicates that courts are not the only, or the final, arena that is used in our society. Society clearly requires arenas in which disputes can be settled, and courts provide an authoritative arena of this type, with a full-time, neutral intervenor to conduct the process of resolution. In the United States, courts are a major part of the political system, and they are available to any citizen for solution of his private disputes, as well as to the state for the resolution of questions about the deviant behavior of individuals within society. However, actual use depends on resources (such as money and time) as much as on the existence of the dispute. These official arenas are generally optional, except for criminal cases, and there are many other arenas in which many disputes are settled informally.[1]

The view that courts are one alternative arena for the settlement of disputes arising in society should emphasize that the

[1] See Austin Sarat and Joel Grossman, "Courts and Conflict Resolution: Problems in the Mobilization of Adjudication," *69 American Political Science Review* 1200 (1975) for a broad discussion of the varieties of arenas.

alternative arenas and procedures are not dramatically different from those offered by courts. The unique qualities of courts may be their authoritativeness, and their governmental position. The judicial process, even if somewhat unique, has been made to include the great amount of bargaining that occurs alongside court litigation, or in place of it. In fact, bargaining has come to play an almost central role in much litigation; bargaining certainly occupies a nearly "official" place in the American criminal process today. This indicates the parallel nature of the conflict resolving procedures of zero-sum and minimax strategies that litigants may pursue simultaneously. It would suggest that these two strategies might not be so diametrically opposed to one another as game theorists would like to make out.

In recent years, courts have not only emerged as major dispute resolving arenas in America, but also have been given additional jurisdiction by legislatures to handle more types of disputes, by various means than in the past. Some legislatures have simply given existing courts additional jurisdiction, and, possibly, additonal resources, and expected that the established court structure will perform the new duties. It is possible for a single court, with a single judge, to perform all the functions and duties that have been itemized in this book. Many such general courts do operate in America today. Single courts handle these disputes possibly because there are not many cases and, thus one court is not overburdened by the variety of disputes that are brought to it.

Beyond giving established courts additional business, some legislatures have sought to reorganize or restructure the judiciary in order to facilitate the handling of new tasks. There have been two patterns of judicial reorganization that are followed and that indicate a major divergence about judicial structures. The first is a consolidation and unification of the courts, to give fewer courts more jurisdiction and to simplify procedures, so that it is possible for one court to treat a variety of problems. A single court is given broad jurisdiction and remedial powers to deal with various problems, and then it may be subdivided into whatever divisions or branches are considered necessary to provide specialized treatment of particular problems that are being given to courts these days. The second, and more common approach is to create additional courts—especially Family Courts and similar arenas—with unique and informal procedures to deal with a new or a different set of problems, which leave the established courts to process the normal judicial work. As a new area of disputes arises, historically, there is pressure for a particular court to handle it. The response to such pressures has often been to create a new court for any major problem rather than spread the pressure of new jurisdiction to an already existing court.[2] These new courts have been grafted onto the existing judicial structure in an ad hoc fashion.

There is the basic question of why and under what circumstances one approach is chosen over the other. It seems clear that large metropolitan areas, with large amounts of judicial business, require large judicial systems—large numbers of courts and judges. There are enough disputes, in a variety of narrow subject matter categories, to justify specialized traditional courts and full-time judges to handle the cases.

One study of local court systems found a high correlation between population and the number of judges on the trial court. However, there was no correlation between population and the number of trial courts of limited jurisdiction.[3] This is explained in part by the fact that recently some states with large populations have eliminated the multiplicity of courts and created a single trial court of general jurisdiction. In addition, some of our large metropolitan areas operate with few, if any, separate courts of limited jurisdiction as described in this book. The single courts in these areas may have separate branches or divisions that functionally divide the work even if it is all within the jurisdiction of one court. Thus, the unifying name of the single court does not prevent functional specialization.

The choice of an approach to judicial structure may be the result of value judgments by the legislator's. In many situations the choice is not consciously made by the legislatures responsible for court systems. There are several factors that can be raised

---

[2] Henry Glick and Kenneth Vines, *State Court Systems* (Englewood Cliffs, N.J.: Prentice-Hall, 1973), p. 24.

[3] *Ibid.,* pp. 33-34.

about the kind of court structure that is desirable. To compartmentalize the system, especially at the trial level, might rigidify it, and prevent its adaptation to new situations. In many respects it appears that unless there is a unification and simplification of procedures, the established courts involved will be of little use as problems change, or as society's needs change. This is part of what happened to the old common law rules of pleading in the mid-nineteenth Century.[4] It essentially became impossible for many to practice law and for others to bring their cases under the old pleading rules because the rules were so complicated and convoluted that few understood them or could utilize them. The modernization of pleadings was done by unifying and simplifying procedures. Whether this analogy applies to court structures as well as court procedures is not possible to tell, but it may be a very close comparison.

Single-court jurisdictions do not permit judicial specialization in a particular type of case and procedure. The judge is much like the general practitioner in medicine—he must be able to treat whatever problem is presented to him. This lack of specialization in some courts and their continued functioning raises the question of whether it is better to allow judicial specialization, or to foster judicial generalization. The answer to this question may depend on whether the reader thinks expert judges are central to the handling of complex and unique cases. How great is the need for specialization and what are its benefits?

In addition, it is important to consider the effect of specialization on procedures. The proliferation of courts to handle problems has facilitated the proliferation and alteration of procedures. The procedures used in these various courts can range from traditionally adversarial to very informal, quite nonadjudicatory in nature. The adversary model may be very useful in theory but, in fact, it has developed that modifications of this model must be made for the actual operation of some of these courts. Some procedural variations from the model have been so

---

[4] David Louisell and Geoffrey Hazard, Jr., *Cases and Materials on Pleadings and Procedure: State and Federal* 3rd ed. (Mineola, N.Y.: The Foundation Press, 1973), pp. 20-38, discusses the transition to modern pleading practice.

great that the court is not supposed to appear like a court, and the judge is not to be a judge but a counselor and advisor to the disputants. This diversity of procedure might suggest that some of the courts of limited jurisdiction are better described not as courts but as conciliation or mediation agencies.

This variety of procedures can develop specialized bars that can practice only in one or several of the unique courts dealt with in this book. It does not appear that these specialized bars have become very formalized, but there is some specialization among attorneys that reflects the unique procedural qualities of some of these courts of limited jurisdiction.

These considerations of trial court organization and procedures also raise questions about the context in which courts operate. The political, social, and economic environment in which courts are set determine their use, their effectiveness, and the functions they perform. Courts in large population centers are very busy, treat numerous people and problems, and may have more impetus to adapt and develop new procedures. Their impact may also be different than smaller courts, with more time to handle individual cases. Such crowded courts may well be more expert in treating the widely diverse subject matter that is presented to courts these days. Such court systems may have a good deal more flexibility in how these cases are handled and, as a result, the success of various "solutions" or "settlements" of the disputes brought to them.

There are two additional considerations about unified or multiple court systems that require further empirical research. The first question relates to whether the unified, single-court system handles as many and as diverse a group of cases as the compartmentalized court structure. It might be expected that the separate-court system would be able to deal with more kinds of cases, reflecting a wider set of social problems than the modern court. At the same time, however, the court, with a unified and somewhat flexible procedure, could treat just as diverse a group of cases as the specialized courts.

Second is the question of the procedures used by the unified court system as it handles the variety of disputes that come to it. Even if that system does not handle as diverse a set of disputes as the multiple system, it can be expected that the unified system would consider enough different kinds of cases that wide adjustments in procedure would be required. The compartmentalized court system may be able to adopt different procedures much easier than a single court dealing with all kinds of problems. The diversity of court procedures seems a worthwhile point to examine for deciding whether unification of trial courts is successful. It is likely that individual judges, in a unified court system, could use various procedures on an ad hoc basis to deal with the diversity of cases which might come before him. However, it is also likely that an individual judge might be less flexible or adaptable to varying procedures and situations than would a number of judges each performing specific and different tasks. The fundamental question about procedures probably involves the degree to which the unified system has subdivided and compartmentalized their operations. The more compartmentalized, the more likely there will be more diverse procedures and specialized operation of any court system.

There is some argument whether the multiplicity of courts described above is a reflection of the past and is on the way out, as courts modernize and attempt to streamline their judicial structures and procedures. One expert observer suggests that the more complicated a judicial system and the more levels that exist within the judicial system, the less modern the system is.[5] If this is the case, then the proliferation of special courts is not modern, and what this book has described is the part of the judicial structure that is least modern and most likely to disappear.[6] However, that study described the hierarchical levels of California courts rather than the proliferation of trial courts of limited jurisdiction.[7] Furthermore, as an example, the recent growth in Family Courts appears to run counter to the presentation of

---

[5] William Blume, "California Courts in Historical Perspective," *22 The Hastings Law Journal* 121, 194 (1970); see also, Henry Glick and Kenneth Vines, *supra* footnote 2, at Table 2-3 and accompanying text.

[6] Henry Glick and Kenneth Vines, *supra* footnote 2, at Table 2-3 suggest that 24 states have traditional and complex judicial systems, while the remainder have, in some degree, more modern judicial structures.

[7] William Blume, *supra* footnote 5.

another source suggesting that state judicial systems are becoming modern by unifying their trial court system.[8]

It is probably more accurate to suggest that the degree of modernity of the court system is not directly related to the number of courts that operate at the trial level, so much as to the kinds of authority, supportive resources, and the outlook of the various members of the judiciary. The choice of one system over the other is not, in fact, as precise as some observers would suggest. Most court systems have some degree of variation on the number and kinds of trial courts. The result is that the decision that one system is "modern" and the other is "traditional" is artificial. This classification is largely a value judgment based on one's preference for a simple, and well-organized structural diagram of court organization.

Whether the court structure is "modern" or "traditional," the trial courts of these systems perform the same variety of functions. The real question is not the court structure but rather the kinds of authority the courts exercise. In this sense, all trial courts have been given additional business and authority by recent legislatures. The array of social-service functions with which courts must deal exist in all court systems, even though some do not have special courts to perform the functions.

As important as the organization of courts are, the external factors such as the means by which judges are selected, the resources made available to courts, and the kinds of cases given to the courts to handle, are crucial to court functioning. The varying quality of judges is a fact of life that is certain to arise no matter what kinds of selection processes are used. However, some kinds of processes tend to select out certain categories of people and make the judgeship attractive or unattractive to them. The result may be that the kind of personnel attracted are not well trained, or are heavily biased, against certain outcomes in the courts. Certainly the lack of adequate supportive staff can hinder the court's performance of social-service functions. Yet often courts are given these kinds of tasks to perform. The expert support personnel necessary for these duties may be absent or only par-

[8] Henry Glick and Kenneth Vines, *supra* footnote 2.

tially adequate, with the result that the effect of such courts is less than expected or anticipated. The increasing diversity of the problems given to courts is an underlying cause for difficulties in the trial court system. Expecting courts to be marriage counseling offices, juvenile counselors, and rehabilitative institutions, within the context of the judicial process, is asking a great deal. Many courts and judges are unable or unwilling to perform these kinds of tasks.

Appellate courts differ substantially from trial courts. They differ in function and, particularly, they differ in procedures from trial courts. Although appellate procedure is derived from the adversary process, the entire process at the appellate level is subject to much less variation from the model than trial courts. The reason for this small amount of variation in appellate process is that the function of appellate courts is very narrow, and not nearly as diverse in subject matter or purpose as at the trial court level. However, many scholars have studied the variations that do occur in appellate court decisions. These turn primarily on the actual decisions or outcomes of appellate courts, and have usually been explained in terms of individual discretion and idiosyncracies. Although these factors also operate at the trial level, this book has focused on the process differences at the trial level, rather then human differences.

The discussion here has been general because the problems and features of the judicial system discussed in this book factor down to these basic considerations. Any particular court, operating at any given time and place, will have its own peculiarities, and its own variations from the outlines presented here. However, it should be possible to understand any trial court in America after this discussion of procedures, functions, and operation. The interesting questions that must remain for study are the empirical explanations of particular attributes of courts and their effects on the results with which people must live after the dispute is settled.

Index